Steven Mezzio, Meredith Stein, Vincent Camp

Cloud Governance

M000222174

Professors of Practice Series

Edited by
Chris Beer

Steven Mezzio, Meredith Stein,
Vincent Campitelli

Cloud Governance

Basics and Practice

DE GRUYTER

ISBN 978-3-11-075526-8
e-ISBN (PDF) 978-3-11-075537-4
e-ISBN (EPUB) 978-3-11-075547-3
ISSN: 2749-9499
e-ISSN 2749-9502

Library of Congress Control Number: 2022943438

Bibliographic information published by the Deutsche Nationalbibliothek
The Deutsche Nationalbibliothek lists this publication in the Deutsche Nationalbibliografie;
detailed bibliographic data are available on the internet at http://dnb.dnb.de.

© 2023 Walter de Gruyter GmbH, Berlin/Boston
Cover image: Hybert Design
Typesetting: Integra Software Services Pvt. Ltd.
Printing and Binding: LSC Communications, United States

www.degruyter.com

Foreword

I am pleased to introduce the book *Cloud Governance: Basics and Practice*, the first volume in a new series titled the *Professors of Practice Series* launched by De Gruyter. The series advocates the importance of balancing theory with real-world practice-driven perspectives, which will help students, scholars, practitioners, and influencers internationally gain additional insights into integrating the book's topic with the external business environment and context.

By way of professional background, I have been a professor of practice at Warwick Business School in London since 2013 and director of the Warwick Business School DBA Program. I am also an executive director of one of the world's leading executive mentoring companies, where I have the privilege of supporting senior business leaders and their organizations. In addition, I have held operational, governance, and leadership roles in a range of organizations internationally. This experience greatly informs my approach to writing and teaching and helps me integrate a practitioner perspective into a lecture theatre.

The Professors of Practice series is a new, original, and timely series of books authored by professors of practice in business schools worldwide and practitioners. Professors of practice are professors or lecturers in higher education who serve as practitioners or influencers in public and private companies, government agencies, consultancy firms, regulators, external auditors, or not-for-profit organizations that span size and geography. Each book in this series draws on theory, practices, and the authors' combination of teaching and practice experience. The books cover critical topics taught in academic settings, combined with real-life examples from an international perspective. This approach helps readers understand both the theoretical and applied nature of the subject matter.

Books in the series will be of interest to a range of cohorts. For instance, business school students; executive education programme participants; teachers and researchers; and business practitioners, including directors, organizational business practitioners, regulators, external auditors, legal and compliance, and learning and development influencers.

The title of this first book in the series is *Cloud Governance: Basics and Practice*. The book combines two independent and complex domains, *the cloud*, and *corporate governance*. Each has organization-wide strategic, performance, risk, business process, and human capital impacts and outcomes. Each is also riddled with confusing jargon and an abundance of inconsistent definitions of terms, frameworks, and complex ecosystems.

The widescale deployment of the cloud rapidly and uniquely infiltrates and impacts the entire organization. While providing valuable opportunities, this organization-wide impact is exacerbating existing risks, creating new and unexpected risks,

https://doi.org/10.1515/9783110755374-202

and materially stressing, disrupting, and transforming long-standing and proven corporate governance practices (e.g., strategies, processes, and competencies).

This disruption shines a bright light on how best to govern the cloud effectively and practically within an organization's overall strategy and governance ecosystem. Governing the cloud responsibly and securely is, therefore, crucial. Cloud governance plays a crucial and central role in responsibly optimizing the strategic opportunities afforded by the cloud while at the same time governing the range of risks emerging from the use of the cloud.

This book combines theory, real-world practices, and the unique educational and practice perspectives of the authors to provide a basic yet comprehensive introduction to the unique combination of *cloud computing* (the cloud) and *corporate governance*. It successfully brings to life the diverse range of opportunities and challenges associated with governing the deployment and enterprise-wide growth and use of the cloud, while explaining and contextualizing the abundance of inconsistent definitions of terms, frameworks, and ecosystems.

The authors of *Cloud Governance: Basics and Practice* bring the following to readers:

- A balanced mix of knowledge, skills, and experience in the relevant domains of corporate governance, cloud governance, organizational strategy, change management, and learning and development; this diversified experience spans industry sectors, international jurisdictions, and public, private, and not-for-profit organizations.
- An effectively balanced, user-friendly presentation of both the *basics* element (e.g., providing user-friendly, practical definitions and explanations of complex jargon) and the *practice element* (e.g., examples of best practices, popular frameworks and standards, and influencer perspectives).
- Easy-to-read chapters that describe the governance implications of the cloud; creatively introducing their "Cloud Governance House" – a unique, simple, and practical cloud governance ecosystem that addresses this complex topic in a simple way.

Cloud Governance: Basics and Practice will appeal to diversified cohorts of international students, operational and risk managers, boards, auditors, and advisors. Understanding the combination of both has emerged as a critical capability for various stakeholders, including students, teachers, researchers, boards, and executives of companies, irrespective of their size and location. It also is an essential companion to those studying and interested in the stand-alone topics of corporate governance or cloud computing.

Professor Chris Beer
Director, Warwick Business School DBA Programme

Contents

Part II: **The Basics of Cloud Governance**

**Part III: The Organizational and IT Context
          of Cloud Governance**

Part V: **Conclusion: Cloud Reflections**

Part I: **Introduction: The Context of Cloud Computing**

Chapter 1
Silver Linings: The Fourth Industrial Revolution and the Utopian Promises of Cloud Computing

Every Cloud Has a Silver Lining.[1]
– Attributed to John Milton, poet

Learning Objectives
- Reflect on the definition of cloud computing
- Understand the impact of the Fourth Industrial Revolution on the growth of cloud computing
- Explain the benefits available from the use of cloud computing capabilities

 ## Key Terms

1. Artificial Intelligence (AI) – "A machine-based system that can, for a given set of human-defined objectives, make predictions, recommendations or decisions influencing real or virtual environments."[2]
2. Cloud-Washing – "The purposeful and sometimes deceptive attempt by a vendor to rebrand an old product or service by associating the buzzword cloud with it."[3]
3. Internet of Things (IoT) – "The network of devices that contain the hardware, software, firmware, and actuators which allow the devices to connect, interact, and freely exchange data and information."[4]
4. Machine Learning – "A branch of AI and computer science which focuses on the use of data and algorithms to imitate the way that humans learn, gradually improving its accuracy."[5]

Chapter Outline

https://doi.org/10.1515/9783110755374-001

1.1 Introduction

Cloud computing (the cloud) is in the vanguard of the global digital transformation; the reimagination of business in the digital age. The reason for this ascribed digital-leadership role is the *promise of the cloud*. That is, the promise of a diversity of unique and compelling benefits potentially available from the use of cloud computing capabilities. As a result, the cloud is ubiquitous, emerging as a mandate of sorts for organizations spanning size, sectors, and geographies.

At the same time, the cloud is an enigma that creates confusing jargon, organizational disruption, and in some cases fuels chaos and thorny problems. For instance, the cloud requires new and reimagined organizational skills, strategies, and processes, while exacerbating existing organizational risks and creating new risks. *Cloud governance*, the topic of this book, is designed to address this dichotomy.

This reference book brings to life the diverse range of opportunities and challenges associated with governing the enterprise-wide use of cloud computing from a practitioner perspective. It is designed to be a basic and practical reference guide with chapter-based self-assessment questions written in a user-friendly manner that should appeal to diversified cohorts of international students, operational and risk managers, boards, auditors, advisors, educators, advisors, and learning and development professionals.

As a starting point, this chapter defines cloud computing and explores the *silver linings* of the cloud. That is, the utopian promises fueling the international proliferation of cloud computing.

1.2 The Fourth Industrial Revolution and Cloud Computing

A Fourth Industrial Revolution is underway globally: a digital revolution that followed the revolutions in water and steam power, electrical power, and electronics and information technology. According to Salesforce, This digital revolution is characterized as follows.

> Digital transformation is the process of using digital technologies to create new – or modify existing – business processes, culture, and customer experiences to meet changing business and market requirements. This reimagining of business in the digital age is digital transformation.[6]

The digital revolution is driven by the rapid, wide-scale deployment of digital technologies, such as in high-speed mobile Internet capabilities, artificial intelligence (AI), and machine learning.

In a 2016 address, Microsoft CEO Satya Nadella advanced the following enduring description of this digital transformation.

> Becoming more engaged with their customers, empowering their employees, optimizing how they run their business operations and transforming the products and services they offer using digital content. The dimensions aren't new, but what has changed is the role that systems of intelligence now play, providing better insight from data and converting that into intelligent action.[7]

Cloud computing is at the vanguard of this digital transformation. As a result, organizations of all sizes, industries, and geographies have substantially and rapidly increased their adoption and use of cloud computing, including reliance on third-party cloud service providers (CSPs).

One driver in this proliferation of cloud computing is the promise of the cloud; the promise of a wide range of unparalleled opportunities provided by the cloud. Such opportunities include streamlining and scaling storage, software, and application support; increasing the speed of data access processing and decision analytics; more productive customer engagement and empowered employees; reducing costs, such as outsourcing costly and difficult-to-update and -manage in-house IT infrastructure. As a result, organizations of all sizes, geographies, and industries are developing their own private cloud or purchasing public cloud services from cloud service providers.

While such potential benefits are compelling, cloud computing disrupts corporate governance. For example, market intelligence reveals critical data, applications and some important roles and responsibilities for IT policies, compliance, risk management, security and IT infrastructure are moving from traditional in-house IT departments to third-party CSPs.

As a result, cloud computing is stressing corporate governance in a number of ways, including further extending the organization's reliance on third-party service providers, exacerbating existing risks, creating new and unexpected operational, cybersecurity, and regulatory risks, and fueling an urgent need for more responsive and resilient enterprise risk management strategies and new skills. This disruptive paradigm is raising concerns and thorny questions from corporate boards, trustees, advisors, managers, regulators, and assurance providers about cloud governance, including strategy, performance, risks, controls, and skills.

1.3 Defining Cloud Computing

The term *cloud computing*, and the more commonly used term, *the cloud* is ubiquitous. Yet, for some, the cloud is an enigma. *What is cloud computing?*

Cloud computing is a simple characterization of a highly complex internet/web-based computer model. A range of definitions of cloud computing appears in the public domain. Table 1.1 presents examples of these definitions.

Table 1.1: Definitions of cloud computing – selected examples.

Source	Definition of Cloud Computing
National Institute of Standards and Technology (NIST)[8]	A model for enabling ubiquitous, convenient, on-demand network access to a shared pool of configurable computing resources (e.g., networks, servers, storage, applications, and services) that can be rapidly provisioned and released with minimal management effort or service provider interaction.
Herbst et al., 2018[9]	Cloud computing is a paradigm under which information and communication technology services are offered on-demand "as a service," where resources providing the service are dynamically adjusted to meet the needs of a varying workload.
Microsoft[10]	Delivery of computing services – including servers, storage, databases, networking, software, analytics, and intelligence – over the internet ("the cloud") to offer faster innovation, flexible resources, and economies of scale. You typically pay only for cloud services you use, helping you lower your operating costs, run your infrastructure more efficiently, and scale as your business needs change.
Salesforce[11]	Delivery of computing services such as software, databases, servers and networking, over the internet. This means end-users are able to access software and applications from wherever they are.
Accenture[12]	A model of computing where servers, networks, storage, development tools, and even applications (apps) are enabled through the internet. Instead of organizations having to make major investments to buy equipment, train staff, and provide ongoing maintenance, some or all of these needs are handled by a cloud service provider.

Who coined the term cloud computing? The origin of the term *cloud computing* continues to be debated. In 2011, *MIT Technology Review* published a story that attributed the first use of the term to Compaq Computer during the late 1990s.

> Some accounts trace the birth of the term to 2006, when large companies such as Google and Amazon began using "cloud computing" to describe the new paradigm in which people are increasingly accessing software, computer power, and files over the Web instead of on their desktops. But *Technology Review* tracked the coinage of the term back a decade earlier, to late 1996, and to an office park outside Houston.

> Inside the offices of Compaq Computer, a small group of technology executives was plotting the future of the Internet business and calling it "cloud computing." Their vision was detailed and prescient. Not only would all business software move to the Web, but what they termed "cloud computing-enabled applications" like consumer file storage would become common.[13]

While these definitions differ, a common thread runs through each: the cloud is a constellation of distinct components and services, including servers, networks, storage, development tools, applications and cloud vendors. These components and services can be scaled on-demand, orchestrated, configured, and enabled by the internet to function as a single cloud ecosystem. Figure 1.1 illustrates a timeline of the evolution of the cloud.

1.4 Silver Linings: The Utopian Promises of Cloud Computing

According to Gartner, "cloud will be the centerpiece of new digital experiences."[14] *Why has the cloud been elevated to such a leadership position in the digital revolution?* One reason is the inherent characteristics of the cloud create unique strategic opportunities. For instance, Table 1.2 presents three dimensions of value associated with the cloud asserted by McKinsey.

According to McKinsey, organizations that pursue a cloud strategy rooted in these value dimensions are more likely to achieve the following benefits.

> First, they execute a well-defined, value-oriented strategy across IT and businesses and install a cloud-ready operating model. Second, they develop firsthand experience with cloud and adopt a much more technology-forward mindset than their peers. And finally, they excel at developing a cloud-literate workforce.[15]

Another reason for the cloud's leadership role in the digital revolution is the long list of financial and operational benefits. Table 1.3 presents examples of

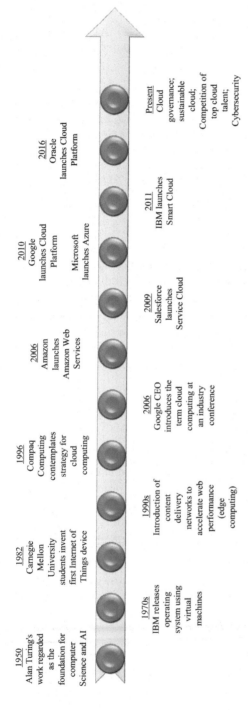

Figure 1.1: High-level timeline of the evolution of the cloud.[16, 17]
Source: Authors.

Table 1.2: Benefits of cloud computing, as adapted from McKinsey.[18]

Cloud Value Dimension	Description
Rejuvenate	Break from traditional legacy approaches by using the cloud to lower costs and risk across IT and core operations.
Innovate	Harness the cloud to accelerate innovation-driven growth and optimize costs, across customer, geography and channel segments.
Pioneer	Early adopters of the cloud are more likely to harness the cloud to experiment with new technologies.

such benefits advanced by the IT Professional's Resource Center (ITPRC), an international hub for IT managers and professionals.

Table 1.3: Top 10 benefits of the cloud, as adapted from ITPRC.[19]

ITPRC's Top 10 Cloud Benefits
1) Cost Savings
2) Greater Scalability
3) Data Backup and Restore
4) Data Security
5) Internet of Things (IoT) Functions
6) Enhanced Collaboration
7) Environmentally Friendly
8) Employee Engagement
9) Real-Time Software Updates
10) Analytics

A range of additional benefits has been advanced in the public domain. For example, cloud-enhanced customer and employee experiences such as mobile payment customer systems in financial institutions; telehealth visits for patients in healthcare; remote working for employees; democratization of application development; cloud orchestration to integrate automated tasks; and processes to perform specific business functions.

1.5 The Dark Side of the Cloud: Cloud Risks

Cloud computing provides a range of compelling benefits to organizations, such as cost savings and greater scalability. At the same time, the cloud disrupts organizations, creating unintended consequences, including skill gaps, exacerbating existing risks, and creating new risks. This disruptive and risk-prone cloud paradigm raises questions from the corporate boards, managers, regulators, and assurance providers concerning the governance of the cloud.

For instance, exaggerating or fabricating the categorization of technology as "the cloud" (i.e., cloud-washing), non-compliance with data privacy and laws, and cybersecurity threats. Table 1.4 presents the top cloud challenges reported by Flexera in their 2022 State of the Cloud Report.

Table 1.4: Top cloud challenges, as adapted from Flexera's 2022 State of the Cloud Report.[20]

Cloud Challenges
– Cloud security
– Managing cloud spend
– Lack of cloud resources and expertise
– Cloud governance
– Cloud compliance
– Managing cloud Bring Your Own License (BYOL) for software
– Cloud migration
– Managing multi-cloud

1.6 Conclusion

The cloud is in the vanguard of the current global digital transformation. The reason for this is the unique and compelling benefits available through the use of cloud computing capabilities. Such benefits include cost savings, efficiency, and democratized access to the cloud that enables innovation. At the same time, the cloud creates unintended consequences, exacerbates existing risks, and creates new risks.

Cloud governance, the topic of this reference book, is designed to address this dichotomy between opportunities and risks. In addition, this reference book unpacks and explains basic concepts and practices associated with cloud computing and cloud governance.

Each of the chapters in this book is interconnected and centered in a cloud governance ecosystem, as depicted in Chapter 6, Figure 6.1. At the same time, it is a reference book with 20 individual chapters that can also be approached as separate, stand-alone articles on specific topics of the cloud that can be read in any order.

Key Questions
1. What is cloud computing?
2. How does the Fourth Industrial Revolution influence the growth of cloud computing?
3. What are the benefits and risks associated with cloud computing?

Chapter 2
The Dark Side of the Cloud: High-Profile Cyber-Attacks

> You know what the Dark Cloud is.
> It's the rapidly growing infrastructure used by cyber criminals to promote
> their evil cause.[21]
> Uri Rivner, Chief Cyber Officer, BioCatch

Learning Objectives
– Gain insights into high-profile cloud cyber-attacks reported in the media
– Awareness of terminology used to describe common types of cloud breaches

 Key Terms

1. Attack Vector – "An attack vector is the means by which a hacker is able to break into a computer system or network to launch an attack. A simple analogy would be that of a mosquito bite that spreads disease by injecting its victims with the virus that it carries."[22]

2. Cyber-Attack – "An attack, via cyberspace, targeting an enterprise's use of cyberspace for the purpose of disrupting, disabling, destroying, or maliciously controlling a computing environment/infrastructure; or destroying the integrity of the data or stealing controlled information."[23]

3. Data Breach – "A data breach is a cyber-attack in which sensitive, confidential or otherwise protected data has been accessed and/or disclosed in an unauthorized fashion."[24]

4. Ransomware – "A form of malware designed to encrypt files on a device, rendering any files and the systems that rely on them unusable. Malicious actors then demand ransom in exchange for decryption."[25]

5. Supply Chain Attack – "An emerging kind of threat that targets software developers and suppliers. The goal is to access source codes, build processes, or update mechanisms by infecting legitimate apps to distribute malware. Attackers hunt for unsecured network protocols, unprotected server infrastructures, and unsafe coding practices. They break in, change source codes, and hide malware in build and update processes."[26]

https://doi.org/10.1515/9783110755374-002

2.1 Introduction

The potential benefits of cloud computing (the cloud) are unique and compelling. However, market intelligence reveals that the cloud also exposes organizations to a wide variety of cyber-attacks, including attack vectors, data breaches, ransomware, and supply chain attacks. This chapter explores high-profile of cloud-related cyber-attacks reported in the media.

2.2 Information Technology Systems and Cyber-Attacks

Information technology systems are subject to cyber-attacks, including data breaches. What is a *cyber-attack*? The National Institute of Standards and Technology (NIST) defines a *cyber-attack* as follows.

> An attack, via cyberspace, targeting an enterprise's use of cyberspace for the purpose of disrupting, disabling, destroying, or maliciously controlling a computing environment/infrastructure; or destroying the integrity of the data or stealing controlled information.[27]

What is a data breach? NIST defines a *breach* as follows.

> The loss of control, compromise, unauthorized disclosure, unauthorized acquisition, or any similar occurrence where: a person other than an authorized user accesses or potentially accesses personally identifiable information; or an authorized user accesses personally identifiable information for an other than authorized purpose.[28]

Media reports and research reveal increases in security attacks, including data breaches. For example, according to Identity Theft Resource Center (ITRC) research,

> For Q3 2021, the number of data compromise victims (160 million) is higher than Q1 and Q2 2021 combined (121 million). The dramatic rise in victims is primarily due to a series of unsecured cloud databases, not data breaches. Also, the total number of cyber-attack-

related data compromises year-to-date (YTD) is up 27 percent compared to FY 2020. Phishing and Ransomware continue to be, far and away, the primary attack vectors.[29]

According to IBM's Cost of a Data Breach Report for 2021, "The average total cost of a data breach increased by the largest margin in seven years. Data breach costs increased significantly year-over-year from the 2020 report to the 2021 report, increasing from $3.86 million in 2020 to $4.24 million in 2021."[30]

2.3 The Dark Side of the Cloud: High-Profile Cyber-Attacks Reported in the Media

The potential benefits of the cloud are unique and compelling. However, market intelligence reveals that cloud computing also exposes organizations to cyber-attacks and data breaches. Examples include breaches in cloud data confidentiality and privacy, unauthorized access to cloud systems, and cloud system availability failures.

This disruptive cloud paradigm raises questions from the corporate boards, managers, regulators, and assurance providers concerning cloud strategy, performance, risks, and controls. Such questions include the scope and location of cloud activities; the implications of dependency on a web of cloud service provider (CSP) vendors; reputation, intellectual property, financial statement, and market trust vulnerabilities; global jurisdiction regulatory compliance; as well as the adequacy of risk management, cybersecurity, audit, and change management.

The reality of cybersecurity risks in a cloud paradigm is evidenced by the growing number of cloud cyber-attacks and cloud breaches revealed by the media. For the purposes of gaining insight into cyber-attacks, this book discusses three randomly selected cloud cyber-attacks reported in the media.

A cloud-related cyber-attack on the company Capital One was considered a *Server-Side Request Forgery* (SSRF) *cyber-attack*. Some estimates suggest that millions of customer accounts were hacked. Table 2.1 presents a summary of the cyber-attack on Capital One.

Table 2.1: Summary of the cloud-related cyber-attack on Capital One, as adapted from BitSite.[31]

Company: Capital One	Capital One is one of the largest banks in the USA.
What was the nature of the cyber-attack?	SSRF Cyber-Attack A server is *tricked* into running commands that it should never have been permitted to run.
How did it happen?	Hackers gained unauthorized access to the organization's network through the cloud and then gained access to customer accounts.
What was the impact of the cyber-attack?	Personal identifiable information data of more than a million customer accounts stored in the cloud was alleged to be compromised.

A *supply chain cyber-attack* on the company SolarWinds was unique in its scope of the attack. As opposed to solely attacking a single company, hackers gained access to the networks, systems and data of the customers of Solar-Winds. Some estimates suggest that approximately 18,000 SolarWinds customers installed malware when the hackers accessed the Solar Winds customer network undetected. Table 2.2 presents a summary of the cyber-attack on Solar Winds.

Table 2.2: Summary of the cloud-related cyber-attack on Solar Winds, as adapted from TechTarget.[32]

Company: Solar Winds	SolarWinds is a provider of software solutions designed to help monitor and manage the performance of customer IT systems.
What was the nature of the cyber-attack?	Supply Chain Cyber-Attack A cyber-attack that targets an organization's network, and in turn gains access to and attacks all other organizations connecting to this same network.
How did it happen?	Approximately 18,000 customers of Solar Winds inadvertently installed this malware that was part of the normal software updates (e.g., software patches, new versions of the software) routinely distributed to customers. The malware was used to gain unauthorized access to systems.
What was the impact of the cyber-attack?	Hackers gained unauthorized access to government and private data and networks.

The cyber-attack on the company Blackbaud was a *ransomware cyber-attack*. Table 2.3 presents a summary of the cyber-attack on Blackbaud.

Table 2.3: Summary of the cloud-related cyber-attack on Blackbaud, as adapted from BankInfoSecurity.[33]

Company: Blackbaud	Blackbaud is one of the largest providers of financial and fundraising software, systems and services to not-for-profit organizations.
What was the nature of the cyber-attack?	Ransomware Cyber-Attack "Ransomware is a form of malware that uses encryption to render files, data, and/or systems unusable. Malicious actors then demand ransom in exchange for realizing the hostage systems, files, and data."[34]
How did it happen?	A data breach. The hackers illegally accessed and removed a copy of a subset of data from Blackbaud's systems.
What was the impact of the cyber-attack?	Some estimates suggest that several million individuals had their personally identifiable information stolen from the illegal and undetected access of Blackbaud's systems.

These media reports of breaches demonstrate the reality of successful cloud-related cyber-attacks.

2.4 Are you Surprised by the Wave of Cloud Cyber-Attacks?

The *dark side of the cloud* should come as no surprise to informed boards of directors, management, cloud risk and security professionals. Cautionary warnings concerning cloud cyber-attack vulnerabilities have been advanced for a decade. For instance, as far back as 2013, McKinsey warned,

> Large institutions, which have many types of sensitive information to protect and many cloud solutions to choose from, must balance potential benefits against, for instance, risks of breaches of data confidentiality, identity and access integrity, and system availability.[35]

In 2019, Gartner advanced the following predictions concerning cloud security:
- "Through 2024, the majority of enterprises will continue to struggle with measuring cloud security risks.
- Through 2025, 90% of the organizations that fail to control public cloud use will inappropriately share sensitive data.
- Through 2025, 99% of cloud security failures will be the customer's fault."[36]

In spite of warnings and best efforts, cloud-related cyber-attacks continue. For instance, in 2022 IBM released a report titled, Cost of a Data Breach Report 2021. The following is only a small sample of the findings reported.

- "Data breach costs rose from USD 3.86 million to USD 4.24 million, the highest average total cost in the 17-year history of this report.
- The average cost was USD 1.07 million higher in breaches where remote work was a factor in causing the breach, compared to those where remote work was not a factor.
- The most common initial attack vector, compromised credentials, was responsible for 20% of breaches at an average breach cost of USD 4.37 million."[37]

If there is a lesson to be learned from the onslaught of cybersecurity attacks that have occurred, it is that despite best efforts to guard against attacks, no organization is immune from becoming a victim of a cloud-related cyber-attack.

2.5 Conclusion

This reference book unpacks and explores the crucial role served by cloud governance in managing cloud risks, including cyber-attacks. This chapter identifies the dark side of the cloud by presenting examples of high-profile cybersecurity attacks.

Key Questions
1. What is the organization doing to be resilient against cyber-attacks?
2. What action is management taking to understand the nature and scope of a relevant cloud-related cyber-attack on other organizations?
3. What is the organization doing to continuously and rapidly improve its cloud governance based on lessons learned from cloud-related cyber-attacks?

Chapter 3
Cloud 101: The Basics of Cloud Computing

> We become what we behold. We shape our tools and thereafter our tools shape us.[38]
> – Attributed to John Culkin, Jr., 1967 American academic,
> former priest, and writer

Learning Objectives
- Understand the basic concepts underlying cloud computing.
- Understand the organizational impact associated with deploying cloud computing.

 Key Terms

1. Cloud Computing – "A model for enabling ubiquitous, convenient, on-demand network access to a shared pool of configurable computing resources (e.g., networks, servers, storage, applications, and services) that can be rapidly provisioned and released with minimal management effort or service provider interaction."[39]

2. Cloud Customer – "The principal stakeholder for the cloud computing service. A cloud consumer represents a person or organization that maintains a business relationship with, and uses the service from a cloud provider."[40] For purposes of this book, the organization is the cloud customer.

3. Cloud Deployment Models – NIST identifies four deployment models: private, community, public, and hybrid.

4. Cloud Service Provider – "Person, organization, or entity responsible for making a service available."[41]

5. Cloud Service Models – NIST identifies three service models that for cloud customers to outsource with different types of service management operations. The three service models are: Infrastructure as a Service (IaaS), Software as a Service (SaaS), and Platform as a Service (PaaS).

6. Cloud Services – Example cloud services available to an organization are:
   - Customer relationship management applications (e.g., call center)
   - Services for managing the production of, and access to, content for web-based applications
   - Platforms for the creation of applications such as dashboards, reporting systems, and data analysis

https://doi.org/10.1515/9783110755374-003

- Services for backup and recovery of file systems and raw data
- Storage for applications, backups, archival, and file storage
- Networks to improve the performance of web-based systems"[42]

7. Cloud Workload – "An abstraction of the actual instance of a functional application that is virtualized or containerized to include compute, storage, and network resources."[43]

Chapter Outline

3.1 Introduction

Any treatise on *cloud governance* requires an understanding of the fundamental technology components of cloud computing (the cloud) and how they interoperate. The purpose of this chapter is to introduce the basics of the cloud, including the various service models and deployment models.

3.2 Defining Cloud Computing

A range of definitions of cloud computing has been advanced. Table 3.1 presents examples of such definitions.

Table 3.1: Definitions of cloud computing – selected examples.

Source	Definition of Cloud Computing
National Institute of Standards and Technology (NIST)[44]	NIST defines cloud computing as a means for enabling on-demand access to shared pools of configurable computing resources (e.g., networks, servers, storage applications, services) that can be rapidly provisioned and released.

Table 3.1 (continued)

Source	Definition of Cloud Computing
European Network and Information Security Agency (ENISA)[45]	ENISA defines cloud computing as an on-demand service model for IT provision, often based on virtualization and distributed computing technologies.
Accenture[46]	Cloud is a model of computing where servers, networks, storage, development tools, and even applications (apps) are enabled through the internet. Instead of organizations having to make major investments to buy equipment, train staff, and provide ongoing maintenance, some or all of these needs are handled by a cloud service provider.

Table 3.2 lists the five key characteristics of cloud computing, according to NIST.

Table 3.2: Key characteristics of cloud computing.

NIST's Key Characteristics of Cloud Computing	Description
Internet Access	Organizations connect to their data and applications via an internet connection.
Measured Service	Cloud is often pay-as-you-go; you only pay for what you use.
On-Demand Self-Service	Services can be requested and obtained rapidly without the need for on-premises hardware.
Shared Resource Pooling	A multi-tenancy model is available; a single application is shared among several users.
Rapid Elasticity	An organization can scale its cloud usage easily to respond to changing needs

Source: NIST.[47]

In basic terms, the cloud provides organizations with the opportunity to outsource some or all of their technology needs to a third-party vendor referred to as a cloud service provider (CSP).

This third-party CSP model creates an opportunity for organizations to eliminate all or a portion of their technology and related activities previously housed within the organization's legacy on-premises centralized IT function. Reducing or eliminating on-premises IT hardware and software applications and relying on CSPs reduces costs associated with buying and periodic maintenance of IT hardware and software applications. Such characteristics of the cloud mark a disruptive and transformational organizational change.

3.3 Outsourcing to Third-Party Cloud Vendors

The concept of outsourcing selected organizational functions, processes or activities to third-party vendors is a common approach to utilizing specialized services, such as payroll processing. In an information technology (IT) context, *CIO Digital Magazine* defines outsourcing as,

> Outsourcing is a business practice in which services or job functions are farmed out to a third party. In information technology, an outsourcing initiative with a technology provider can involve a range of operations, from the entirety of the IT function to discrete, easily defined components, such as disaster recovery, network services, software development or quality assurance testing.[48]

The use of cloud computing vendors is an example of a popular trend in outsourcing IT products and services.

One of the unique and transformational features of cloud computing is the use of third-party cloud service providers (CSPs). According to the NIST, a CSP is,

> A person, an organization; it is the entity responsible for making a service available to interested parties. A Cloud Provider acquires and manages the computing infrastructure required for providing the services, runs the cloud software that provides the services, and makes arrangements to deliver the cloud services to the Cloud Consumers through network access.[49]

Market estimates suggest that over 500 vendors operate in some capacity as a CSP offering a range of cloud services. Amazon AWS, Microsoft Azure, Google Cloud Platform, Alibaba Cloud, Oracle, and IBM are examples of CSPs.

Another category of cloud vendor is a cloud managed service provider (MSP). An MSP assists organizations with managing cloud activities, including managing the organizations' relationships with CSPs. The term "cloud services" refers to a wide range of services delivered by CSPs. The major components of these services are cloud service models and cloud deployment models.

Important differences emerge in a cloud paradigm, as compared to activities historically outsourced. One major difference relates to the roles and responsibilities for decisions concerning how the data and the applications in the cloud are used in the organization. That is, the cloud service vendor (i.e., the CSP) is responsible for supplying and maintaining the hardware and software infrastructure and operating environment on behalf of the organization buying the services. However, the CSP is not responsible for making decisions on how and why the organization deploys the CSP-owned hardware and software. The Society for Computers and Law offers an analogy to explain this concept.

> Rent a computer, which you use yourself to process data; the rental company may have supplied the computer complete with a third party's application software, but the third party could not be said to be 'processing' data for you, when you use the computer to process data.[50]

Another difference is terminology. For instance, the terms third-party service vendor and outsourcing have been replaced by cloud service providers (CSPs) and cloud services, respectively.

3.4 Cloud Service Models

Cloud service models represent CSP offerings to deliver cloud services to organizations. The organization's cloud strategy would determine which cloud service model or models management selects. Table 3.3 presents the three major cloud service models.

Table 3.3: Three major cloud service models.

Cloud Service Model	Description
Infrastructure as a Service (IaaS)	The CSP hosts, delivers, and manages the basic computing infrastructure of servers, software, storage, and network equipment. Organizations only pay for what they use.
Software as a Service (SaaS)	The CSP delivers and manages the infrastructure, operating system, and programming tools and services, which the customer can use to create applications.
Platform as a Service (PaaS)	The CSP delivers and manages one or more applications and all the resources (e.g., operating system and programming tools) and underlying infrastructure, which the customer can use on-demand.

Source: NIST.[51]

Table 3.4 describes other cloud service models that are growing in popularity.

Table 3.4: Additional cloud service models gaining popularity.

Cloud Service Model	Description
Desktop as a Service (DaaS)	Gartner defines this service as "an offering that provides users with an on-demand, virtualized desktop experience delivered from a remotely hosted location. It includes provisioning, patching, and maintenance of the management plane and resources to host workloads."[52]
Business Process as a Service (BPaaS)	Gartner defines this service as "the delivery of business process outsourcing services that are sourced from the cloud and constructed for multi-tenancy. Services are often automated, and where human process actors are required, there is no overtly dedicated labor pool per client. The pricing models are consumption-based or subscription-based commercial terms. As a cloud service, the BPaaS model is accessed via internet-based technologies."[53]
Cloud Management Platforms	Gartner describes these types of platforms as "integrated products that provide for the management of public, private, and hybrid cloud environments. The minimum requirements to be included in this category are products that incorporate self-service interfaces, provision system images, enable metering and billing, and provide for some degree of workload optimization through established policies."[54]

Source: Gartner's IT Glossary.

New cloud service models continue to emerge and increase in popularity as organizations continue to expand their use of the cloud.

3.5 Cloud Deployment Models

An important strategic decision concerning the use of cloud computing is the selection of a cloud deployment model. According to NIST, cloud deployment models describe how the cloud is operated and who has access to the cloud service resources.[55] Table 3.5 lists popular cloud deployment models.

The decision to adopt a specific cloud deployment model is based on a range of variables. For example, the type of cloud environment, the location of the servers providing the services, scale, access, and the relationships between the infrastructure and users. Table 3.6 illustrates adoption rates of cloud services based on the Flexera 2022 State of the Cloud Report.

Table 3.5: Cloud computing deployment models, as adapted from NIST.[56]

Cloud Deployment Model	Description
Single and Multi-Public Cloud	– Available to the public – Owned and operated by a CSP – Multi-cloud means multiple public clouds
Single and Multi-Private Cloud	– Established for one organization; may involve multiple customers within that organization – Maybe on or off-premises – Protected by powerful firewalls
Community Cloud	– Available to the public – Shared by several organizations and supports a specific community that has shared requirements – May be managed by the organization or a third party – May exist on or off-premises – Industry cloud is a type of community cloud. According to InfoWorld, an industry cloud is "a bundle of cloud services, tools, and applications that focus on the most important use cases in a specific industry. The most common industry clouds are designed for the retail, healthcare, government, and finance sectors."[57]
Hybrid Cloud	– A composite of two or more of the three deployment models (private, community, or public) – Bound together by technology that enables data and application portability

Table 3.6: Types of cloud services.

Types of Cloud Services used by Organizations	Percent of Organizations Surveyed (N=753)
– Deploying a multi-cloud strategy	89
– Deploying a hybrid cloud strategy	80
– Using at least on private cloud	79
– Using cloud managed service providers (MSPs)	57
– Running workloads in the public cloud	50

Source: The Flexera 2022 State of the Cloud Report.[58]

3.6 The Organizational Impact of Cloud Computing

Adopting cloud computing at scale can introduce fundamental and transformative changes to how organizations acquire, access, and leverage technology resources. In addition, the cloud has fostered the compression of timeframes designed to acquire, measure, and utilize feedback loops to guide future performance. Some of these changes create opportunities and exacerbate challenges, which can be transformational and disruptive.

Cloud Opportunities and Challenges

The cloud creates a range of strategic opportunities. Table 3.7 presents perspectives on possible opportunities afforded by the cloud.

Table 3.7: Perspectives on the opportunities of cloud computing. Adapted from McKinsey,[59] ITPRC,[60] and Salesforce.[61]

Adapted from McKinsey	Adapted from ITPRC	Adapted from Salesforce
1) Cost optimization: applications, maintenance, IT infrastructure	1) Cost Savings	1) Cost Savings
2) Improved business resiliency and governance	2) Greater Scalability	2) Security
3) Risk reduction	3) Data Backup and Restore	3) Flexibility
4) Digitalize core business operations	4) Data Security	4) Mobility
5) Business model transformation and growth	5) IoT Functionality	5) Insight
6) Agility, democratized access to computer power	6) Enhanced Collaboration	6) Increased Collaboration
7) Innovation-driven growth	7) Positive (Environmental Social Governance (ESG) Impact	7) Quality Control
8) Accelerated product development	8) Employee Engagement	8) Disaster Recovery
9) Hyper-scalability	9) Real-Time Software Updates	9) Loss Prevention
10) Cloud facilities expanded use of technology	10) Big Data Analytics	10) Automatic Software Updates
11) Positioned and enabled to adopt new technologies		11) Competitive Edge
		12) Sustainability

The cloud also creates a range of challenges. Table 3.8 presents perspectives on possible challenges associated with deploying the cloud.

Table 3.8: Perspectives on cloud challenges. Adapted from Conosco,[62] Flexera,[63] Forbes.[64]

Adapted from Conosco	Adapted from Flexera	Adapted from Forbes
1) Security	1) Security	1) Getting It Right
2) Cost	2) Lack of Resources/	2) People and Processes:
3) Legacy Applications	Expertise	Change and Adaptation
4) Downtime	3) Managing Cloud	3) Having a Defined Strategy
5) Vendor Lock-in	Spend	and Business Objectives
6) Technical Knowledge	4) Governance	4) Time, Cost and Security
	5) Managing Software	5) Not Getting Caught Up in The
	Licenses	Hype
	6) Compliance	6) Connecting Legacy Systems
	7) Central Cloud Team/	with Cloud Applications
	Business Unit	7) Modifying the Architecture of
	Responsibility	Cloud Services
	Balancing	8) Translating Security Posture
	8) Cloud Migration	to the Cloud
	9) Managing Multi-Cloud	

A cloud strategy, a cloud migration plan, and a cloud change management plan are crucial to capitalizing on cloud opportunities, achieving desired outcomes, and managing challenges.

Impact of the Cloud on the Organizational Structure

The experience and outcomes of cloud computing, especially over the last 10-15 years, have demonstrated how cloud computing introduces multiple and simultaneous changes to an organization. These changes extend beyond the walls of the traditional IT organization and beyond the walls of the organization.

For instance, the cloud is pressuring organizations to rethink how some of their key operations (e.g., strategy and on-premises IT) and governance functions (e.g., risk management, strategy, compliance) collaborate, interoperate, and share responsibilities with each other and with CSPs. The cloud is also introducing new roles, new responsibilities, prompting the need for hiring and contracting resources with cloud expertise, and highlighting the need to re-skill/upskill employees. Stein, Mezzio et al. (2019) provided the following perspective: "Organizations need to fully understand current processes to assess the scope of needed change and develop effective deployment and change management strategies."[65]

3.7 Conclusion

Understanding the basics of cloud computing and its inexorable growth is fundamental to appreciating the impact it has had on organizations of all sizes regardless of geographic location and industry sector. Deploying the cloud at scale also disrupts and transforms organizational governance strategies, processes, and functions.

Key Questions
1. What is cloud computing?
2. How is cloud computing different from previous technologies?
3. What are CSPs?
4. What are the major cloud service models?
5. What are the major cloud deployment models?
6. What are some of the organizational opportunities and challenges of cloud computing?

Part II: **The Basics of Cloud Governance**

Chapter 4
Cloud Strategy

> Greatness is not where we stand, but in what direction we are moving.[66]
> – Oliver Wendell Holmes, jurist, and legal scholar

Learning Objectives
- Recognize the distinction between a cloud strategic plan and a cloud migration plan
- Understand the factors that can influence a cloud strategic plan and a cloud migration plan
- Understand the linkage of cloud strategy, performance management, and governance
- Recognize cloud strategy and planning challenges and enablers

 Key Terms

1. Root Cause Analysis –"The process of discovering the root causes of problems in order to identify appropriate solutions."[67]
2. Workloads – A collection of applications that interoperate and work together to achieve a designed outcome.

4.1 Introduction

Organizations are striving to strategically optimize the spectrum of potential beneficial outcomes from cloud computing. At the same time, organizations need to manage the disruption and transformation created by the cloud. According to CloudCheckr,

https://doi.org/10.1515/9783110755374-004

> Cloud adoption represents a major IT transformation, a shift in culture, and a new way of financing your infrastructure. It presents new cost and security challenges, requiring governance and control across the organization. It also needs a proactive team to take ownership and direction of the migration process.[68]

In this context, a *cloud strategy*, including a *cloud migration and deployment plan*, is crucial to achieving desired cloud outcomes, cloud performance management, and cloud governance.

However, according to research by Gartner, many organizations are adopting some form of cloud computing without a credible cloud strategy and without an enterprise-wide cloud migration plan.[69] This chapter discusses the nature, content, role, enablers, and challenges associated with designing and deploying a cloud strategy.

4.2 An Evolving Cloud Strategy

Organizations design strategies at a range of levels. For instance, organization-wide, functional strategies (e.g., human resources), and technology strategies (e.g., cloud computing) just to name a few. At a basic level, a strategy consists of a vision (e.g., increase profitability); goals and objectives (e.g., reduce IT costs); desired outcomes (e.g., reduce IT costs by 20%); organizational performance (i.e., increase productivity) and performance management (e.g., use of key performance indictors).

Cloud Strategies Continue to Evolve

Over the past decade, there has been a continued evolution of cloud strategies. For instance, a *cloud-first* strategy and a *cloud-only* strategy. This evolution reflects changing technologies, dynamics, regulations, security breaches, and lessons learned.

The *cloud-first* strategy has been a popular approach for cloud adoption for the past decade. This strategy is rooted in the notion that the cloud should be the first consideration when considering IT transformation. For instance, the following describes the rationale for the U.S. Department of Interior's earlier cloud-first policy.

> The Cloud First Policy was intended to accelerate the pace at which the Federal Government realized the value of cloud computing by requiring agencies to evaluate safe, secure, cloud computing options before making any new investments.[70]

More recently, the cloud-first strategy was joined by a so-called *cloud-smart* strategy.

A cloud-first strategy emphasizes selecting the cloud as a priority (i.e., *first*) above all other options when considering replacements for legacy in-house information technology and applications. According to Gartner, a cloud-*smart* strategy differs by focusing on an approach that is customized to the unique characteristics of the organization.

> The dynamic nature of cloud requires organizations to shift their approach from cloud-first, which prioritizes cloud adoption and legacy modernization above other considerations, to cloud-smart, which balances cloud adoption with the organization's unique circumstances, goals and business value.[71]

KPMG suggests the following macro-level approach for creating a cloud-smart strategy.
- "Defining the cloud as the foundation for digital business
- Scaling cloud across the enterprise
- Aligning talent to build a culture of digital collaboration"[72]

A cloud-smart strategy may include the following questions: *Which infrastructure is best suited for migration to the cloud? Which services? Which applications?*

Defining a Cloud Strategic Plan and Cloud Migration Planning

According to Gartner, "a *cloud strategy* is a concise point of view on the role of cloud within the organization. It is a living document, designed to bridge between a high-level corporate strategy and a cloud implementation/adoption/migration plan."[73] A cloud strategy is designed in a manner similar to any other organizational strategy.

For instance, a cloud strategy would include a vision as to how cloud computing will be deployed within the organization. This vision would include:
- Measurable expected outcomes linked to strategic objectives
- A roadmap for organizational performance to migrate from legacy technology to cloud-based technology, applications, products, and services
- A plan to maintain the equilibrium between the cloud and advanced technologies (e.g., artificial intelligence)

A *cloud migration plan*, also referred to as a cloud adoption or deployment plan, while integral to a cloud strategy is separate and distinct. According to VMware, "a cloud migration plan is the high-level plan an organization adopts to move existing on-premises and/or co-located application workloads and their associated data into the cloud."[74]

Why is this distinction between cloud strategy and cloud migration planning important? A cloud migration plan is designed at a more tactical level. According to McKinsey,

> IT leaders need to weigh the pros and cons of migrating each application or data asset. This often requires extensive dialogue with both cloud-services providers and software vendors so that companies can understand how their offerings are likely to evolve.

> Another key area of focus is managing cybersecurity during and after the transition. Companies should take stock of cloud-service providers' security resources and determine how to adapt their own cybersecurity practices to balance speed and protection.[75]

Migration plans may include multiple migration sub-plans. For instance, data migration, storage migration, application migration, and CSP-selection migration sub-plans.

A range of stakeholders may be responsible for collaborating to create a cloud strategic plan and a cloud migration plan. Such stakeholders may be exclusively internal to the organization, or consist of a combination of internal and external stakeholders. For instance, the Chief Operating Officer (COO), the Chief Information Officer (CIO), the Chief Technology Officer (CTO), and the Chief Financial Officer (CFO). This team may be supported by the legal function, the risk management function, and the internal audit function. Third-party vendors may also contribute to the cloud strategy.

4.3 Cloud Strategic Goals, Objectives and Expected Outcomes

A range of sources inform the decision making and design of a cloud strategy. For instance, the use of a CSP and the nature, scope, and scale of cloud services. As with any other organizational functional-level strategy it is crucial for the cloud strategy to align with the organization-wide business strategy.

Strategic Objectives and Desired Outcomes from Cloud Computing

A range of targeted outcomes from the cloud serve a major role in a cloud strategy. For instance, Table 4.1 presents ITPRC's perspective on the top 10 benefits expected from the cloud.

Table 4.1: Top 10 benefits of the cloud, as adapted from ITPRC.[76]

ITPRC's Top 10 Cloud Benefits	Rationale
1) Cost Savings	CSPs offer centralized IT resources on demand on a pay-as-you-go basis. Such service offerings reduce or eliminate in-house IT infrastructure costs.
2) Greater Scalability	The cloud is scalable; no need to invest in hardware to increase capacity (e.g., storage or computing resources). Instead, negotiate changes with the CSP.
3) Data Backup and Restore	Most CSPs automatically back up and encrypt customer data to the cloud.
4) Data Security	CSPs have built-in security features like role-based authentication, access control, and encryption that can help keep your data secure.
5) IoT Functionality	The cloud can collect IoT data generated by multiple IoT sensors and store it in a single central location where users can monitor it in real-time.
6) Enhanced Collaboration	Cloud data and file storage facilitate remote team collaborations from their devices no matter where they are; they can access and share files from any location and collaborate in real-time.
7) Sustainability/ ESG-Impact Focused	Hosting workloads in the cloud provides an opportunity for organizations to decrease energy consumption by eliminating an on-site data center.
8) Employee Engagement	The cloud supports employee engagement by making remote working possible and providing instant access to IT resources.
9) Real-Time Software Updates	CSPs automatically update software, eliminating the in-house efforts and costs to monitor and update software.
10) Big Data Analytics	The cloud enables the processing of big data analytics and machine learning to develop insights and contribute to decision-making.

The ITPRC benefits are oriented toward the tactical operational benefits of the cloud. In addition to tactical operational benefits, the cloud may also contribute to more macro-level strategy and innovation-oriented benefits. For instance,

Table 4.2 presents strategy and innovation-oriented benefits advanced by McKinsey.

Table 4.2: Benefits of cloud computing, as adapted from McKinsey.[77]

McKinsey's Dimensions of Cloud Value	Associated Cloud Value Drivers
Rejuvenate Break from traditional legacy approaches by using cloud to lower costs and risk across IT operations.	– Cost optimization: applications, maintenance, IT infrastructure – Improved business resiliency and governance – Risk reduction – Digitalize core business operations
Innovate Harness the cloud to accelerate innovative growth and optimize costs across customers, channel segments, and geography.	– Business model transformation and growth – Agility, democratized access to computer power – Innovation-driven growth – Accelerated product development – Hyper-scalability
Pioneer Early adopters of the cloud are more likely to harness the cloud to experiment with other emerging technologies.	– Cloud facilitates expanded use of technology – Positioned and enabled to adopt new technologies

4.4 Developing an Organization-Wide Cloud Strategic Plan

A cloud strategic plan conveys how, why, and when an organization will invest in, introduce, deploy, or escalate existing or new cloud initiatives in order to achieve a targeted set of beneficial outcomes. Numerous frameworks exist to serve as guides for developing a strategic plan. For example, *Harvard Business Review* suggests that most strategic plans consist of the following three major components.

> Strategic plans all tend to look pretty much the same. They usually have three major parts. The first is a vision or mission statement that sets out a relatively lofty and aspirational goal. The second is a list of initiatives—such as product launches, geographic expansions, and construction projects—that the organization will carry out in pursuit of the goal. This part of the strategic plan tends to be very organized but also very long. The length of the list is generally constrained only by affordability. The third element is the conversion of the initiatives into financials. In this way, the plan dovetails nicely with the annual budget.[78]

Gartner created a framework for developing a cloud strategic planning document consisting of 10 major components. Table 4.3 presents these components.

Table 4.3: Framework for developing a cloud strategic plan, as adapted from Gartner.[79]

Major Components of a Cloud Strategy	Guidance
1) Executive Summary	Summarize how the plan demonstrates business value.
2) Cloud Baseline:Terms of Reference	Identify all terms and associated definitions that appear within the cloud strategy to ensure all stakeholders understand the definitions.
3) Business Baseline:Strategic Objectives Mapped to Expected Outcomes and Risks	Present why the organization is migrating to the cloud. – Present what the business is trying to accomplish, and whether it aligns with existing data center/business strategies. – Map the strategic business goals to the potential benefits of the cloud and to associated potential risks.
4) Service Strategy	Define overall service strategy for meeting the organization's technology requirements. – Decisions on if and when to use a CSP versus build or maintain capabilities on premises or elsewhere (public versus private cloud). – Identify benefits and challenges with multi-cloud/hybrid/ public/private alternatives.
5) Financial Considerations	Evaluate and understand the financial impact of migrating from an in-house technology model to a model using CSP pay-as-you-go and/or subscription models.
6) Principles	Explicitly state key principles, such as the following: – Cloud First, Cloud Smart or other cloud strategy. – Key vendor-oriented considerations (skills, cost, etc.). – Leveraging a multi-cloud model and best of breed.
7) Current State Assessment	Inventory and understand the current state of the organization's technology/workloads, including ownership, dependencies and security requirements for the most critical/most expensive.

Table 4.3 (continued)

Major Components of a Cloud Strategy	Guidance
8) Cloud Security	Security is a shared responsibility (e.g., organization and CSP). Identifying roles and responsibilities in detail is critical. Many of the cloud security controls are enabled by an array of configuration options unique to individual CSPs. − While many of the traditional IT security principles and practices apply equally to the cloud, the policies, governance, and assurance requirements may differ. − The security differences created by the cloud should be integrated into the cloud strategy.
9) Supporting Elements/Enablers	A strategy must be aligned with supporting enablers such as staffing, data center, architecture, and, a Cloud Center of Excellence.

10) Exit Strategy from CSP Contracts	It is crucial to have a CSP exit strategy.
	 − Some regulators (e.g., some EU and financial services regulators) mandate the creation of a documented exit strategy.
	 − The exit strategy should focus on answering *what, why, and how* questions, including consideration of the following.
	   − Data ownership
	   − Backup
	   − Getting back your data
	   − Portability

The content of a cloud strategic plan will vary based on the unique attributes of the organization and the nature and scope of the cloud initiative. For example, size, industry sector, and the level of organizational capabilities with cloud computing.

Box 4.1 describes a Capability Maturity Model advanced by Carnegie Mellon University. Such models can help with identifying capability needs (e.g., a cloud-enabled workforce) that will in turn inform cloud strategic goals and objectives.

4.5 Cloud Strategy Challenges and Enablers

As with all strategic plans, a range of factors *enable* effective execution of the cloud strategy. Other factors *challenge* the effectiveness of cloud strategic plans. Predicting the future, an inherent characteristic of all strategies, impacts both the enablers and the challenges.

For instance, cloud strategy predications and assumptions involve key assumptions associated with cloud technology, CSP service levels, risk analysis, organizational performance and much more. Such predications and assumptions are generally based on research and analysis of the previous practices and experiences of other organizations (i.e., best practices and bad practices).

The complexity, lack of long-term experience with the cloud, and the relatively nascent and rapidly changing state of the cloud however increases the uncertainty over such predications. As a result, designing the necessary enablers and managing challenges is a complex process.

Challenges to Cloud Strategy

Many cloud influencers identify cost management, governance (e.g., security risks and compliance risks), and unprecedented levels of reliance on third-party CSPs as part of their cloud top challenges. A number of additional thorny issues associated with human capital, organizational performance, and governance also challenge cloud strategies.

In 2020, the International Data Group (IDG), a provider in market intelligence, conducted a cloud computing survey of over 550 IT professionals. Table 4.4 summarizes the section of the survey results concerning major cloud-related challenges.

Table 4.4: Top cloud challenges, as adapted from 2020 IDG Cloud Computing Survey.[80]

Cloud Challenges, as Reported by IDG	Description
Controlling cloud costs	– Failure to properly measure return on investment (ROI). – Buy-as-you-go and subscription services not managed properly.

Table 4.4 (continued)

Cloud Challenges, as Reported by IDG	Description
Data privacy and security challenges	– Trusting sensitive and proprietary data to CSPs. – Some or all of the organization's technology, applications, software, and data no longer fully reside within the boundaries of the organization. – Delay by the CSP in the notification or lack of notification of a data breach.
Securing/protecting cloud resources	– Cloud misconfigurations. – Lacking transparency into exact location of data storage and processing.
Governance/compliance	– Challenges identifying and complying with multi-jurisdiction (e.g., industry and geography) regulatory requirements. – Inability to demonstrate compliance with regulatory requirements.
Lack of cloud security/management/ development expertise	– Skill gaps for existing employees and inability to access to top talent. – New skills needed to manage and oversee CSP performance. – Understanding the technical and governance issues associated with cloud technology, public cloud service models, and cloud deployment models is essential.
Integrating cloud resources with on-premises systems	– Moving legacy systems to the cloud. – Isolated and segmented cloud deployments.
Migrating data or applications to the cloud	– Hybrid cloud models are complex and require different performance and governance strategies. – Failure to plan for cloud portability and interoperability.
Managing cloud resources	– Failure to appropriately remove data from multiple clouds. – Lack of clear ownership of cloud-generated data. – Inadequate records management, preservation, retention, and disposal policies.

Table 4.4 (continued)

Cloud Challenges, as Reported by IDG	Description
Cultural resistance to cloud adoption	– Ineffective organizational change management for cloud adoption. – Lack of skills and experience to execute strategy.
Mismatch between cloud service offerings and business requirements	– Shared responsibility: CSP standards may not align fully with the organization's requirements. – Organization's performance (e.g., technology and governance) highly dependent on CSPs.
Cloud performance and reliability	– Lack of performance monitoring mechanisms. – Interruption of cloud services due to critical subcontractor failure. – Loss of direct control over and access to the cloud infrastructure. – The performance of the cloud and/or the performance of the CSP may not be in accordance with policies, cloud strategy, and cloud governance requirements. – Lack of real-time monitoring/transparency/ timely alerts by CSP and remediation for outages.

Enablers of Cloud Strategy

Identifying and creating enablers of cloud strategy execution are numerous and varied. Cloud strategy enablers can be categorized at a macro level and at a more tactical micro level. Table 4.5 presents examples of macro-level enablers.

Table 4.5: Enablers of cloud strategy – selected examples.

Macro-Level Cloud Strategy Enablers	Overview
Cloud Center of Excellence (CCoE)	According to TechTarget, – "A CCoE is a multidisciplinary team of experts within an organization. – The team develops and leads a strategy to support successful, uniform cloud adoption. – It also helps business units implement cloud technologies that are secure, efficient and cost-effective."[81]
Cloud Migration Plan	– Integral to the cloud strategic plan, the cloud migration plan is a detailed plan for moving on-premises IT systems to the cloud. – It is a more tactical-level plan (e.g., at the level of each individual application or data set).
Cloud Performance Management	– Provides visibility into the value proposition of cloud adoption. – Such a system is designed to align cloud strategic objectives with expected outcomes and key performance measures (KPIs). – Such KPIs would be monitored, reported and responded to if cloud performance is not meeting expectations.
Flexible Cloud Strategy	– Avoid sticking to a fixed strategy in the face of substantial changes in the competitive and technology environment. – Leverage processes improvements attained through maturity and adoption of best practices and the wisdom generated through the concepts of lessons learned and root cause analysis. – These minor tweaks to process, measurement and communication would be additive to the perceived and real success of the organization on its cloud journey.

Tactical-oriented variables can also contribute to enabling the execution of cloud strategies. Table 4.6 presents *CIO Insight's* perspective on cloud strategy enablers.

Table 4.6: Best practices for cloud implementation, as adapted from *CIO Insight*.[82]

Nine Cloud Enablers	Overview
1) Cloud Governance	Governance over cloud performance, security, compliance.
2) Voice of Cloud Users and Key Stakeholders	Identify and focus on business, technology and support needs and expectations (e.g., access, availability, skills, business needs, etc.).
3) Five Essentials	− On-Demand Self-Service − Broad Network Access − Resource Pooling: Resource consumption can be set to provide more or less at different points of time. − Rapid Elasticity: Provision of scalable services. − Measured Services: Cloud usage is monitored, controlled, reported.
4) Promote Automation to Key Stakeholders	Promote engagement and use of the cloud through examples of how the cloud can contribute to business productivity and efficiency.
5) CSP/Service-Level Management	Manage and govern CSPs and service-level requirements and performance.
6) Govern the Migration to the Cloud	Migrate at a pace that facilitates continuous evaluation of strategy viability, operational and CSP performance, stakeholder feedback, risks and controls.
7) Focus on Enterprise Performance Capabilities	Ensure CSP provides for enterprise-wide capabilities, such as agility and managed/monitored services.
8) CSP Credentials	Ensure CSPs are sufficiently qualified for all aspects of the purchasing relationship.
9) Avoid Over-Committing to One Cloud Category	In terms of private versus public cloud, avoid initially using a private cloud until internal demand increases to the point where a public cloud is needed.

4.6 Conclusion

A *cloud strategic plan*, including a *cloud migration plan*, is crucial to achieving targeted cloud outcomes, performance management, and governance. As with all strategic plans, a cloud strategy and the migration plan should be iterative. That is, continuously monitored and tested by assessing stakeholder and process impacts. This enables greater insights into the validity of initial assumptions, leading to timely refinements with each periodic iteration.

Key Questions
1. What is a cloud strategic plan and how does it differ from a cloud migration plan?
2. How are the strategies for deploying the cloud evolving?
3. What are the key factors influencing the development of the cloud strategy?
4. What are the challenges and enablers of a cloud strategy?

Box 4.1: Capability Maturity Model
A cloud computing strategy should address the organizational capabilities needed to adopt cloud technologies. To support the development of these capabilities, an organization should evaluate the current level of maturity against benchmarks and set prioritized goals for continuous improvement.

Carnegie Mellon University's Software Engineering Institute advanced the Capability Maturity Model (CMM) for organizations to improve and institutionalize their software process. Carnegie Mellon states that "higher degrees of institutionalization translate to more stable processes that are repeatable, produce consistent results, and over time are retained during times of stress."[83] Table 4.7 lists the levels of the Carnegie Mellon Capability Maturity Model and provides examples in context of the cloud.

Table 4.7: Levels of a maturity model, as adapted from Carnegie Mellon University's Software Engineering Institute.

Capability Maturity Model Level[84]	Description	Cloud Examples
Initial	– Lack of organization-wide capabilities – Inconsistent use – No clear stakeholder engagement – No documentation	– No cloud strategy – Fragments cloud use by business unit or by individual employee efforts – Allocates resources discretely (e.g., single workload or project) – No service level agreements – Gaps in cloud skills exist

Table 4.7 (continued)

Capability Maturity Model Level[84]	Description	Cloud Examples
Repeatable	– Approach is not systematic	– Maintains weak cloud security controls – Lacks an understanding of the cloud-shared responsibility model
Defined	– Standard process exists – Some familiarity among stakeholders	– No comprehensive cloud asset inventory exists
Managed	– Monitor and control process – Stakeholder buy-in – Evaluate performance	– Documents cloud strategy – Maintains a strong cloud security program – Documents and enforces service-level agreements (SLAs) – Conducts internal audits of the cloud – Upskills employees on the cloud – Obtains reasonable assurance that CSP complies with international regulations
Optimizing	– Continuous and routine monitoring	– Documents and uses cloud strategy to inform decisions – Establishes Cloud Center of Excellence – Continuously evaluates CSP performance using cloud key performance indicators – Matures incident response capabilities to prevent, detect, and correct cloud breaches – Oversees and communicates financial impact of the cloud – Institutes strong cloud governance

Another resource for organizations to benchmark their maturity is the Open Alliance for Cloud Adoption, which maintains a cloud maturity model.[85]

Chapter 5
Cloud Performance Management

A majority of the obstacles for adoption and growth of cloud computing are related to the basic performance aspects, such as availability, performance, capacity, or scalability.[86]
– Computer Measurement Group, a nonprofit organization of IT professionals

Learning Objectives
- Explain the basic objectives and elements of performance management
- Explain cloud performance management and cloud key performance indicators
- Understand the linkage of cloud strategy and cloud performance management
- Understand that challenges and enablers to cloud performance management

 **Key Terms**

1. DevOps – A compound term combining the terms development (i.e., Dev) and operations (i.e., Ops). Represents the collaboration of information technology operations and capabilities, including software and system development, security, quality, engineering and configuration.
2. Performance Latency – Measurement of the time it takes for data to travel over a network to a designated destination, and return a receipt acknowledgement to the sender.
3. Performance Throughput – The amount of data received or sent over a communication channel (e.g., network).

Chapter Outline

https://doi.org/10.1515/9783110755374-005

5.1 Introduction

Organizations adopt cloud computing to realize a range of strategic beneficial outcomes. For example, technology cost savings and improved operational efficiency. Migrating to the cloud and future operations are, however, replete with issues that challenge cloud success.

In this context, *cloud performance management* plays a pivotal role. Specifically, a role in monitoring, measuring, and responding to best and good practices, as well as shortfalls in progress made on the cloud strategy, including the strategic outcomes expected from the cloud. This chapter discusses the objectives, components, and practices of cloud performance management, including performance indicators.

5.2 Defining Organizational Performance Management

At the organizational level, Gartner defines *performance management* as "the combination of methodologies and metrics that enables users to define, monitor and optimize outcomes necessary to achieve organizational goals and objectives."[87] Performance management consists of an integrated chain of components and activities. Table 5.1 presents examples of some of these components.

Table 5.1: Performance management frameworks – selected examples.

Source	Performance Management Components
Adapted from Otley[88] (1999)	– Objectives – Strategies and plans for the attainment of objectives – Target setting (e.g., outcomes expected from objectives and strategies) – Stakeholder (e.g., employees) performance incentive and reward structures – Information feedback loops (e.g., *actual* progress on performance results against *expected* strategic outcomes)
Adapted from Boston Consulting Group[89] (2017)	Five critical components of a best-in-class performance management system: – Relevant KPIs – Data taxonomy – Integrated management reporting – User-friendly reporting dashboards – Real-time business intelligence/analytics

Numerous performance management frameworks have been advanced over many decades. At a basic level, such frameworks are generally informed by diagnostic questions, such as the questions presented in Table 5.2.

Table 5.2: Performance management framework diagnostic questions – selected examples.

Framework Phase	Category	Performance Management Framework Diagnostic Questions	Example
Strategy and Performance Planning	Strategy	What is our vision/goal?	Migrate to the cloud
	Objectives and Desired Outcomes	What are we trying to achieve?	Reduce infrastructure technology costs by 20 percent.
	Organizational Performance	How will we achieve it through organizational performance, including designing structures and incentivizing behavior?	Cloud vendor performance.
Assess Performance Progress	Measure and Monitor Progress	Are we making progress toward achieving objectives and desired outcomes?	Comparison of actual performance to desired outcomes through the use of cloud performance measures, such as technology cost metrics.
Improve Performance	Respond with Corrective Actions	If we are not making progress, how do we respond (i.e., what to do differently)?	Respond by correcting performance if performance does not meet expectations.

Source: Authors.

Performance management can be applied to any level in a business. For example: the overall organization, a business function, system, an employee, a vendor, or an initiative. McKinsey asserts performance management is essential to the success of a business.

> Through both formal and informal processes, it helps them align their employees, resources, and systems to meet their strategic objectives. It works as a dashboard too, providing an early warning of potential problems and allowing managers to know when they must make adjustments to keep a business on track.[90]

Understanding and optimizing the inherent *strategy-performance management relationship* is crucial the effectiveness of performance management.

5.3 The Strategy-Performance Management Relationship

According to Poister (2003), "Performance management can also be considered part of strategic management on a more practical level."[91] *Why is that?* An inherent and circular strategy-performance management relationship of sorts exists. A relationship whereby the key performance indicators (KPIs) that are integral to performance management play a key role. KPI.org defines KPIs as,

> KPIs are the critical (key) indicators of progress toward an intended result. KPIs provide a focus for strategic and operational improvement, create an analytical basis for decision making and help focus attention on what matters most. As Peter Drucker famously said, "What gets measured gets done."
>
> Managing with the use of KPIs includes setting targets (the desired level of performance) and tracking progress against that target. Managing with KPIs often means working to improve leading indicators that will later drive lagging benefits. Leading indicators are precursors of future success; lagging indicators show how successful the organization was at achieving results in the past.[92]

Two important roles are served by KPIs in the strategy-performance management relationship.

In the first role, KPIs are designed following the design of a strategy and serve in a *strategy-outcome measurement role*. Once the strategy is executed through organizational day-to-day performance, the associated KPIs serve as an early-warning system, reporting progress made on expected strategic outcomes.

In the second role, KPI results circle back to the original strategy to serve in a *strategy-validation role*. If the results of selected KPIs reflect a lack of progress on expected outcomes, the root cause may be the result of a failure in organizational performance (e.g., employees or CSPs fail to perform their role properly). An unachievable strategy, however, may also be the root cause of failing to make progress on the strategy. In this case, KPIs play a crucial role in raising questions about the viability of the strategy or viability of one or more of the strategic objectives.

5.4 Performance Management and Information Technology

As with all functional-level or process-level strategies, it is crucial for an organization's information technology (IT) strategy to include an *IT performance management* process. According to NIST, an objective of *IT performance management* is to measure the success of IT system investments and their impact on strategic outcomes.[93] Implicit in this definition is the relationship between a) *IT performance* (e.g., speed of transaction processing), b) a related KPI (e.g., number of transactions processed per second), and c) a pre-defined expected or targeted outcome of the KPI (minimum of 100 transactions processed per second). Table 5.3 defines key terms in this relationship.

Table 5.3: Definitions of IT performance management, IT performance, and KPIs.

Source	Term	Definition
TechTarget	IT Performance Management	"IT performance management is the supervision of an organization's information technology (IT) infrastructure to ensure that key performance indicators (KPIs), service levels and budgets are in compliance with the organization's goals. The term encompasses purchasing decisions, the standardization of IT equipment and guidance on capital and human resources."[94]
TechTarget	IT Performance	"IT performance encompasses areas such as general system performance, server virtualization and cloud management, application performance monitoring (APM), network management and automation (or self-learning) management."[95]
Gartner	IT Key Performance Indicator (KPI)	"A key performance indicator (KPI) is a high-level measure of system output, traffic or other usage, simplified for gathering and review on a weekly, monthly or quarterly basis. Typical examples are bandwidth availability, transactions per second and calls per user. KPIs are often combined with cost measures (e.g., cost per transaction or cost per user) to build key system operating metrics."[96]

An organization-wide IT performance management framework and KPIs may be used as a benchmark for designing a performance management process for strategies associated with components of the IT strategy. For example, an organization-wide cloud strategy.

5.5 Cloud Performance Management and Key Performance Indicators

According to Techopedia, "Cloud performance management is the practice of assessing various metrics and benchmarks for cloud systems. It is used to determine how well a cloud system is functioning and what improvements can be made to the system."[97] IT and other business performance management frameworks may be used as a guide for designing a cloud performance management process.

The performance indicator component of the strategy-performance management relationship is particularly important to strategies that are new to the organizations (e.g., cloud migration). Table 5.4 presents examples of generic categories of KPIs that may be customized for use as cloud KPIs.

Table 5.4: Categories of generic key performance indicators – selected examples.

Source	Categories of Generic KPIs

Adapted from Investopedia[98]	Business Performance
	– Financial KPIs
	  Measure, and monitor financial metrics, such as cost and return on investment.
	– Business Process KPIs
	  Measure, and monitor operational performance, such as productivity and efficiency.

Adapted from HarvardBusiness Review[99]	Customer Performance Indicators – Impact and outcome metrics that *customers* care about – For example, website availability and first-time resolution of a web issue.

Adapted from BMC.com[100]	IT Performance
	– IT Infrastructure
	  Such as infrastructure downtime, the number of workloads processed, capital and expense cost, resource availability.
	– IT Solutions and Services
	  Such as service uptime, availability, reliability, cost per user, and network outages.
	– IT Service Desk Employees
	  Such as service availability rate, and first call problem resolution rate.
	– Security
	  Such as data breaches, network infringements encountered and deflected, security policy adherence, security training drills, and results.

Performance indicators are helpful for designing business and general IT-oriented cloud performance measures. However, according to Herbst, et al. (2018), the cloud introduces a unique set of unprecedented changes that differ from other technologies.

To make informed choices between competing cloud service providers, permit the cost-benefit analysis of cloud-based systems, and enable system DevOps to evaluate and tune the performance of these complex ecosystems, appropriate performance metrics, benchmarks, tools, and methodologies are necessary.

This requires re-examining old system properties and considering new system properties, possibly leading to the re-design of classic benchmarking metrics such as expressing performance as throughput and latency (response time).[101]

As a consequence, the design of cloud KPIs will require customization. This customization should accommodate the unique characteristics of the cloud. For instance, CSP service-level metrics, changes in employee and customer experience metrics, and cloud-risk metrics.

The nature and scope of KPIs used to measure cloud progress and performance will vary based on the nature and priority of strategic objectives and desired outcomes expected from cloud deployment. Such variables include business process and financial-oriented objectives (e.g., cost savings or greater efficiency), and the cloud maturity level of the organizations (e.g., beginner, intermediate or advanced cloud user). Table 5.5 presents examples of cloud metrics in order of survey respondent ranking reported by Flexera in their 2022 State of the Cloud Report.

Table 5.5: Top cloud initiatives/metrics, as adapted from Flexera 2022 State the Cloud Report.[102]

Top Cloud Initiatives/Metrics	Percentage of Respondents
Cost savings	59
Migrating more workloads to the cloud	57
Move from on-premises software to SaaS	42
Progress on a cloud-first strategy	40
Better financial reporting on cloud cost	38
Automate policies for governance	36
Expand use of containers	35
Manage software licenses in the cloud	33
Expand use of public clouds	33
Expand use of public cloud services (IaaS/PaaS)	31
Implement continuous integration and continuous deployment in the cloud	29
Enable centralized IT to broker cloud services	15
Expand use of cloud managed service providers (MSPs)	12
Expand use of cloud marketplaces	7

Cloud deployment model and service/delivery model-based performance metrics will also be necessary. The nature and scope of performance measures would depend on the deployment models in place (i.e., public, private hybrid cloud) and the cloud service/delivery models. Such service models include Business as a Service, Software as a Service (SaaS), Infrastructure as a Service (IaaS) and Platform as a Service (PaaS).

According to NetApp, "Cloud performance metrics enable you to effectively monitor your cloud resources, to ensure all components communicate seamlessly."[103] Such KPIs are commonly linked to the strategic objectives of cloud *availability*, *performance*, *capacity*, *reliability*, and *scalability*, customized to each cloud model and service. Table 5.6 presents examples of cloud service/delivery objectives and KPIs.

Table 5.6: Cloud service objectives and KPI examples, as adapted from Altarawneh et al., 2019 [104] and Flexera's State of the Cloud Report (2021).[105]

Cloud Service Objective	Service Objective Definition Adapted from Technopedia and TechTarget	Examples of Cloud KPIs
Availability	The ability of a user to access information or resources in a specified location and in the correct format.[106]	Service and System Availability – Mean time between failure – Mean time to repair
Performance	Measures the time and throughput performance of applications. Measures CSP service levels.[107]	Elapsed Time and Throughput – Response time for service – Completion time for tasks – Number of transactions or requests per specified unit of time
Capacity	The maximum amount of data that may be transferred between network locations.[108]	– Service bandwidth – Clock speed of the processor – Storage capacity
Reliability	Reliability includes the following. – The app or service is up and running – Access from any device at any time from any location – No interruptions or downtime – Connection is secure – Able to perform the tasks needed[109]	Percentage of time service or system is working properly over a time period

Table 5.6 (continued)

Cloud Service Objective	Service Objective Definition Adapted from Technopedia and TechTarget	Examples of Cloud KPIs
Scalability	The ability of a process, network, software, or organization to grow, adapt to, and manage increased demand.[110]	– Ability to support a defined or projected growth scenario – Yes or no metric or a metric that defines the upper limit of scalability – Manage software licenses – Move on-premises software to SaaS – Migrating more workloads to the cloud – Progressing on a cloud-first strategy – Expanded use of containers – Increase use of public clouds
Cost	"Cloud sprawl is the uncontrolled proliferation of cloud resources and is to blame for many cloud bill spikes."[111]	– Cost savings – Improved financial analysis of cloud cost

For all such categories, cloud KPIs are designed to evaluate *actual* progress on performance results against *expected* strategic outcomes. Performance indicators would be developed, reported, monitored, and responded to by designated employees at designated intervals.

5.6 Challenges and Enablers of Cloud Performance Management

A number of challenges and enablers impact the effectiveness of cloud performance management. Such challenges and enablers will vary based on the unique characteristics of the organization and the cloud deployment and service strategy, models, and services.

For instance, the uncertainty over the actual number and location of cloud resources and activities across the organization challenges design of a comprehensive and accurate cloud performance management process. According to Symantec's 2019 Cloud Security Threat Report,

> We found that the complexity in the way the cloud is used creates serious visibility prob-
> lems for IT. Tracking these cloud workloads is a universally recognized problem. Ninety
> three percent of survey respondents report they have issues keeping tabs on all their
> cloud workloads. And the problem will continue to grow rapidly.[112]

An inaccurate and outdated baseline of all cloud resources and activities will render cloud performance management ineffective. A cloud management process, including an accurate and real-time cloud inventory, is therefore crucial to effective cloud performance management.

Another example is the inherent complexity of the cloud, which also challenges efforts to measure and manage cloud performance and success. Securing the proper cloud skills and big data analysis skills and tools can help mitigate this challenge. Such skills and support can be hired, contracted with consultants, and/or leveraged from MSPs and CSPs.

The inherent complexity of the cloud also challenges cloud performance management. That is, deciding on what levels of cloud performance should be measured. McKinsey suggests using a framework that consists of the following three major levels.

1) Measure the big picture of the initiative using a small number of KPIs to measure the highest-level strategic goals or ambitions (e.g., use the cloud to improve customer service and reduce infrastructure costs).
2) Measure the journey of the initiative using a series of cascading progress-level metrics (e.g., measuring milestone achievements of the cloud migration plan).
3) Capture, analyze and report progress using all measures to provide transparency and incentivize future performance.[113]

A lack of or inadequate cloud governance-related KPIs is another challenge to comprehensively managing cloud performance. For instance, the common problem of cloud misconfigurations is a major threat to cloud governance, contributing to cloud risk. Security Intelligence defines misconfigurations as,

> Cloud misconfigurations come about when a user or team specifies settings that fail to
> provide adequate security for their cloud data. In the absence of strong security meas-
> ures, attackers can leverage those misconfigurations in an effort to steal cloud data.[114]

Measuring, monitoring, and responding to a comprehensive set of KPIs focused on cloud risks, controls, and incidents are essential contributors to cloud governance. To that end, active participation in the performance management process by the various risk, controls and governance capabilities across the organization is essential.

Many other challenges and enablers should be considered. Securing the relevant knowledge, skills and abilities will contribute to designing an effective cloud performance management process to address challenges and enablers. For instance, expertise in the areas of cloud KPIs; big data analytics, data visualization and reporting tools; market and industry intelligence on best practices and challenges. Creating a cloud center of excellence that includes the performance management process may also be a viable option.

5.7 Conclusion

A diversity of compelling benefits are available through the cloud. At the same time, the cloud creates unintended consequences, exacerbates existing risks, and creates new risks. Optimizing such benefits and managing associated risks requires an agile and trusted process for managing the success, and long-term sustainability of the cloud journey.

Performance management is integral to organizational strategy, success, and governance. Cloud performance management and associated KPIs provide an early warning of the risks of failing to achieve the expected beneficial outcomes from the cloud.

Key Questions
1. What are the basic objectives and elements of cloud performance management?
2. What are the basic objectives and elements of cloud KPIs?
3. Why is the linkage between cloud strategy, cloud governance, and cloud performance management important?
4. What are some of the challenges and enablers to cloud performance management?

Chapter 6
The Basics of Cloud Governance

The more we study the major problems of our time
the more we come to realize that they cannot be understood in isolation.[115]
– Fritjof Capra, physicist

Learning Objectives
- Recognize some of the inherent complexities and uncertainties associated with defining and implementing effective organizational governance
- Understand how cloud governance aligns with cloud strategy, cloud performance, overall organizational strategy, and overall organizational governance
- Explore conceptualizations of a cloud governance business process ecosystem

 Key Terms

1. Business Process Ecosystem – "a mix of human and non-human species – to operate and maintain itself in a region of emergent complexity, a region bounded by stasis and chaos."[116]
2. Lifecycle Process – The lifecycle of the cloud begins on the maturity path when an organization decides to adopt the cloud and follows its growth into a mature technology that drives digital transformation for the business.

Chapter Outline

https://doi.org/10.1515/9783110755374-006

6.1 Introduction

Organizational governance plays a crucial role in optimizing cloud strategic objectives, achieving performance, and managing risk. The organizational disruption and change effects of the cloud, however, stress corporate governance in a number of ways.

This chapter explores how cloud governance is defined; the crucial linkages of cloud governance to cloud strategy; cloud performance; organization-wide strategy and governance; and cloud-shared responsibilities. This chapter also advances and discusses a basic conceptualization of a cloud governance business process ecosystem.

6.2 Defining Corporate Governance

The *Oxford Advanced Learner's Dictionary* states that the word *governance* is derived from the Greek "kubernan," which means "to steer."[117] *Webster's Dictionary* defines governance as "the act or process of governing or overseeing the control and direction of something (such as a country or an organization)."[118]

Defining Corporate Governance

This chapter focuses on governance in an organizational setting, often referred to as *corporate governance*. Table 6.1 presents several definitions of corporate governance.

Table 6.1: Definition of corporate governance – selected examples.

Source	Definition of Corporate Governance
The Future of Corporate Governance: A Personal Odyssey[119]	Corporate governance describes the way trust is shown, power exercised, and accountability achieved in corporate entities for the benefit of their members, other stakeholders, and society.

Table 6.1 (continued)

Source	Definition of Corporate Governance
Organisation for Economic Co-operation and Development[120] (OECD)	Corporate governance involves a set of relationships between a company's management, its board, its shareholders and other stakeholders. Corporate governance also provides the structure through which the objectives of the company are set, and the means of attaining those objectives and monitoring performance are determined.
International Finance Corporation (IFC) of the World Bank Group[121]	Corporate governance focuses on how companies are directed, governed, and controlled. It defines relationships between a company's management, its board, its shareholders, and other stakeholders.
Institute of Chartered Accountants in England and Wales[122]	The purpose of corporate governance is to facilitate effective, entrepreneurial and prudent management that can deliver the long-term success of the company. Corporate governance is the system by which companies are directed and controlled. Boards of directors are responsible for the governance of their companies. The shareholders' role in governance is to appoint the directors and the auditors and to satisfy themselves that an appropriate governance structure is in place.
Investopedia[123]	Corporate governance essentially involves balancing the interests of a company's many stakeholders, such as shareholders, senior management executives, customers, suppliers, financiers, the government, and the community. Since corporate governance also provides the framework for attaining a company's objectives, it encompasses practically every sphere of management, from action plans and internal controls to performance measurement and corporate disclosure.

Defining IT Governance

Information Technology (IT) governance is an integral component of corporate governance. That is, organizational governance should govern both business objectives and IT objectives in an integrated manner. Table 6.2 presents two enduring definitions of IT governance.

Table 6.2: Definition of IT governance – selected examples.

Source	Definition of IT Governance
Van Grembergen[124]	IT governance is the organizational capacity exercised by the board, executive management and IT management to control the formulation and implementation of IT strategy, in this way ensuring the fusion of business and IT.
Mitre[125]	IT governance is an integral part of overall corporate governance enterprise governance and consists of the leadership and organizational structures and processes that ensure that the organization's IT sustains and extends the organization's strategies and objectives.

A range of IT governance frameworks are available to help integrate the unique governance considerations associated with IT into an overall corporate governance strategy. For example, the International Organization for Standardization created Standard 38500:20015, *Information Technology – Governance of IT for the Organization,* "to promote effective, efficient, and acceptable use of IT in all organizations by:
- Assuring stakeholders that, if the principles and practices proposed by the standard are followed, they can have confidence in the organization's governance of IT.
- Informing and guiding governing bodies in governing the use of IT in their organization.
- Establishing a vocabulary for the governance of IT."[126]

Table 6.3 presents the six principles for IT governance advanced in Standard ISO 38500:20015.

Table 6.3: Principles for IT governance, as adapted from ISO 38500:2015.[127]

ISO 38500:2015 IT Governance Principles	Overview
Principle 1: Responsibility	Individuals and groups within the organization understand and accept their responsibilities in respect of both supply of, and demand for IT. Those with responsibility for actions also have the authority to perform those actions.
Principle 2: Strategy	The organization's business strategy takes into account the current and future capabilities of IT; the strategic plans for IT satisfy the current and ongoing needs of the organization's business strategy.
Principle 3: Acquisition	IT acquisitions are made for valid reasons, on the basis of appropriate and ongoing analysis, with clear and transparent decision making. There is appropriate balance between benefits, opportunities, costs, and risks, in both the short term and the long term.
Principle 4: Performance	IT is fit for purpose in supporting the organization, providing the services, levels of service and service quality required to meet current and future business requirements.
Principle 5: Conformance	IT complies with all mandatory legislation and regulations. Policies and practices are clearly defined, implemented and enforced.
Principle 6: Human Behavior	IT policies, practices and decisions demonstrate respect for human behavior, including the current and evolving needs of all the "people in the process."

6.3 Strategy and Governance Misalignments

A crucial role served by organizational governance protocols is *governing* the achievement of strategic objectives, execution of organizational performance, and mitigation of associated risks. According to the OECD, "Corporate governance also provides the structure through which the objectives of the company are set, and the means of attaining those objectives and monitoring performance are determined."[128]

Yet, cases of *strategy-governance misalignments* persist. That is, a silo approach is, at times, taken in the development and execution of organizational strategy, and the development and execution organizational governance. *Why is that?* Capasso and Dagnino (2012) provided the following perspective on such a question that continues to be relevant today,

> Notwithstanding the received body of studies, respectively, in the corporate governance field and in the strategic management domain, current business practice brings to light a myriad

of intriguing cases and instances in which the relationship between the entrepreneurial role (or strategy formulation and execution) and the governance function underscores the existence of uncertain situations and dangerous juxtapositions, which can turn out hazardous conflicts of interest suitable to jeopardize the virtuous running of the firms' value creation process as a whole.

Why is it so? In our understanding, the basic reason why the fundamental relationship between corporate governance and strategic management has not been heretofore explained in detail lays in the condition that corporate governance and strategic management have suffered from artificial separation. This artificial separation has been driven by the "silo view" of corporate governance and strategic management.[129]

A case in point on recognizing the importance of the strategic-governance alignment is the Committee of Sponsoring Organizations of the Treadway Commission's (COSO) enterprise risk management (ERM) framework titled *Enterprise Risk Management – Integrating with Strategy and Performance*. This COSO ERM framework explicitly states the importance of integrating risk management with governance in strategy setting and performance management.[130]

Crucially, organizational *strategy*, including cloud strategy, should integrate business objectives and risks and information technology (IT) objectives and risks. In turn, organizational *governance*, including cloud governance, should integrate both business objectives and risks and IT objectives and risks.

6.4 Defining Cloud Governance and Conceptualizing a Cloud Governance Business Process Ecosystem

This reference book focuses on basic concepts and real-world practices of cloud governance. This section presents working definitions of *cloud governance*, and a basic, macro-level conceptualization of a *cloud governance business process ecosystem*. The topics of each of the individual chapters of this book represent individual and interconnected components of this ecosystem.

Defining Cloud Governance

Numerous definitions of cloud governance exist. Table 6.4 presents the touchstone definition of cloud governance selected for this reference book.

This definition captures the business-side and the IT side of cloud strategy and, therefore, corporate and cloud governance. Moreover, this definition integrates some of the crucial enablers of effective cloud governance. For instance, accountability; responsibility (e.g., policies); strategy (e.g., value); risk management,

Table 6.4: Definition of cloud governance.

Source	Definition of Cloud Governance
Thuraisingham[131]	Cloud computing governance is a view of IT governance focused on accountability, defining decision rights and balancing benefit or value, risk, and resources in an environment embracing cloud computing. Cloud computing governance creates business-driven policies and principles that establish the appropriate degree of investments and control around the lifecycle process for cloud computing services.

environmental and IT context influences; fit for purpose (e.g., adequate resources); and building stakeholder trust.

Conceptualizing a Cloud Governance Ecosystem

Leveraging this definition of cloud governance as a springboard, we created a high-level conceptualization of a *cloud governance business process ecosystem.* Our definition of a cloud governance business process ecosystem is broadly based on the definition advanced by Vidgen and Wang (2006),

> "a mix of human and non-human species – to operate and maintain itself in a region of emergent complexity, a region bounded by stasis and chaos. Further, managers must recognize that they are embedded within the ecosystem and that they are themselves shaped by, as well as shaping, the ecosystem."[132]

This cloud governance ecosystem model was also influenced by the Technological, Organizational and Environmental (TOE) theoretical framework advanced by DePietro et al. (1990).[133] This cloud governance business process ecosystem consists of the following major elements.

1. Alignment of organizational strategy and performance with cloud strategy and performance
2. Alignment of organizational governance with cloud governance
3. Shared responsibility relationships for cloud governance necessitated by the cloud
4. Organizational governance functions with newfound cloud governance roles
5. Integration of the influence of context on cloud governance
   - Technological context influencing the cloud
   - Organizational context influencing the cloud
   - Environmental context influencing the cloud

Creating a conceptualization of a cloud governance ecosystem is in a way a *wicked problem*. Part of the problem is that confusion, uncertainties, and disagreements often emerge among key stakeholders over the role and application of corporate governance in practice. According to *Harvard Business Review*,

> How corporations govern themselves has become a matter of broad public interest in recent decades. Amid this many commentators and experts still disagree on such basic matters as the purpose of the corporation, the role of corporate boards of directors, the rights of shareholders, and the proper way to measure corporate performance.[134]

Another part of the problem is that theories and concepts associated with corporate governance are in many ways complex, nebulous, confusing and difficult to translate into real-world practice.

In this context, the authors of this book acknowledge that the cloud ecosystem advanced in this book is not intended to be a holistic and micro-level view. Instead, it is designed to create a macro-level practical starting point to gain a basic understanding of cloud governance, which is a complicated and contentious topic.

Table 6.5 conceptualizes each of the components of the cloud governance ecosystem advanced in this chapter. Figure 6.1 visually depicts the relationships among the cloud ecosystem components.

Table 6.5: Conceptualization of cloud governance ecosystem.

Cloud Governance Ecosystem Component	Overview
1. Cloud Governance Working Definition	Cloud computing governance is a view of IT governance focused on accountability, defining decision rights, and balancing benefit or value, risk, and resources in an environment embracing cloud computing. Cloud computing governance creates business-driven policies and principles that establish the appropriate degree of investments and control around the lifecycle process for cloud computing services.[135]

Table 6.5 (continued)

Cloud Governance Ecosystem Component	Overview
2. Cloud-Shared Responsibility Model	A conceptual model that defines, divides, and allocates distinct responsibilities for assigned elements of cloud governance to the four distinct cohorts of organizational stakeholders. – Authorized Cloud-Democratized Employees – Employees Engaged in Shadow Cloud Activities – Third-Party Cloud Vendors – Organizational Governance Functions
3. Organization's Governance Functions	The following governance functions are disrupted and transformed by the cloud: – The Board of Directors – Compliance – Security – Incident Response – Enterprise Risk Management – Risk Assessment – Internal Audit – Third-Party Assurance
4. Technological Context	"Represents the internal and external technologies related to the firm."[136]
5. Organizational Context	"Related to the resources and the characteristics of the firm."[137]
6. Environmental Context	"Refers to the arena in which a firm conducts its business."[138]

Source: Authors.

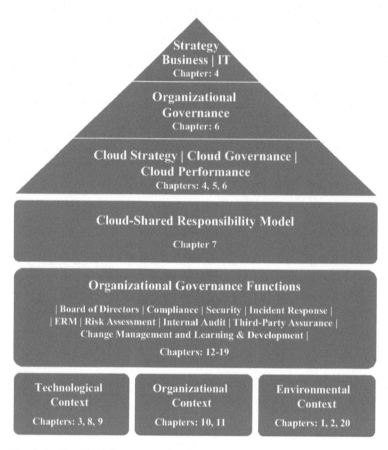

Figure 6.1: The Cloud Governance House: A Perspective on the Cloud Governance Ecosystem.
Source: Authors.

These cloud governance ecosystem components are depicted in a Cloud Governance House. The foundation of the Cloud Governance House is the operating context of cloud governance (i.e., technological, organizational and environmental context). The roof of the house is the organization's strategy (i.e., interrelated business strategy, IT strategy and cloud governance strategy). The rooms of the house are the cloud shared-responsbility model and the organizational governance functions (e.g., the board, compliance, internal audit, etc.).

6.5 Conclusion

Cloud governance plays a crucial role in optimizing cloud strategic objectives and managing cloud risks. Yet, theories and concepts associated with corporate governance are in many ways complex, nebulous, confusing, and difficult to translate into real-world practice. A practical definition of cloud governance and a customized characterization of the major components comprising an organization's cloud governance ecosystem can reduce such bewilderment and consternation.

Key Questions
1. How do academia and practice define cloud governance?
2. How does context influence cloud governance?
3. What are some of the inherent complexities and uncertainties associated with defining and implementing effective organizational governance?
4. Why is it essential for cloud governance to align with cloud strategy, overall organizational strategy, and organizational governance?

Chapter 7
Cloud Computing and the Shared Responsibility Model

The price of greatness is responsibility.[139]
– Winston Churchill, former Prime Minister of the United Kingdom

Learning Objectives
- Understand the concept of a shared responsibility model in the context of cloud computing
- Consider the practical implications of deploying a cloud-shared responsibility model

 Key Terms

1. Democratization of IT – Describes a paradigm where employees outside of the organization's centralized IT department are empowered to engage directly with cloud activities, including outsourcing CSP services.
2. IT Governance Protocols – "The system by which the current and future use of IT is directed and controlled."[140]
3. On-premises/in-house IT Department – The utilization of internal resources to operate the technology functions instead of outsourcing technology services to a vendor.
4. Shadow IT – Represents employees throughout the organization who are not authorized to adopt, create, and deploy cloud and other IT activities and do so under the radar and outside of the ownership of the in-house centralized IT department.

Chapter Outline

https://doi.org/10.1515/9783110755374-007

7.1 Introduction

The cloud disrupts and transforms the manner in which technology, applications, and data are deployed, accessed, managed, and governed. A major element of this disruption is the emergence of a cloud-shared responsibility model. This chapter defines a cloud-shared responsibility model and discusses the impact of shared responsibilities on cloud governance.

7.2 Market Definitions of a Cloud-Shared Responsibility Model

Deployment of the cloud at scale disrupts an organization's traditional IT operations, including IT governance. The primary reason for this disruption is the shifting of certain important responsibilities from the organization's on-premises IT functions to third-party CSPs.

An on-premises (i.e., in-house) IT department or function represents an organization's centralized internal resources that are primarily responsible for deploying, managing, and governing the organization's IT operations (e.g., infrastructure, software, applications and data). In the context of the cloud, some cloud responsibilities are now located partly in-house and some are allocated to third-party vendors (e.g., CSPs). This paradigm shift is commonly referred to in the cloud domain as a *shared responsibility model*.

A range of definitions of cloud-shared responsibility models have been advanced in practice. Table 7.1 presents examples of these definitions.

Table 7.1: Definitions of a cloud-shared responsibility model – selected examples.

Source	Definition of a Cloud-Shared Responsibility Model
TechTarget[141]	A cloud security framework that dictates the security obligations of a cloud computing provider and its users to ensure accountability.
Threatscape[142]	A globally accepted cloud security framework that reflects the security obligations and responsibilities of your cloud provider and those that belong to you, the customer.
Cloud Security Alliance[143]	Your security team maintains some responsibilities for security as you move applications, data, containers, and workloads to the cloud, while the provider takes some responsibility, but not all.

Two common threads running through these definitions are the sharing of responsibilities between the organization (i.e., cloud customer) and the third-party CSP, with an emphasis on cloud *security*.

7.3 Expanded Conceptualization of a Cloud-Shared Responsibility Model

In the context of cloud governance, this book posits a conceptual definition of a *cloud-shared responsibility model* that encompasses more than just third-party cloud vendors. Instead, this book posits cloud-shared responsibility as conceptual model that defines, divides, and allocates distinct material responsibilities for cloud governance to the following four cohorts of organizational stakeholders.

1) Democratized Employees Outside of the IT Function Authorized to Engage with the Cloud

Democratized IT, including the cloud, represents organizational employees outside of the in-house IT function authorized to engage directly with cloud activities, including outsourcing CSP services. According to *Harvard Business Review*, "Companies that want to compete in the age of data need to do three things: share data tools, spread data skills, and spread data responsibility."[144]

In such circumstances, management should define shared responsibilities between employees and establish associated cloud governance policies and functions (e.g., centralized IT department, compliance department, etc.). In this context, a cloud-shared responsibility model would create policies and define roles and responsibilities for employees interacting directly with the cloud and with CSPs.

2) Employees Engaging in Unsanctioned (i.e., Shadow) Cloud Activities

Shadow IT activities, including cloud activities, represents the unauthorized and unknown use of cloud activities by organizational employees outside of the purview of the centralized IT function and organizational governance functions. According to Gartner, most organizations grossly understate the number of shadow IT applications already in use.[145]

In such circumstances, management should define shared responsibilities between employees and establish associated cloud governance policies and functions (e.g., centralized IT department, compliance department, etc.).

3) Organizational Governance Functions with Cloud-Governance Responsibilities

Most organizational governance functions are responsible for selected elements of IT governance. For example, the compliance, security, and ERM functions often coordinate and collaborate on efforts to share responsibilities for managing risks to strategic IT objectives (e.g., data privacy).

The rapid deployment of the cloud at scale has heightened the need for such shared responsibilities. As a result, management must transform the organization's governance functions to account for these shared responsibilities to address the unique complexities brought about by the cloud.

4) Third-Party Cloud Vendors (e.g., CSP)

A CSP relationship *extends* organizational boundaries. According to Deloitte, "Executives extend the enterprise every time they use a cloud service, outsource a business process, or otherwise spread operations beyond the traditional four walls of their organization."[146] This paradigm is commonly referred to as the *extended organization*.

The deployment of the cloud at scale often involves the procurement of services from CSPs and other third-party vendors and therefore substantial and rapidly *extends* an organization's governance processes beyond the boundaries of the organization. This cloud-extended organization creates a complex web of distributed, interconnected, and interdependent shared-responsibility stakeholders, including employees (i.e., first party), customers (i.e., second party), vendors, and their hired subcontractors (i.e., third, fourth, and fifth parties). Figure 7.1 depicts this complex web of extended relationships.

To share and harmonize in-house IT cloud responsibilities with a CSP, an organization needs to determine: 1) Which responsibilities will be allocated to the CSP, 2) Whether the CSP is qualified to take on these roles, 3) Whether the CSP can be trusted to take on these roles responsibly and reliably, and 4) Whether the CSP will provide evidence of accountability.

Who has Overall and Primary Responsibility for Cloud Governance?

In spite of deploying a shared responsibility model for cloud governance with third-party vendors (e.g., CSPs), the organization (i.e., the cloud customer) – not the CSP – has the primary responsibility for the governance of the cloud. According to Lane et al. (2017),

> While most cloud service providers promise that "reasonable" care is undertaken to minimize the risks to data security and privacy, the onus of doing due diligence of a cloud service provider's security practices is very much the responsibility of the organisation itself.[147]

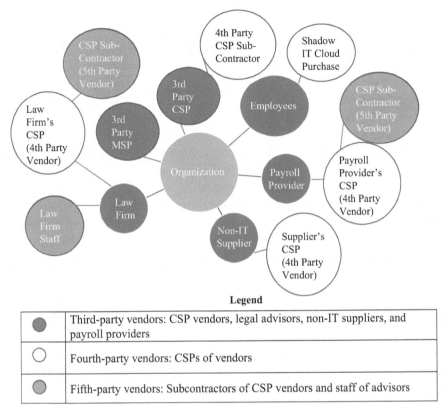

Figure 7.1: Extended-enterprise: web of data sharing in the cloud computing domain. Source: Authors.[148]

Both the CSP and the organization are responsible for monitoring the integrity, availability, and operations of the cloud. The organization, however – not the CSP – has the primary responsibility and will be held fully accountable by regulators and other key stakeholders for the proper operation, performance, and governance of the cloud.

7.4 Implications of Deploying a Cloud-Shared Responsibility Model

A cloud-shared responsibility model disrupts an organization's IT governance protocols that have been fortified and successfully used over many years. *Why is that?*

According to Nollkaemper (2018), "shared responsibility is generally regarded as having the potential to address responsibility gaps in situations of concerted action."[149] *Concerted action*, in this case, is defined as jointly planning a coordinated strategy of shared responsibilities to meet predefined and agreed-upon objectives and outcomes. In this context, a cloud-shared responsibility model is crucial for defining distinct responsibilities among the organizational stakeholders (e.g., CSPs) and for reducing responsibility gaps.

Large-scale shared responsibilities generally do not exist under a traditional, in-house IT department that limits its engagement in third-party outsourcing. A new cloud-shared responsibility model, therefore, requires a clear distinction and definition of roles and responsibilities between the organization and key stakeholders sharing responsibilities with the organization (e.g., CSPs). According to the CSA, "Defining the line between your responsibilities and those of your providers is imperative for reducing the risk of introducing vulnerabilities into your public, hybrid, and multi-cloud environments."[150]

Management should be sensitive to grey areas to avoid misinterpretation and inadequately execute the cloud's shared responsibilities. Moreover, irrespective of shared responsibility with third-party vendors, the organization has overall and primary responsibility for cloud governance. Organizations are therefore held fully accountable and liable for cloud governance, including compliance with laws and regulations.

7.5 Conclusion

Deployment of the cloud at scale using CSPs creates a need for greater reliance on a shared responsibility model for cloud governance. The extent of such shared responsibilities did not exist in a pre-cloud model when IT systems were primarily owned, operated, and governed by the organization and located entirely on-premises. Instead, some responsibilities are now *shared* with CSPs, as well as organizational employees, and organizational governance functions with cloud responsibilities.

Organizations must identify key stakeholder cohorts that will share responsibilities for cloud governance, define responsibilities, and hold these cohorts accountable for their share of cloud governance. Crucially, the organization has overall and primary responsibility for cloud governance, irrespective of shared responsibility arrangements with third-party vendors.

Key Questions
1. What are example definitions of a cloud-shared responsibility model?
2. What are the practical implications to consider of deploying a cloud-shared responsibility model?

Part III: **The Organizational and IT Context of Cloud Governance**

Chapter 8
Cloud Vendors and the Organization's In-House IT Function

> As consumers, we have so much power to change the world
> by just being careful in what we buy.[151]
> – Emma Watson, English actress and activist

Learning Objectives
- Understand how the cloud impacts an organization's in-house IT function
- Identify the role of cloud vendors
- Understand the criteria used to select cloud service providers (CSPs), managed service providers (MSPs), and managed security service providers (MSSPs)
- Awareness of mechanisms available to govern cloud costs and return on investment (ROI)

 Key Terms

1. Availability – "The time that the data center is accessible or delivers the intend IT service as a proportion of the duration for which the service is purchased."[152]
2. Cloud Management – "A combination of software, automation, policies, governance, and people that determine how cloud computing services are made available. Cloud management is how administrators control and orchestrate all the products and services that operate in a cloud: the users and access control, data, applications, and services."[153]
3. Cloud Native – "An approach to designing, constructing, and operating workloads that are built in the cloud and take full advantage of the cloud computing model."[154]
4. Concentration Risk – "Risk that may arise from relying on a single third party for multiple activities"[155]
5. At Scale – "At the required size to solve the problem. At scale typically refers to handling larger volumes."[156]
6. Exit Strategy – "A corporate plan developed to ensure that the cloud services that support business activities can be replaced or replicated efficiently, without significant disruption."[157]

https://doi.org/10.1515/9783110755374-008

7. Hyperscaler – "Companies who have built global networks of data centers that support an increasingly large share of the cloud service market."[158]
8. Reliability – "The probability that the system will meet certain performance standards in yielding correct output for a desired time duration."[159]
9. Scalability – "The ability to support more users, concurrent sessions, and throughput than a device can handle."[160]
10. Service Roadmap – A timeline for the development, delivery, and evolution of a solution.
11. Vendor Lock-in – Occurs when organization using a cloud product or service cannot easily transition to a competitor CSP.

Chapter Outline

8.1 Introduction
8.2 The Impact of the Cloud on the Organization's In-House IT Function
8.3 Cloud Vendors
8.4 Criteria for Selecting a Cloud Vendor
8.5 Cloud Service-Level Agreements
8.6 Conclusion

8.1 Introduction

Procuring cloud services from third-party vendors (e.g., CSPs) disrupts an organization's in-house IT function. This chapter discusses the impact that cloud strategy has on the role of the in-house IT function. This chapter also explores selection criteria organizations may use to procure cloud services from third-party cloud vendors (e.g., CSPs).

8.2 The Impact of the Cloud on the Organization's In-House IT Function

Transitioning to the cloud disrupts an organization's in-house IT function. Fuzes (2018) portrays a traditional on-premises (i.e., in-house) IT function as follows.

> Traditionally, companies owned the IT systems they used. They built their own data center, purchased the hardware (servers, storage) and software components for different layers of the software architecture, and developed customized solutions according to their business needs. The IT systems were usually installed within the premises of the customer. Hence this is called the on-premise model.[161]

Deploying the cloud at scale transforms the *pre-cloud* in-house IT function. *Why is that?* According to Choudhary and Vithayathil (2013),

> As more services are procured from cloud vendors, the need for functions within the IT department that serve to administer, monitor, and maintain the IT infrastructure will be considerably diminished or even eliminated.[162]

How does the in-house IT function change? According to Deloitte,

> There is a fundamental mindset shift from an IT command-and-control center model to a customer-centric IT-as-a-service model where IT is supporting a customer-centric, product-focused operating model. This marks a shift from centralized operations support to embedded operations capabilities.[163]

An *IT-as-a-service* model describes the procurement of cloud services from a CSP to provide all or a portion of the organization's IT needs.

The Cloud and IT-Democratized Front-Line Employees

An *IT-as-a-service* model often empowers front-line employees with the authorization to engage directly with the cloud activities, including procuring vendor services (e.g., CSPs). According to Choudhary and Vithayathil (2013),

> Under cloud computing, the IT department may need to increase the focus on adding value to the incoming cloud-based services. The mission of the IT department would transition to determining the means by which the IT personnel can ensure that enhancements to cloud-based services fit the current and future needs of the consuming units.[164]

Harvard Business Review echoes this sentiment with the idea that business unit managers "should have authority of *what* services are delivered and IT should have authority of *how* the services are delivered."[165]

Impact of the Cloud on the Role and Skills of the CIO and the In-House IT Function

The cloud transforms the role and skills of the in-house IT function. For instance, the leadership of the in-house IT function (e.g., Chief Information Officer) will often play a substantial role in identifying actions necessary to harmonize the IT function with the cloud strategy. According to K2 Partnering Solutions, a global technology recruitment firm, "CIOs must develop more managerial and strategic skills to drive the organization's cloud computing solutions. The CIO will be the person in charge of expanding a multi-cloud strategy, which means they must consider aspects such as security, service integration, and cost."[166] Figure 8.1 presents a summary of some of the major evolutionary changes over time in the role served by a CIO role – adapted from Deloitte.

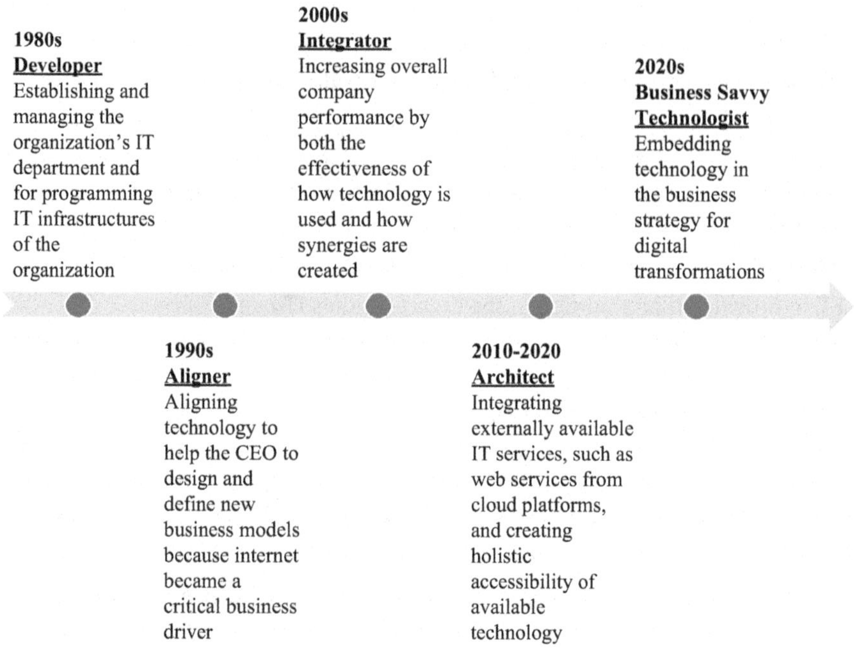

1980s
Developer
Establishing and managing the organization's IT department and for programming IT infrastructures of the organization

2000s
Integrator
Increasing overall company performance by both the effectiveness of how technology is used and how synergies are created

2020s
Business Savvy Technologist
Embedding technology in the business strategy for digital transformations

1990s
Aligner
Aligning technology to help the CEO to design and define new business models because internet became a critical business driver

2010-2020
Architect
Integrating externally available IT services, such as web services from cloud platforms, and creating holistic accessibility of available technology

Figure 8.1: CIO role, by decade, as adapted from Deloitte.[167, 168]

See Box 8.2 for additional insights on the cloud and the future of CIOs.

The in-house IT function may also take the lead or have a seat at the table in key decisions and material changes resulting from deploying the cloud at scale, including the following.

– Designing the cloud strategy
– Selecting a CSP vendor
– Adding incremental value to cloud services procured from CSPs
– Facilitating the cloud integration, deployment, change management, and training
– Determining and enforcing cloud governance responsibilities shared with CSPs

According to *CIO Digital Magazine*, "The cloud may provide the largest push yet for IT professionals to take on more business skills. IT professionals who want to keep their jobs will need to contribute to the business in new ways, and that means becoming technology strategists."[169]

8.3 Cloud Vendors

A cloud ecosystem is often comprised of a range of vendors providing distinct cloud services. Table 8.1 lists examples of the cloud vendor roles and services.

Table 8.1: Categories of cloud vendors.

Cloud Vendor Type	Cloud Roles and Services

Full-Service CSPs, including Hyperscalers	Market estimates suggest that over 500 vendors operate in some capacity as full-service CSPs offering public, private, and hybrid cloud services.
	Hyperscalers are CSPs that have a large share of the cloud market.
	  – Hyperscalers are portrayed in the market as industry leaders because of their unique market share, which in turn enables them to offer services that improve scalability, interoperability, and compliance capabilities with evolving regulatory requirements.
	  – Hyperscalers include Amazon AWS, Microsoft Azure, Google Cloud Platform, Alibaba Cloud, Oracle, IBM, and Tencent Cloud.

Managed Private CSP	According to Red Hat, private cloud providers serve customers a private cloud that's deployed, configured, and managed by someone other than the customer. It is a delivery option that helps enterprises with understaffed or under skilled IT teams provide better private cloud services and cloud infrastructure to users."[170]

Table 8.1 (continued)

Cloud Vendor Type	Cloud Roles and Services
Managed Service Providers (MSP)	MSPs help organizations manage cloud services, including managing CSPs. Such MSP vendors provide organizations with continuous, regular management, maintenance, and support. Examples of MSP-related services include: – Network monitoring – System management – Human resources – Assessing service-level compliance by CSP – Data backup and disaster recovery (storage only) – Email server hosting – Patch management – Hardware updates – Software installations
Managed Security Service Provider (MSSP)	According to Gartner, an MSSP "provides outsourced monitoring and management of security devices and systems. Common services include managed firewall, intrusion detection, and vulnerability scanning."[171]

Source: Authors.

8.4 Criteria for Selecting a Cloud Vendor

A cloud strategy often defines cloud deployment and cloud service model objectives. The primary cloud services provided by vendors include PaaS, SaaS, and IaaS. Other services include Desktop as a Service, Cloud Business Process Services, and Cloud Management and Security Services.

A number of criteria inform management's decision concerning which cloud vendor or vendors to select. Tables 8.2 and 8.3 list examples of selection criterion.

Table 8.2: Definitions of Cloud Industry Forum's selection criteria.

Cloud Industry Forum's Vendor Selection Criteria[172]	Cloud Governance Implications
Certifications and Standards	– CSP provides evidence to adhere to industry best practices, and compliance with standards and frameworks.

Table 8.2 (continued)

Cloud Industry Forum's Vendor Selection Criteria[172]	Cloud Governance Implications
Technologies and Service Roadmap	– Quality and availability of CSP technology services and deployment models align with the organization's cloud strategy. – CSP provides a comprehensive cloud service roadmap. A service roadmap answers "three essential questions: Where are we now? Where do we want to go? and How can we get there?"[173]
Data Security, Data Governance, and Business Policies	– Poorly designed policies can lead to poor fiscal performance, compliance, regulatory fines and penalties, and destruction of reputation and stakeholder trust. – Management should understand the proposed location and transfer process of data across jurisdictions, regions, states, and countries. – For example, to reduce the risk of a cloud data breach, management and the CSP must have safeguards in place to protect personally identifiable information.
Service Dependencies and Partnerships	– CSP relationships extend responsibilities outside of the protective boundaries of the organization. – CSP relationships are further exacerbated when the primary CSP vendor outsources an organization's cloud activities to other vendors, creating fourth- and fifth-party vendor risks.
Contracts, Commercials and SLAs	– The organization – not the CSP – has the primary responsibility and accountability for the proper operation, performance, and governance of the cloud. Management must understand the scope of services and responsibilities that vary based upon the CSP. – To efficiently manage cloud performance, an SLA should specify terms about data rights, data usage, and legal protections. – For example, management should leverage data usage monitoring tools.

Table 8.2 (continued)

Cloud Industry Forum's Vendor Selection Criteria[172]	Cloud Governance Implications
Reliability and Performance	– CSP products and services should be reliable. However, downtime is inevitable. Management should ensure performance monitoring and reporting tools are available to manage service disruptions. – Management should understand the frequency and impact of failures on its users. For example, the reliability performance level could be that the cloud application is available 99.99 percent of the time during business hours and 99 percent of the time on nights and weekends. – A cloud *service outage* is an unexpected period of time during which cloud services are unavailable to the customer. If a CSP experiences an outage, then the organization can lose revenue and suffer damage to its reputation. For example, on October 4, 2021, Facebook and Instagram were unavailable for six hours. Facebook lost $60 million (USD) during that downtime.[174]
Migration Support, Vendor Lock-In and Exit Planning	– Vendor lock-in occurs when an organization using a cloud product or service cannot easily transition to a competitor CSP. – For example, management should understand the CSP data ownership and retrieval rights upon term end.
Business Health and Company Profile	– Management places substantial reliance on CSPs for meeting cloud strategic objectives, cloud governance, executing cloud operations, and cloud performance. Organizations should perform due diligence to understand whether a CSP is a sustainable business that will continue to exist in the future.

Table 8.3: Definitions of Accenture's selection criteria.

Accenture's Vendor Selection Criteria[175]	Cloud Governance Implications
Technical Capabilities	– If management wants to deploy high-performance computing and big data analytics, then the organization will want a CSP that can meet these requirements.

Table 8.3 (continued)

Accenture's Vendor Selection Criteria[175]	Cloud Governance Implications
Ease of Integration	– The organization's cloud strategy should align with how well the CSP's products can integrate their future technology offerings.
Organizational Capability	– If management does not consider the relevance, redundancy, and adequacy of the internal IT staff competencies and CSP support, then the organization will lack experienced personnel, impacting cloud performance on business objectives.
Security and Resilience	– Organizations must protect their data, perform continuous oversight, and have a comprehensive cloud security program that describes and defines the framework to achieve effective cloud security.
Regulation and Compliance	– Management should have visibility and be aware of the location of CSP servers to comply cloud security laws, regulations, and policies. – CSPs must demonstrate their ability to comply with regulatory requirements. – There is a significant cost of non-compliance with cloud-related regulations.
Cost	– Cost is an important consideration to decide which cloud vendor to select. – CSPs offer a bundle of services and pricing models. – Management should use calculation tools to govern cloud cost.

Such criteria assist management with selecting the vendor that best meets the business needs and aligns with the organization's cloud strategy.

8.5 Cloud Service-Level Agreements (SLA)

A cloud service-level agreement (SLA) represents terms agreed upon between a customer (e.g., an organization) and a cloud vendor (e.g., CSP). An SLA is an essential component of both a service relationship and cloud governance relationship between the organization and its vendor. According to Thomas Trappler (2010), "cloud agreements often entail developing and managing a complex long-term relationship with a vendor. In such relationships it is critical that the vendor understand the client's expectations and that the client has a means for ensuring that the vendor meets requirements."[176] Table 8.4 presents example definitions of an SLA.

Table 8.4: Definition of an SLA – selected examples.

Source	Definition of an SLA
U.S. NIST[177]	"Cloud consumers need SLAs to specify the technical performance requirements fulfilled by a CSP. SLAs can cover terms regarding the quality of service, security, remedies for performance failures. A CSP may also list in the SLAs a set of promises explicitly not made to consumers, i.e., limitations, and obligations that cloud consumers must accept."
New Zealand's Communications Security Bureau[178]	"A well-written SLA provides both the consumer and the CSP with clarity and certainty regarding which party is responsible for what, in terms of security, performance, system availability, and service management. Further, an SLA must also specify the penalties and remedies the Provider will incur, should they not meet the agreed-upon service levels."
European Commission's Joinup[179]	"The contract instrument used to govern the relationship between the cloud consumer and the CSP. The SLAs differ according to the each CSP, such that while they may contain similar functionality features, the individual terms and conditions applying to each service may be both complex and expressed in a manner unique to the CSP."
Gartner[180]	"An SLA sets the expectations between the service provider and the customer and describes the products or services to be delivered, the single point of contact for end-user problems, and the metrics by which the effectiveness of the process is monitored and approved."

Framework for Designing an SLA

A wide range of frameworks are available to guide the creation of vendor service-level agreements. Table 8.5 illustrates a cloud vendor SLA framework suggested by the Cloud Standards Consumer Council.

Table 8.5: Cloud vendor SLA frameworks, as adapted from the Cloud Standards Consumer Council.[181]

Step	Objective
1.	Understand Roles and Responsibilities
2.	Define Business Level Agreement
3.	Understand Service and Deployment Models
4.	Define Performance Metrics
5.	Meet Security and Privacy Requirements
6.	Manage Requirements
7.	Prepare a Disaster Recovery Plan
8.	Understand the Disaster Recovery Plan
9.	Develop Governance Requirements and Processes
10.	Create an Exit Agreement

CSP Service-Level Targets

The SLA should also include service-level targets. Examples of measurable service levels include *reliable performance levels* and *availability of cloud services*. Table 8.6 presents examples of performance and availability level service targets.

Table 8.6: Examples of reliability and availability service-level targets.

Category	Service-Level Target Examples
Reliable Performance Levels	Outage: CSP will respond immediately and will attempt to resolve the issue in 2 hours
	End-user impacted: CSP will respond within 20 minutes and will attempt to resolve the issue within 12 hours
	Potential for performance issue if not addressed: CSP will respond within 30 minutes and will attempt to resolve the issue within 24 hours
Availability Performance Levels	99.99%; annual downtime is 50 minutes; 4 minutes per month
	99%; annual downtime is 3 days per year; 7 hours per month
	95%; downtime is 18 days per year; 2 days per month

Source: Authors.

Financial Governance Protocols

The SLA should also include financial governance protocols. Transitioning to cloud services using a third-party vendor can be a costly undertaking. Flexera's 2022 State of the Cloud Report found that 421 respondents are spending $600,000 (USD) up to $12 million (USD) annually on cloud services. Sixty respondents to the Flexera survey each reported spending more than $60 million (USD) annually on cloud services. Flexera's survey also showed that organizations waste 32 percent of cloud spend.[182]

In addition, the lack of financial governance protocols can result in cloud costs spiraling out of control. For example, in 2018, Pinterest spent $190 million on AWS, $20 million more than it expected.[183] See Box 8.1 for a case study about Pinterest. To mitigate such financial risks, organizations must have financial governance protocols in place to manage cloud costs and to measure the return on investment (ROI). Table 8.7 presents Flexera's suggested activities to govern cloud cost.

Table 8.7: Financial governance measures.

Examples of Cloud Financial Governance Measures
– Govern IaaS/PaaS usage/cost
– Optimize SaaS usage/cost
– Govern software licenses in IaaS and PaaS
– Define cloud cost management policies
– Charge back cloud costs (to business units)
– Report and analyze cloud cost
– Own cloud budgets
– Optimize cloud spend
– Forecast cloud cost, post-migration

Source: 2022 Flexera State of the Cloud Survey.[184]

MSPs and CSPs offer a range of tools to help plan, track, and manage cloud costs. Example tools include billing reports and alerts, cost calculators, and detection capabilities for usage anomalies. Gartner recommends the use of the following cost performance metrics.
– Trending patterns daily, monthly, quarterly and annually
– Actual versus planned spending
– Percentage of the overall spending
– Top spenders and least spenders, by business unit
– Estimated spending waste[185]

Analyzing and measuring the ROI in the cloud is also essential to managing cloud performance. Measuring the ROI of cloud investments is a complex and iterative process. For instance, VMware suggests the following considerations:

> Cloud ROI is impacted by initial outlay, the speed with which returns occur, and cost decreases that occur as a result of the investment. ROI has both tangible and intangible components – a complete ROI picture must include factors such as overall corporate value, customer goodwill, and brand value in the marketplace, to name a few.[186]

If agreed-upon service-level and other performance targets are not met, then the CSP generally offers remedies to the organization. For example, a credit towards a portion of the monthly service fee.

Remedies for When CSPs do not Meet Performance Levels

The SLA should also include remedies for when CSP service-level performance problems emerge. In such situations, the organization and the CSP should work together to understand the root cause of the problem, the impact, and the action plan to correct the issue.

If the CSP is unable to resolve the issue, then management should consider seeking remedies from the CSP. In addition, the organization should modify the SLA as necessary to address these issues should they arise again in the future.

Exit Strategy

In some cases, an organization dissatisfied with the performance of their CSP may decide to cancel their existing services with the CSP and transfer the services to a new CSP. This is often referred to as an *exit strategy*. Deloitte offers the following advice concerning the design of an exit strategy from the CSP,

> Estimate the exit cost, and build it into the business case. Ask the vendor directly how they facilitate customer data out of their repository, their extract formats, their charging mechanisms for exit activities and termination, and what migration tools they are using. Build this assessment into the vendor evaluation criteria.[187]

It is important for an organization to document clear and specific exit strategy terms in the SLA.

8.6 Conclusion

The deployment of the cloud at scale disrupts and transforms an organization's in-house IT function. Part of the reason for this disruption is the use of CSPs. Management should evaluate and respond to the impact of the cloud on the pre-cloud strategy and operation of the in-house IT function. Management should also assess vendor qualifications to select the most suitable vendors. Once hired, the organizations should monitor cloud vendor service-level performance and hold vendors accountable for service failures.

Key Questions

1. What is the difference between the following third-party cloud vendor categories: CSP, MSP, and MSSP and what roles do they serve?
2. What impact does the cloud have on the roles of the in-house IT function?
3. What criteria should be considered when selecting a cloud vendor?

Box 8.1. Case Study: AWS and Pinterest about Vendor Selection and Concentration Risk
Pinterest, the image-sharing and social media service company, has an agreement with AWS to provide the cloud computing infrastructure to host the website, mobile application, and internal tools used for operations. According to the company's December 31, 2020, Form 10-K annual filing with the U.S. Security and Exchange Commission, Pinterest is required to maintain a substantial majority of their monthly usage of certain compute, storage, data transfer and other services on AWS. Pinterest identified a business concentration risk that "any transition of the cloud services currently provided by AWS to another CSP would be difficult to implement and would cause us to incur significant time and expense."[188] Pinterest and AWS have an enterprise agreement governing Pinterest's use of cloud services. Under the agreement, Pinterest is required to purchase at least $750 million (USD) of cloud services from AWS through July 2023.[189]

Box 8.2. Future of the CIO
Chief Executive Officers are increasingly asking their Chief Information Officers (CIOs) to lead the organization's digital transformation. According to McKinsey "CIOs are shifting their role to become true working partners to the business and focusing increasingly on how technology can drive business outcomes."[190] According to McKinsey "the role of technology as a business and innovation partner to design a tech-forward business strategy (for example, tech-enabled products and business models), integrate tech management across organizational silos, and deliver excellent user experiences."[191]

In context of the cloud, McKinsey emphasized that "CIOs have a crucial role in getting the business to focus on the far bigger prize: the new businesses, innovative practices, and new sources of revenue that cloud either enables or accelerates."[192] Lastly, the CIO as the business savvy technologist, must effectively communicate with other management executives and the board of directors. The CIO must be able to clearly articulate how cloud technology can drive business outcomes without IT jargon.

Chapter 9
Cloud Sprawl, Cloud Inventory and Cloud Management

Behind every cloud is another cloud.[193]
Judy Garland, American actress

Learning Objectives
- Understand the reasons for, and implications of cloud sprawl
- Understand the definition and purpose of a cloud inventory
- Understand the definition and purpose of cloud management
- Explain the role of a real-time inventory and organization-wide management of the organization's cloud assets and activities in cloud strategy, performance, governance and in managing CSPs

Key Terms

1. Cloud Access Security Broker – "On-premises, or cloud-based security policy enforcement points, placed between cloud service consumers and CSPs to combine and interject enterprise security policies as the cloud-based resources are accessed."[194]
2. Cloud Asset Inventory – An inventory of the cloud activities that includes the cloud service type, locations (e.g., jurisdictions, regions, countries, states) of cloud servers, cloud licenses, and risk level of data stored in the cloud.
3. Shadow IT – IT devices, software, and services outside the ownership or control of IT organizations.

Chapter Outline

https://doi.org/10.1515/9783110755374-009

9.1 Introduction

It is crucial for management to have visibility into cloud activities to execute an effective cloud strategy, manage cloud performance, and support cloud governance. Some organizations however are unclear about the nature, scope, and locations of their cloud activities. A cloud asset inventory and management process can provide management with valuable and timely visibility into the nature, scope, and locations of all cloud activities. This chapter discusses the need for the organization to create and continuously update a cloud asset inventory.

9.2 Cloud Sprawl: *Where is My Cloud*?

Some organizations are unclear about the nature, scope, and locations of their cloud activities. *Why is that*? Cloud sprawl is a primary reason. According to TechTarget, "cloud sprawl is the uncontrolled proliferation of an organization's cloud instances, services or providers. Cloud sprawl typically occurs when an organization lacks visibility into or control over its cloud computing resources."[195] One major reason for cloud sprawl is the inherently dynamic, scalable, and distributed nature of cloud deployment. The ability to be nimble, agile, and scale substantially and rapidly is a major benefit of deploying cloud computing. At the same time, however, cloud sprawl often results, which in turn increases the risk of losing track of cloud resources and activities throughout the organization.

Another reason is the democratization and decentralization of IT-enabled by cloud computing. Regardless of size, industry, or geography, growing numbers of non-IT employees are empowered to independently contract with CSPs for cloud products and services. Such employee empowerment can create "shadow IT." Gartner refers to shadow IT as "IT devices, software, and services outside the ownership or control of IT organizations."[196] Gartner's research shows that "most organizations grossly understate the number of shadow IT applications already in use."[197] Binadox, an IT company, reports that "shadow IT grows out of pure necessity when employees are looking for ways to solve specific work-related tasks."[198]

Shadow IT puts the organization at risk of violating cloud security laws, regulations, and policies. The global landscape of cloud applications makes it difficult for organizations to protect data and comply with privacy laws. Shadow IT can also create financial risk for the organization because there is a significant cost of non-compliance with cloud-related regulations. For example, in 2021, Amazon disclosed a fine of €746 million ($877 million USD) under the European

Union's General Data Protection Regulation (GDPR) for a compliance failure associated with a privacy issue.[199]

Another major contributor is the extended organization. With the increase in the use of third-party CSP vendors, management extends responsibilities for cloud activities outside of the protective boundaries of the organization. This complicates real-time visibility into cloud activities across the enterprise. CSP relationships are further exacerbated when the primary CSP vendor outsources an organization's cloud activities to other vendors, creating fourth- and fifth-party vendor risks.

9.3 Cloud Inventory

The factors contributing to cloud sprawl create a crucial need for organizational visibility into and control over its cloud computing resources. The Chief Risk Officer Forum reports that for management to understand the IT risk landscape, "organizations must identify relevant information assets. Once identified, appropriate details such as asset type, owner, and location should be entered into an appropriate asset register."[200] In the context of cloud computing, a cloud inventory can play a crucial role.

What is a cloud inventory? A cloud inventory is an inventory of the major components and locations of cloud resources, including the following:
- Hardware
- Software licenses
- Data
- Locations (jurisdictions, regions, countries, states) of cloud servers
- Access rights
- Prioritization of critical outage points
- CSPs

A comprehensive and real-time cloud asset inventory system is a key element of cloud strategy, performance measurement, governance, compliance, security, and overall operational oversight. Importantly, an incomplete or out-of-date inventory can be equally, if not riskier than the lack of a complete, accurate and up-to-date cloud inventory.

How do you create a cloud inventory? It is a complex task and will be based on the unique characteristics of the organization and the unique nature and scope of cloud deployment. A number of questions need to be addressed concerning cloud deployment, including the following:

- How many CSPs is the organization contracted to do business with?
- Are service-level agreements in place with all CSPs?
- Do the primary CSP vendors outsource cloud activities to subcontractors?
- How many cloud software licenses does the organization have?
- What countries are the CSP servers located in that house the data?

In addition, some cloud experts suggest using a range of native cloud tools and also leveraging CSP capabilities. For example, management could create a cloud inventory three ways. Management can deploy an asset discovery tool; deploy a Cloud Access Security Broker (CASB); and flag suspicious IT-related purchases and survey the organization.

Asset Discovery Tool

An asset discovery tool can assist in the identification of cloud activities across the enterprise. Asset discovery tools can help management monitor when new, risky, and high volumes of cloud services are being used. According to Tripwire, a cybersecurity firm, an organization will benefit from deploying an asset discovery tool in many ways such as

> Using accurate data harvested from an asset discovery tool, an organization can then start to map assets to relevant information such as owner, location, contracts, and projects that are associated with the assets. Having IT assets mapped will give an organization more fleshed-out asset reports that contain insights into security risks and overall assets operational costs.[201]

Cloud Access Security Broker (CASB)

The asset discovery tool may not identify all the cloud activity being used across the organization. To cast a wider net, management can also deploy a CASB. In 2012, Gartner coined the term CASB and defined it as "on-premises, or cloud-based security policy enforcement points, placed between cloud service consumers and CSPs to combine and interject enterprise security policies as the cloud-based resources are accessed."[202] A CASB can provide management the visibility into the organization's usage of cloud applications. A CASB can help management monitor network traffic to minimize cloud data leaks and recognize threats from malicious actors. Table 9.1 describes the four types of primary services provided by a CASB, as adapted from the Cloud Security Alliance.[203]

Table 9.1: Primary security services provided by CASBs. Source: Cloud Security Alliance.

Primary Types of CASB Services	Definition of CASB Services
Visibility	Identifies all the cloud services (including Shadow IT) used by an organization's employees.
Data Security	Enforces data security policies. Monitors user activity to block or limit access.
Threat Protection	Protects cloud services from unwanted users or applications. Monitors events to identify irregular behavior, permission violations, or configuration changes that indicate a compromised account.
Compliance	Offers policy controls and remediation that enforce cloud compliance in real time for regulations such as GDPR, the Sarbanes-Oxley Act (SOX), and the Health Insurance Portability and Accountability Act (HIPAA). Provides historical event data for retrospective compliance auditing.

Flag Suspicious IT-Related Purchases and Survey the Organization

Another source of information for management to create a cloud asset inventory is for the accounting department to flag suspicious IT-related purchases. In smaller organizations, management could also survey business units to request what cloud services they purchased. Management could also take a proactive approach and raise employee awareness with cybersecurity training and communicating policies that describe that employees should not purchase cloud products without the IT department's approval.

9.4 Cloud Management

A cloud inventory is central to a broader, organization-wide cloud operations management process, herein referred to as cloud management. Red Hat defines cloud management as:

A combination of software, automation, policies, governance, and people that determine how cloud computing services are made available. Cloud management is how administrators control and orchestrate all the products and services that operate in a cloud: the users and access control, data, applications, and services. It's about giving admins the ability to access the resources they need, automate those processes that they want to, and make adjustments as needed, while also monitoring usage and cost. It's also how admins maintain flexibility and scalability, while being able to adapt quickly when things change.[204]

A cloud management process can inform the cloud strategy, help measure and monitor cloud performance, create a stronger cloud security program, ensure cloud compliance, and provide assurance that internal controls are operating effectively. Table 9.2 summarizes how a cloud asset inventory can inform cloud management objectives.

Table 9.2: Summary of how a cloud asset inventory can inform cloud management objectives.

Cloud Management Objective	Description
Cloud Strategy	The organization's cloud strategy describes why, how, and where it strategically wants to deploy cloud computing services across the enterprise.
Cloud Performance	Flexera's 2022 State of the Cloud Report found that the top three performance measures that organizations track are "cost efficiency/savings, delivery speed of product/ services and cost avoidance."[205] Management could use the results of the cloud inventory to create and monitor such measures. A cloud inventory can contribute to measuring operational performance, as well as CSP performance.
Cloud Security	Organizations must protect their data, perform continuous oversight, and have a comprehensive cloud security plan that describes and defines the security framework and program established to achieve effective cloud security. The global landscape of cloud applications makes it difficult for organizations to comply cloud security laws, regulations, and policies. There is a significant cost for non-compliance with cloud-related regulations. A cloud inventory can help management track cloud resources and activities and manage cybersecurity risk.

Table 9.2 (continued)

Cloud Management Objective	Description
Cloud Compliance	Certain governments have implemented various data protection laws for their citizens. For example, certain jurisdictions require a CSP to disclose customer data in the course of a government investigation, monitor electronic communications sent through the systems of a CSP, or require a CSP to access and disclose the data on the servers they own in in that jurisdiction. The cloud asset inventory will help management identify where the data resides, which is important for organizations to comply with international laws and regulations.
Assurance, Risk Management, and Internal Controls	Management can use the cloud asset inventory to oversee whether their internal controls to safeguard the assets are effective. Management cannot protect against a threat if management does not know a risk is exists.

Source: Authors.

Some organizations leverage third-party cloud management platforms as part of the cloud management process. Platforms can contribute to managing data, content, and applications. Platforms provide insight into a range of critical performance indicators. For instance, platforms can illustrate how and when each part of the cloud infrastructure is being used, how cloud applications are performing (e.g., lagging, unavailable, underutilized), security vulnerabilities, and which CSP activities do not align with organizational standards and policies.

9.5 Responsibilities: Cloud Inventory and Cloud Management

What function should be responsible for creating and managing a cloud inventory? The organization has options for which functional unit should be responsible for creating and managing a cloud inventory, such as the following:
- Cloud Center of Excellence
- Chief Information Security Officer function
- Chief Operating Officer function
- Third-party Managed Service Provider (MSP) or CSP

In this capacity, the designated functional unit would play a crucial role in integrating and communicating with governance stakeholders, including the board of directors, compliance, security, ERM, CSPs, and assurance providers. The organization's legal department would also play a role because the legal department should maintain the records of contracts and service-level agreements with all CSPs. The contracts and SLAs are a source of information for management to create the cloud inventory.

9.6 Conclusion

A lack of transparency creates substantial risk to cloud strategy, performance, compliance, governance, and security. It is essential to cloud governance for management to have access to real-time, accurate information about the extent to which the organization is deploying and using the cloud. An overall cloud management process, including a cloud inventory provides an organization with valuable and timely visibility into the nature, scope, and locations of all cloud resources and activities.

Key Questions
1. What is a cloud inventory?
2. Why is it important to have a cloud inventory?
3. How do you create a cloud inventory and who maintains it?
4. How do you define cloud management?
5. What are the major elements of cloud management?
6. Who is responsible for cloud inventory and cloud management?

Chapter 10
Sustainable Cloud: The Relationship Between the Cloud and ESG

> Companies have historically driven financial, security, and agility benefits through cloud, but sustainability is becoming an imperative.[206]
>
> – Accenture

Learning Objectives
- Define sustainable cloud
- Understand the relationship between cloud computing and sustainability

---

 Key Terms

1. Carbon Neutral – "A current state which is achieved when the greenhouse gas emissions associated with an entity, product or activity are reduced and offset to zero for a defined duration."[207]
2. *Carbon Neutral* Protocol – Designed to support initiatives to reduce carbon emissions for the global economy to become net zero.[208]
3. Data ethics – "Concepts of right and wrong in relation to the collection and dissemination of both structured and unstructured data, particularly as these actions relate to personal information."[209]
4. Environmental Social Governance (ESG)
   - Environmental: The environmental factor covers such risks as the water crisis, carbon footprint, and renewable energy.
   - Social: The social factor covers topics such as supplier conduct, community relations, employee satisfaction, and workforce diversity.
   - Governance: The governance factor covers the composition of the board of directors, audit committee structure, executive compensation, conflicts of interest, bribery, corruption, safety management, and whistleblower programs.
5. Sustainability – "Meeting the needs of the present without compromising the ability of future generations to meet their own needs."[210]
6. Sustainable Cloud – A sustainable cloud is the organization's use of the cloud and its positive impact on the water crisis, carbon footprint, renewable

https://doi.org/10.1515/9783110755374-010

energy, data ethics, and supplier conduct. A sustainable cloud includes how an organization must govern the material ESG impacts and outcomes associated with cloud deployment. A sustainable cloud also includes the idea that the cloud will continue to provide long-term value to the organization.

7. Sustainability Reporting – A practice for "organizations to measure, understand and communicate their economic, environmental, social and governance performance, and then set goals, and manage change more effectively."[211]

Chapter Outline

10.1 Introduction
10.2 Sustainable Cloud
10.3 Environmental Factors and the Cloud – The E in ESG
10.4 Social and Governance Factors and the Cloud – The S and the G in ESG
10.5 ESG Reporting and the Cloud
10.6 Conclusion

10.1 Introduction

The United Nations defines sustainability as "meeting the needs of the present without compromising the ability of future generations to meet their own needs."[212] Sustainability considerations are increasingly driven by strategies that transcend all organizational functions, processes, and activities. Cloud computing is no exception.

This chapter discusses two important ways that cloud computing impacts an organization's sustainability strategies. First, how the deployment and use of cloud computing, including the use of third-party CSPs, impact sustainability (e.g., carbon emissions, water consumption, and data ethics). Second, opportunities for organizations to leverage the unique capabilities afforded by the cloud to improve ESG data generation, analysis, and reporting.

10.2 Sustainable Cloud

Today, the purpose of a business has transformed from a historical business purpose focused solely a shareholder or owner value to a purpose with broader stakeholder value. Stakeholders include owners, vendors, employees, customers, and society. This stakeholder-centered business purpose balances the integration of three objectives referred to as the triple bottom line (TBL). This TBL consists of people (i.e., society), the planet (i.e., environment), and profits.

An organization's deployment and use of the cloud impact its TBL and its sustainability strategy. According to Accenture,

> Cloud has moved from "nice-to-have" to "must-have." The cloud can deliver a double helix effect of shareholder and stakeholder value – simultaneously reducing costs and carbon emissions if approached from a sustainability perspective. Leading to a greener planet and a boost in profitability.[213]

To that end, an organization will strive to operate a so-called sustainable cloud.

A sustainable cloud points to how an organization's use of the cloud materially impacts ESG strategies and outcomes in two important ways. One way is how an organization's use of the cloud impacts areas such as carbon emissions, energy reduction, water consumption, data ethics, and supplier conduct. Another way is for organizations to procure cloud solutions to measure, monitor, and report ESG performance.

10.3 Environmental Factors and the Cloud – The *E* in ESG

The World Economic Forum's Global Risks Report 2021 ranks climate change as a catastrophic risk, forecasted to have short-term and long-term threats to the world.[214] In the context of cloud computing, there are environmental factors that management should consider, such as carbon emissions. According to PwC's 2021 U.S. Cloud Business Survey, such sustainability considerations extend to the use of third-party CSPs,

> While most companies recognize that moving their data to a third-party CSP can help them reduce their carbon footprint, some are also looking at how to incorporate their CSP's emissions in their carbon reduction.[215]

Increasingly, CSPs are asserting their dedication to providing energy efficient cloud solutions. Table 10.1 presents examples of such public assertions, by select CSPs.

Organizations that are engaging CSPs should structure service-level agreements (SLAs) to include the reporting of CSP greenhouse gas emissions and other significant environmental and climate change related performance metrics for the duration of the contract. For example, the *CarbonNeutral* Protocol suggests an example metric to track "if document storage is outsourced to a cloud-based service, [then management could] request the figure for CO_2e

Table 10.1: Examples of environmental stewardship commitments by CSP.

CSP	Environmental Stewardship Commitments
Salesforce	Salesforce delivers a carbon-neutral cloud to their global customers. In September 2021, Salesforce achieved 100 percent renewable energy for its operations. It is a net zero company across its value chain.[216]
Google	Google is carbon neutral and matches 100 percent of the energy consumed by their global operations with renewable energy. By 2030, Google Cloud's goal is to run on carbon-free energy, 24/7, at all of their data centers.[217]
AWS	AWS is committed to achieving 100% renewable energy usage for their global infrastructure by 2025.[218]
Microsoft	Microsoft Azure is committed to achieving 100% renewable energy by 2025.[219]
Oracle	Oracle is committed to achieving its goal of 100% renewable energy use at all Oracle Cloud regions by 2025.[220]
IBM	In February 2021, IBM announced a new goal to achieve net zero greenhouse gas emissions by 2030.[221]

emitted per gigabyte per year."[222] The Protocol is designed to support initiatives to reduce carbon emissions for the global economy to become net zero.

Another example of an environmental impact is water conservation. The 2020 Global Risks Report defines the water crisis as a "significant decline in the available quality and quantity of fresh water, resulting in harmful effects on human health and/or economic activity."[223] An organization consumes water to cool in-house data centers. The Uptime Institute's Global Data Center Survey 2020 suggests that organizations with in-house data centers should adopt a mitigation strategy to "assess water risks and develop a water resiliency plan."[224] Most CSPs have initiatives in place to improve their water efficiency and reduce the use of potable drinking water to cool their data centers.

10.4 Social and Governance Factors and the Cloud – The *S* and the *G* in ESG

In addition to environmental impacts, the cloud also has social and governance implications. That is, the cloud also impacts the *S* (i.e., social responsibility) in ESG, and the *G* (i.e., governance responsibility) in ESG.

From a social responsibility perspective, organizations are increasingly being held responsible for working conditions (e.g., safety, fair compensation, safety, human rights) existing at their third-party vendors (e.g., payroll processors and

CSPs). An organization's governance policies should also extend to third-party vendors, including data ethics policies. The Institute of Internal Auditors describes data ethics as "concepts of right and wrong in relation to the collection and dissemination of both structured and unstructured data, particularly as these actions relate to personal information."[225] Internationally, government regulations place emphasis on data ethics such as the European Union's General Data Protection Regulation and the U.S. healthcare-focused privacy law.

In the context of the cloud, organizations should examine environmental stewardship, social responsibility, and governance issues during their due diligence process when selecting CSPs. SLAs should include all such commitments and requirements. Organizations should also expect to see periodic reporting of evidence of CSP adherence to ESG-related commitments and responsibilities.

10.5 ESG Reporting and the Cloud

The U.S. Securities and Exchange Commission (SEC) requires public companies to disclose selected ESG matters in their annual Form 10-K and other financial filings. The European Union Sustainable Finance Disclosure Regulation also imposes mandatory disclosure of selected ESG-related obligations.[226] Beyond regulatory requirements, organizations are rapidly increasing their range of voluntary communication of their sustainability strategies, commitments impacts, and outcomes. For instance, organizations are using dedicated ESG web pages, social media, and stand-alone sustainability reports.

Internationally, standard-setting organizations have advanced a number of distinct sustainability reporting frameworks. The frameworks guide organizations on how to disclose the impact and outcomes of their business operations on sustainability practices, such as cloud usage. For example, The Global Reporting Initiative, Climate Disclosure Standards Board, and the Greenhouse Gas Protocol (GGP) guide the preparation of ESG disclosures and communications. The GGP advances accounting standards for organizations to measure, manage, and report greenhouse gas emissions from their operations and supply chains. Table 10.2 defines the three types of emissions for ESG reporting.

The cloud can serve as a powerful tool for organizations to gain greater transparency and access to ESG data analysis and reporting. Table 10.3 presents examples of CSP product offerings to help organizations measure, manage, and report ESG metrics.

Table 10.2: Description of emission type for ESG reporting, as adapted by GGP.[227]

Type of Greenhouse Gas Emission	Description
Scope 1 Emissions	Direct greenhouse gas emissions from owned or controlled sources such as from a cloud data center.
Scope 2 Emissions	Indirect greenhouse gas emissions from the generation of purchased energy.
Scope 3 Emissions	All indirect greenhouse gas emissions (not included in scope 2) that occur in the supply chain of the reporting organization. Scope 3 emissions includes both virtual and physical suppliers, emissions from the product lifecycle of the reporting organization, and emissions resulting from activities like employee travel.

Table 10.3: Summary of example product offerings to help organizations report carbon emissions data.

Products for Sustainability Reports	Product Description
Google Cloud Platform[228]	Provides Scope 1 emissions data for the reporting organization to view carbon-free energy scores by regions of the Google Cloud Platforms.
Microsoft Cloud for Sustainability[229]	Measures and monitors the environmental footprint of the organization and its supply chain that use the Microsoft Azure product to report Scope 1, 2, and 3 emissions.
AWS Data Exchange[230]	Tracks and reports Scope 1, 2, and 3 sustainability data. Provides the reporting organization access to third-party ESG data sets that assess the sustainability performance of companies. Access allows customers visibility into the supply chain.
Moody's ESG Solutions[231] (Moody's is a global risk assessment firm, not a CSP)	Using cloud technology provides data to monitor and analyze ESG performance. Access to reporting tools for documenting ESG performance. Maps ESG data across supply chains.
Salesforce Sustainability Cloud[232]	Tracks, analyzes, and reports environmental data for Scope 1, 2, and 3 emissions. Allows the reporting organization to connect and collaborate with suppliers about emission reduction targets. See Box 10.1 for the Salesforce case study.

10.6 Conclusion

Organizations have a responsibility to ensure value creation for shareholders and stakeholders while acting on the world's social and environmental challenges that are important to internal and external stakeholders. It is crucial for management to consider ESG factors in the context of the cloud. There is an important relationship between cloud computing and sustainability. One part of the relationship is how the cloud materially impacts the organization's ESG strategies and outcomes. Another part of the relationship is how management can leverage the cloud to improve ESG reporting.

Key Questions
1. What is a *sustainable cloud*?
2. What is the relationship between cloud computing and sustainability?
3. What are the ESG factors that are material considerations about the cloud?
4. What is the role of the cloud in an organization's ESG impacts and outcomes?
5. What is the role of the cloud in data analysis and reporting ESG impacts?

Box 10.1: Salesforce Case Study

Salesforce is an American cloud-based software company focused on customer relationship management. In September 2021, Salesforce achieved 100 percent renewable energy for its operations. It is a net zero company, including its supply chain. Salesforce's 2021 Climate Action Plan describes the company's vision on how to continue as a carbon neutral company.[233]

Salesforce uses its cloud platform called Sustainability Cloud 2.0, to track its progress and lower the company's carbon footprint. Salesforce also sells its Sustainability Cloud product to customers. Customers can use Sustainability Cloud to track and reduce carbon emissions. Organizations which use Sustainability Cloud can obtain data for customized ESG reporting. This ESG data can be used for reports to boards of directors, third-party audits, investors, and financial filings. Salesforce's Sustainability Cloud product claims that it will provide Scope 3 reporting to connect and collaborate with suppliers about emission reduction targets. Salesforce states that their Sustainability Cloud product can provide forecasting and scenario planning. Salesforce markets that Sustainability Cloud allows customers to purchase and manage carbon credits and educate employees about climate policies and sustainability.

Chapter 11
Cloud-Driven Change Management and Learning

> The greatest danger in times of turbulence is not the
> turbulence – it is to act with yesterday's logic.[234]
> – Peter Drucker, author

Learning Objectives
- Understand the role of change management in large-scale migration to the cloud
- Differentiate between *cloud management* and *cloud organizational change management*
- Appreciate the need for a cloud-enabled workforce
- Understand the role of learning and development in large-scale migration to the cloud

---

 Key Terms

1. At Scale – A large-scale event or action that is extensive and organization-wide in scope, involving a large number of people, processes, systems, and/or functions in an organization.
2. IT Service Management (ITSM) – "How IT teams manage the end-to-end delivery of IT services to customers. This includes all the processes and activities to design, create, deliver, and support IT services."[235]

Chapter Outline
11.1 Introduction
11.2 Cloud-Driven Organizational Change
11.3 Cloud-Driven Change Management
11.4 A Gap in Cloud Skills: Toward a Cloud-Enabled Workforce
11.5 Cloud-Related Learning and Development Considerations
11.6 Conclusion

11.1 Introduction

Large-scale deployment of the cloud requires new skills, unleashes reengineering needs, and requires changes to existing organizational governance protocols.

https://doi.org/10.1515/9783110755374-011

Effectively managing these and other cloud-related changes is crucial to achieving cloud strategy, performance, and governance objectives. This chapter discusses organizational change management, learning and development, and related cloud governance considerations associated with the large-scale deployment of the cloud.

11.2 Cloud-Driven Organizational Change

Large-scale adoption of the cloud (i.e., deploying the cloud at scale) represents a large-scale *organizational change.* According to *Harvard Business Review,*

> Organizational change refers to the actions in which a company or business alters a major component of its organization, such as its culture, the underlying technologies or infrastructure it uses to operate, or its internal processes.[236]

Organizational change spans a continuum, with incremental adaptive change at one end and large-scale transformational change at the other end. Table 11.1 defines each of these end-points.

Table 11.1: Definitions of adaptive and transformation change, as adapted from Harvard Business School.[237]

Change	Overview
Adaptive Change	Small, incremental adjustments that organizations make to adapt to daily, weekly, and monthly business challenges. Often related to fine-tuning existing processes, products, and company culture, without fundamentally changing the organization as a whole.
Transformational Change	Refers to a dramatic and at times sudden (e.g., pandemic response) evolution of some basic structure of the business itself (e.g., strategy, culture, organization, physical structure, supply chain, or processes).

Smaller-scale adoption of cloud applications and services generally represents an *adaptive* change. Large-scale deployment of the cloud, however, represents a *transformational* organizational change. The following discussion presents four examples of how the cloud uniquely drives transformational change.

1. The Cloud Changes the On-Premises IT Function in an Organization

Procuring cloud services from third-party cloud vendors (e.g., CSPs) disrupts and transforms the *pre-cloud* on-premises (i.e., in-house) IT function. According to *CIO Digital Magazine*, "the effect on IT organizations is that they have had to quickly transition from managing legacy infrastructure to becoming experts in orchestrating cloud technologies and integrating them with their existing infrastructure."[238]

One major factor causing such a transformation of the in-house IT function is the use of CSPs. According to Choudhary and Vithayathil (2013), "As more services are procured from cloud vendors, the need for functions within the IT department that serve to administer, monitor, and maintain the IT infrastructure will be considerably diminished or even eliminated."[239]

Another major factor causing the disruption of the in-house IT function is the democratization of IT, including the cloud. According to Accenture,

Technology democratization places powerful capabilities with people in operations, maintenance, the contact center, and back-office functions. It augments, not replaces, existing technology approaches to innovation. A new decentralized approach adds a grassroots layer to innovation, where staff are free to innovate on their own, in their own timeframes, without the need for specialized IT resources.[240]

An organizational change management strategy should respond to these and other transformative impacts of the cloud on the pre-cloud in-house IT function.

2. The Cloud Disrupts Organizational Governance

Deploying the cloud at scale transforms organizational governance. A primary driver is a substantial increase in the reliance on a *shared responsibility model* for cloud governance. The following stakeholders are often involved in cloud-shared responsibility model.

- Employees – Democratized IT Organizational employees authorized to directly engage in cloud activities (e.g., work directly with CSPs)
- Employees – Shadow IT Activities Shadow cloud activities represent the unsanctioned and unknown use of cloud activities by front-line organizational employees outside the purview of the centralized IT function and organizational governance functions
- Organizational Governance Functions with IT and cloud-related roles (e.g., the compliance function and the internal audit function)
- Third-Party Cloud Vendors (e.g., CSPs and MSPs)

Transformation of the compliance function is an example of a cloud-driven change to an organizational governance function. According to Lucidchart,

> With the cloud in use, your organization may have to set new internal policies for employees and should consider how changing compliance should be managed. If, for example, your organization is subject to PCI, GDPR, or HIPAA compliance, part of your change management would involve anticipating how these regulations impact your cloud transition and use.[241]

Management must transform organizational governance functions and protocols to properly integrate and respond to a cloud-shared responsibility model.

3. A New *Cloud Management* Process is Needed

Another cloud-driven change is the creation of a new *cloud management* process. In-house IT functions, cloud-shared responsibility models, and cloud governance protocols (e.g., compliance function) must be transformed to properly integrate and respond to a new cloud management process.

Red Hat defines cloud management as "A combination of software, automation, policies, governance, and people that determine how cloud computing services are made available."[242] In the IT domain, cloud management is an element of an IT Service Management (ITSM) process. ITSM activities involve day-to-day, end-to-end delivery of IT operations and services (e.g., software updates). Alternatives for deploying cloud management include the use of third-party cloud management platforms and creating a Cloud Center of Excellence.

4. The Cloud Creates a Cloud Talent Gap

A gap in *digital skills* is a significant impediment and risk for organizations. In its 2021–2023 Emerging Technology Roadmap survey results of approximately 400 global organizations, Gartner reported, "Talent shortages are a rising and significant challenge for successful adoption of emerging technologies."[243] Gaps in cloud skills are a major part of the overall gap in digital skills.

11.3 Cloud-Driven Change Management

The deployment and operation of an effective *organizational change management* strategy and process are crucial to cloud governance. According to Lucidchart,

> Effective change management smooths the transition to the cloud and gives organizations better insight throughout the process. Given the monumental changes associated with moving to the cloud, you need a change management strategy to manage risk and minimize wasted effort or cost.[244]

Numerous definitions of change management exist. Table 11.2 presents three examples.

Table 11.2: Definition of change management – selected examples.

Source	Definition of Change Management
American Society for Quality (ASQ)[245]	The methods and manners in which a company describes and implements change within both its internal and external processes. Including, preparing, and supporting employees, establishing the necessary steps for change, and monitoring pre- and post-change activities to ensure success.
Prosci[246]	The application of a structured process and set of tools for leading the people side of change to achieve the desired outcome.
TechTarget[247]	A systematic approach to dealing with the transition or transformation of an organization's goals, processes, or technologies. The purpose of change management is to implement strategies for effecting change, controlling change, and helping people to adapt to change.

Organizational change management is inherently complex, time consuming, costly, and risky. According to the Enterprisers Project,

> Executing a successful change management effort is one of the toughest challenges for an organization, regardless of how much money, brainpower, talent, and resources you may have at your disposal.[248]

A major part of the challenge is the risk of not fully and effectively achieving the outcomes expected from deploying the cloud. Leveraging well-established change management frameworks can contribute to effective cloud adoption.

Change Management Frameworks

Many frameworks exist for managing wide-scale transformational change in organizations. Tables 11.3 and 11.4 present two examples.

Table 11.3: Change management model, as adapted from ASQ.[249]

ASQ Change Management Model	
Step	Description
1. Leadership	Includes sponsors providing leadership resources and support.
2. Why the Need for Change?	Includes socializing and securing consensus and collective buy-in for the need for change from organizational stakeholders.
3. Vision for the Change	Clearly defining outcomes expected from the change that are agreed to by key stakeholders of the organization.
4. Commitment to the Change	Securing commitment from key stakeholders of the organization for the necessary resources needed for change and commitment to success.
5. Monitoring the Change	Monitoring the progress and success of the change, including the use of key performance measures.
6. Start-to-Finish of the Change and Beyond	Ensuring the change is completed and endures through change enablers, including learning and development, so that employees are skilled and prepared for the new environment.
7. Anchor the Change	Reinforcing and anchoring the change to the DNA of the organization.

Organizations often supplement change frameworks with IT-specific change frameworks, such as the Information Technology Infrastructure Library (ITIL). IBM defines ITIL as,

A library of best practices for managing IT services and improving IT support and service levels. One of the main goals of ITIL is to ensure that IT services align with business objectives, even as business objectives change.[250]

Table 11.5 presents an overview of the ITIL 4 Framework.

While such generic change management frameworks are valuable starting points, the cloud introduces unique elements of complexity and uncertainties. Organizations will need to customize such generic change management frameworks to accommodate the unique organizational impact of cloud-driven change.

Table 11.4: Eight-step process for leading change, as adapted from Kotter.[251]

The Kotter 8-Step Process for Leading Change	
Steps	**Overview**
1. Create a sense of urgency	Help others see the need for change through a bold, aspirational opportunity statement that communicates the importance of acting immediately.
2. Build a guiding coalition	A volunteer army needs a coalition of effective people – born of its own ranks – to guide it, coordinate it, and communicate its activities.
3. Form a strategic vision and initiatives	Clarify how the future will be different from the past and how you can make that future a reality through initiatives linked directly to the vision.
4. Enlist a volunteer army	Large-scale change can only occur when massive numbers of people rally around a common opportunity. They must be bought-in and urgent to drive change – moving in the same direction.
5. Enable action by removing barriers	Removing barriers such as inefficient processes and hierarchies provides the freedom necessary to work across silos and generate real impact.
6. Generate short-term wins	Wins are the molecules of results. They must be recognized, collected, and communicated – early and often – to track progress and energize volunteers to persist.
7. Institute change	Press harder after the first success. Your increasing credibility can improve systems, structures, and policies. Be relentless with initiating change after change until the vision is a reality.
8. Sustain acceleration	Articulate the connections between the new behaviors and organizational success, making sure they continue until they become strong enough to replace old habits.

Table 11.5: Overview of the ITIL 4 Framework, as adapted from Diligent.[252]

The Dimensions of the ITIL 4 Framework
For Consideration When Designing and Delivering an IT Service or Product

Dimensions	Overview
1. Organizations and People	Focuses on the structure and governance of the organization and the people involved in every aspect of the service. This includes suppliers, customers, employees, and managers. Organizations should consider how teams are connected, the level of training, and the type of organizational culture.
2. Information and Technology	Focuses on tools, technology, and information needed to support both product delivery and IT governance and management. Considerations may include the capabilities and capacity of the support service and the technology required for the service.
3. Partners and Suppliers	Focuses on external suppliers and partners that help organizations deliver products and services. The comparison of in-house versus outsourced capabilities is a key part of this dimension. Organizations should consider and compare the cost of outsourcing, as well as reliability, performance, and capacity.
4. Value Streams and Processes	Focuses on how services and products are delivered on the service value chain, and the operating model to deliver services or products. It can be used for an incident response as well as product development.

11.4 A Gap in Cloud Skills: Toward a Cloud-Enabled Workforce

A cloud-enabled workforce is essential to cloud performance success, including effective cloud governance. According to Deloitte, "A critical success factor is to have staff with the skills required to maintain cloud-based systems."[253] Yet, gaps in cloud skills persist. According to Gartner, "Talent shortages are a rising and significant challenge for successful adoption of emerging technologies."[254] The cloud is no exception.

Gaps in Cloud Skills

Organizations and CSPs are concerned with attracting and retaining talent in the cloud domain. Some organizations are leaning in to contribute to filling this gap. For instance, in 2020, Amazon announced its commitment to training 29 million people in cloud computing by 2025. In November 2021, Amazon opened their *AWS Skills Center* in Seattle, Washington, a free cloud computing training center open to the public.[255]

In spite of such efforts, the cloud skills gap continues to persist and widen. A case in point is reflected in the results of a survey conducted by North Carolina State University and Protiviti. Survey results were based on 1,453 respondents in global C-suite and board positions who were asked for their views on top organizational risks. Results indicated that the number four risk for 2022, and the projected number one top risk for 2031, is that the "adoption of digital technologies requires new skills or significant efforts to upskill/reskill existing employees."[256]

Gaps in digital skills include gaps in cloud skills. For example, in their 2022 Planning Guide for Cloud and Edge Computing, Gartner asserted,

> The lack of cloud skills has reached crisis levels. This is often the real barrier to cloud adoption. Businesses are missing out on opportunities for cost savings and superior technology because their IT organizations lack the skills to support cloud services.[257]

Gaps in cloud skills also challenge organizational governance functions. For instance, members of the board of directors need an adequate level of cloud literacy to effectively exercise their cloud governance responsibilities.

Toward a Cloud-Enabled Workforce

What is a cloud workforce? With respect to roles, a cloud workforce consists of several cohorts of stakeholders that directly or tangentially play a role in the cloud. For instance, the in-house IT function; frontline business employees; the board of directors; and CSPs. *What is a cloud-enabled workforce?* A cloud-enabled workforce consists of roles and skills a cloud workforce must be equipped with to drive cloud success.

Why is a cloud-enabled workforce crucial to cloud success? According to Deloitte, the people side of the cloud is essential to achieving strategic outcomes expected from the cloud.

> The challenge, however, is what we call the "cloud adoption plateau" – a stall in cloud adoption and true organizational transformation – that limits what organizations are able

to achieve with cloud. Organizations may experience this plateau when they move too quickly to migrate work (applications and processes) to the cloud without developing the right operating model, skills, leadership support, and new ways of working.

In essence, they haven't re-architected work for the cloud. These shortfalls have a business cost and an innovation cost – this is where HR leaders have an important opportunity to work with IT and business leaders to help overcome them. That means creating a cloud-enabled organizational structure and workforce that is ready to support the organization's cloud transformation strategy, close innovation gaps, and enable sustained cloud ROI.[258]

How does an organization achieve a cloud-enabled workforce? Transforming into a cloud-enabled workforce is a component of *the people-side* of change management. According to Prosci, "The application of a structured process and set of tools for leading the people side of change to achieve a desired outcome."[259] As an illustration, Table 11.6 presents perspectives on cloud-enabling an in-house IT function.

Table 11.6: Perspectives on cloud-enabling an in-house IT function.

Source	Perspectives on Cloud-Enabling an In-House IT Function
Lucidchart[260]	A move to the cloud will require teams to develop or hire new skills and create a new culture and strategy in the way teams approach IT.
Cloud Standards Customer Council[261]	Cloud computing and related technologies like blockchain, data science, and artificial intelligence are transforming the nature of IT, resulting in skill shortages in some domain areas and staffing surpluses in other traditional IT domains. As businesses consolidate data centers and relocate or virtualize workloads on-premises or via external cloud service providers, the need for certain data center positions (e.g., facility monitoring/management, server setup, configuration, etc.) sharply diminish. A new set of domain skills around process automation, architecture, resource optimization, and cost management are required to drive cloud-based initiatives. A solid understanding of infrastructure, middleware, and application concepts in the context of the enterprise business model are critical.

Organizations facing gaps in cloud skills have a continuum of options available to build a cloud-enabled workforce. Five examples are presented in Table 11.7.

Table 11.7: Options for addressing gaps in cloud skill – selected examples.

Option	Overview
Permanent Hires	Hire employees with the requisite cloud skills to create a cadre of employees with the skills needed to address the full spectrum of cloud competencies (e.g., cloud strategy, deployment, scaling operations, technology, governance, etc.). A major challenge of this option is the high demand for digital talent globally and the limited supply. This option also needs substantial time to scale.
Temporary Rotations	Temporary role rotations for full-time employees through technology/cloud-related functional roles to shadow specialists and gain hands-on experience.
Temporary Staffing	Hiring temporary employees with the requisite cloud skills on a contract basis contributes to addressing immediate-term and short-term cloud-resource needs. The benefits of this outsourcing-type model are the ability to secure resources with the precise level of skills needed, just-in-time. A major challenge of this approach, however, is that it is not a permanent solution to embedding cloud skills into the organization for the long term.
Reliance on Vendors (e.g., MSPs and CSPs)	Organizations are increasingly relying on vendors to supplement shortages in skills and resources. Benefits include real-time access to skills and resources. Challenges of this option include cost.
Learning and Development (L&D)	Designing learning interventions to develop cloud skills for existing employees. A major benefit of this option is employees with critical institutional knowledge add requisite cloud skills to their competencies. A major challenge ensuring L&D interventions can be practically applied to the workplace. Such development initiatives are often the responsibility of an organization's learning and development function.

Source: Authors.

11.5 Cloud-Related Learning and Development (L&D) Considerations

Learning and development (L&D) interventions are integral to a cloud-enabled workforce and to effective change management strategies. Numerous definitions of organizational L&D exist. Table 11.8 presents examples.

Table 11.8: Definitions of learning and development – selected examples.

Source	Terminology	Definition
Association of Talent Development (ATD)[262]	Learning and Development (L&D)	The term "learning and development" encompasses any professional development a business provides to its employees. It is considered to be a core area of human resources management and may sometimes be referred to as training and development, learning and performance, or talent development.
Academy to Innovate HR (AIHR)[263]	L&D	L&D is one of the core areas of human resource management. L&D is a systematic process to enhance an employee's skills, knowledge, and competency, resulting in better performance in a work setting. Specifically, learning is concerned with the acquisition of knowledge, skills, and attitudes. Development is the deepening of knowledge in line with one's development goals. The goal of learning and development is to develop or change the behavior of individuals or groups for the better, sharing knowledge and insights that enable them to do their work better, or cultivate attitudes that help them perform better.
ATD[264]	L&D Function	A function within an organization that is responsible for empowering employees' growth and developing their knowledge, skills, and capabilities to drive better business performance. The function may be organized centrally, either independently or sitting under human resources (HR); decentralized throughout different business units; or it may be a hybrid (sometimes referred to as federated) structure.

Learning and Development (L&D) Frameworks

Several frameworks exist to assist with developing and customizing an organization's cloud-related L&D strategy. Tables 11.9 and 11.10 present examples.

Such learning frameworks may be used to develop a customized cloud learning strategy and related processes. For instance, defining cloud learner needs, designing, developing, and delivering cloud training.

Table 11.9: Overview of the ACADEMIES framework, as adapted from McKinsey.[265]

The McKinsey ACADEMIES Framework: Dimensions of a Strong L&D Function		
#	Step	Overview
1.	Alignment with business strategy	The learning strategy supports professional development and builds capabilities across the company, on time, and cost-effectively. In addition, the learning strategy can enhance the company culture and encourage employees to live the company's values.
2.	Co-ownership between business units and HR	L&D functions establish a governance structure in which leaders from both groups share responsibility for defining, prioritizing, designing, and securing funds for capability-building programs. Executives help embed the learning function and all L&D initiatives in the organizational culture. The involvement of senior leadership enables full commitment to the L&D function's longer-term vision.
3.	Assessment of capability gaps and estimated value	Take a deliberate, systematic approach to capability assessment, leveraging a comprehensive competency or capability model. After identifying essential capabilities for functions or job descriptions, assess how employees rate in each of these areas. L&D interventions should seek to close these capability gaps.
4.	Design of learning journeys	Continuous learning opportunities take place over a period of time and include L&D interventions such as fieldwork, pre-, and post-classroom digital learning, social learning, on-the-job coaching and mentoring, and short workshops. The main objectives are to help people develop the required new competencies in the most effective and efficient way and to support the transfer of learning to the job.

Table 11.9 (continued)

The McKinsey ACADEMIES Framework: Dimensions of a Strong L&D Function		
#	**Step**	**Overview**
5.	Execution and scale-up	Successful execution of L&D initiatives on time and within budget is critical to sustaining support from business leaders. Many new L&D initiatives are initially targeted to a limited audience. Successful execution of a small pilot, such as an online orientation program for a specific audience, can lead to an even bigger impact once the program is rolled out to the entire enterprise.
6.	Measurement of impact on business performance	A learning strategy's execution and impact should be measured using key performance indicators (KPIs). – Business Excellence KPI: How closely aligned all L&D initiatives and investments are with business priorities. – Learning Excellence KPI: Whether learning interventions change people's behavior and performance. – Operational Excellence KPI: How well investments and resources in the corporate academy are used.
7.	Integrate L&D into HR processes	L&D has an important role in recruitment, onboarding, performance management, promotion, workforce, and succession planning.
8.	Enabling of the 70:20:10 learning framework	70 percent of learning takes place on the job, 20 percent through interaction and collaboration, and 10 percent through learning interventions such as classroom training.
9.	Systems and learning technology applications	Significant enablers for just-in-time learning are technology platforms and applications.

Designing Cloud-Specific L&D Programs

Numerous options are available to develop and deliver cloud training programs. One option is purchasing cloud training programs and courses from third-party education vendors (e.g., open-enrolment programs). Table 11.11 presents examples of such courses.

Table 11.10: Overview of the ADDIE framework, as adapted from AIHR.[266]

Step	Overview
1. Analyze	– Target audience – Needs analysis – Desired outcomes
2. Design	– Learning objectives – Learning intervention alternatives – Communication strategies
3. Development	– Determine instructional strategies – Determine delivery methods – Development of the learning interventions
4. Implementation	– Training program implementation – Communications
5. Evaluation	– Have all learning objectives been met? – Have expected learning outcomes been realized? – Do the learning interventions and objectives need improvements?

The advantage of purchasing cloud training programs and courses from third-party education vendors is time savings and access to courses developed with input from cloud experts and learning experts. A major disadvantage is off-the-shelf courses may not be fully responsive to the unique attributes of an organization and may not fully meet learner needs.

Organizations may also develop their own cloud courses and programs through their in-house L&D function. The advantage of this option is that courses and programs will be customized to the unique characteristics of the organization and can be modified as necessary. Creating customized courses, however, is time-consuming, costly, and requires access to specialized cloud technical skills and specialized skills in training.

Some organizations choose a combination of all options available to create a cloud-enabled workforce. Regardless of the approach, it is essential to prioritize and integrate the people-side of cloud transformation into organizational change management strategies. Organizations are at the early stage of designing and delivering L&D content using the cloud-driven Metaverse for an immersive training experience.

Table 11.11: Cloud L&D program topics, as adapted from Arcitura.[267]

Arcitura Cloud Fields of Practice	Knowledge and Proficiency
Cloud Professional	Cloud computing concepts, models, and business considerations, and proficiency in fundamental technology and security-related areas of cloud computing.
Cloud Technology Professional	Identification, positioning, and utilization of modern cloud technologies and associated security considerations.
Cloud Architect	Technology architecture that underlies cloud platforms and cloud-based IT resources and solutions, and has mastered the hands-on application of design patterns, principles and practices used to engineer and evolve such environments.
Cloud Security Specialist	Common threats and vulnerabilities associated with cloud-based environments, and in establishing security controls and countermeasures via the mastery of cloud security patterns and practices.
Cloud Governance Specialist	Defining, establishing, and evolving governance controls and frameworks specifically for cloud-based IT resources and platforms in support of organizational and technological governance requirements.
Cloud Storage Specialist	Mechanisms, devices, technologies, practices, and overall assessment criteria pertaining to cloud storage technologies and services.
Cloud Virtualization Specialist	Technologies, mechanisms, platforms, and practices based upon and associated with contemporary virtualization environments and cloud-based virtualization architectures.

11.6 Conclusion

Large-scale deployment of the cloud disrupts and transforms organizations. Cloud-driven transformational changes include governance protocols, strategies, systems, processes IT, operations, and skills.

Such cloud-driven transformations lead to the need for effective organizational change management strategies and methods. Effective organizational change management, including a cloud-enabled workforce, is essential to achieving cloud strategic performance outcomes and to effective cloud governance.

Key Questions
1. What is cloud-driven change management?
2. What is a cloud-enabled workforce?
3. What is cloud-related learning and development?

Part IV: **Governance Functions Disrupted
and Transformed by the Cloud**

Chapter 12
Cloud Risk Management

> By failing to prepare, you are preparing to fail.[268]
> – Benjamin Franklin, inventor, writer, and founding father of the U.S.

Learning Objectives
- Awareness of the general approach to managing risks
- Understand the definition of cloud risk
- Recognize the risks created by the cloud
- Understand the high-level processes available to identify, assess, and mitigate cloud risks
- Recognize common control activities to mitigate cloud risks

 Key Terms

1. Cloud Risk – The effect of uncertainty to achieve cloud objectives. Cloud objectives may include realized cost savings, innovation, efficiency, and improved decision making.
2. Control Activities – "The actions established through policies and procedures that help ensure that management's directives to mitigate risks to the achievement of objectives are carried out."[269]
3. Risk – "The effect of uncertainty on objectives."[270]
4. Risk Assessment – "estimating the likelihood that each risk event will occur, and the potential impact of the consequences."[271]
5. Risk Management – "To determine possible uncertainties or threats, to protect against resulting consequences and to permit the achievement of business objectives."[272]
6. Risk Mitigation – "Prioritizing, evaluating, and implementing the appropriate risk-reducing controls/countermeasures recommended from the risk management process."[273]

Chapter Outline

https://doi.org/10.1515/9783110755374-012

12.1 Introduction

The benefits of digital advancements create compelling opportunities. At the same time, such advances introduce risks related to the successful adoption and utilization of technology. Cloud computing is no exception. This chapter discusses what can go wrong in the cloud by exploring the myriad of cloud-related risks.

12.2 Defining Risk Management

The process for managing cloud risk is crucial to achieving strategic, operational, security, and compliance objectives of cloud computing. There is a wide range of definitions of the general concept of *risk management*. Table 12.1 presents four example definitions.

Table 12.1: Definition of risk management – selected examples.

Source	Definition of Risk Management
NIST[274]	The process of managing risks to organizational operations (including mission, functions, image, or reputation), organizational assets, or individuals resulting from the operation of an information system, and includes: – the conduct of a risk assessment – the implementation of a risk mitigation strategy; and – employment of techniques and procedures for the continuous monitoring of the security state of the information system.
ENISA[275]	To determine possible uncertainties or threats, to protect against resulting consequences, and to permit the achievement of business objectives.
Germany's BSI-Standard 200-3[276]	The complete process for identifying, assessing, and evaluating risks.
ISO 31000[277]	Coordinated activities to direct and control an organization with regard to risk.

While these definitions vary, each definition either implicitly or explicitly encompasses a process for managing risk that includes identifying, assessing, and responding to risks. Table 12.2 presents definitions of each of these steps in the risk management process.

Table 12.2: High-level steps in a risk management process flow.

Steps in a Risk Management Process Flow	Description
1) Identify Risks	– Designed to produce a comprehensive population of risks. The essential question is: What are the risks to achieving cloud objectives? – Such risks may be organized and reported by category (e.g., strategy risk, compliance risks, security risks).
2) Assess Risks	– Designed to assess and prioritize each risk identified. The essential questions are, what is the likelihood of a risk occurring and how severe could the impact be? – An organization can assess risks based on the likelihood of risks occurring and their potential impact on strategy. Typically, organizations use qualitative or quantitative techniques. – Management then prioritizes risks to focus their attention and resources on risks with the greatest potential likelihood and severity of impact.
3) Respond to Risks	– Once management identifies and assesses the risks, the essential question is if the risk does occur, how should management plan to respond? – Responses to risk vary. Examples include, avoiding the risk by eliminating it; ignoring the risk; reducing the risk; transferring the risk.

Source: Authors.

12.3 Defining Cloud Risk

Cloud computing is inherently risky. The International Organization for Standardization (ISO) defines risk as the "effect of uncertainty on objectives."[278] In the context of the cloud, *objectives* represent the strategic objectives underlying the use of the cloud in an organization. Example cloud objectives may include realized cost savings, innovation, efficiency, and improved decision-making.

12.4 Identifying Cloud Risk

Once management defines cloud objectives, a logical next step in a risk management process is to identify specific cloud risks. Identifying cloud risks is a complex and iterative process. A range of techniques is available in the public domain to assist with the risk identification process. For instance, the European Network and Information Security Agency (ENISA)[279] and the Project Management Institute[280] advance a variety of techniques that organizations can use to identify potential risks. Table 12.3 lists the commonly used risk identification techniques.

Table 12.3: Commonly used techniques to identify risk.

Risk Identification Technique	Description
Brainstorming	Bring a group together to creatively identify risks.
Delphi	Individuals separately identify risks. Then, a group of experts collectively review and finalize the list of risks.
Interviewing	Ask key stakeholders questions to help identify risks.
Focus Groups	A facilitator guides a group discussion about risk. The group could be from the same unit or from different units of the organization.
Survey	Develop survey questions designed for stakeholders to answer questions about their area of responsibility to identify risks.
Documentation Reviews	Review documentation such as an audit report or process flow chart to identify risk.
Environmental Scanning	Analyze information about trends and relationships in an organization's internal and external environment.
Scenario Planning	According to Deloitte, "scenario planning helps organizations perceive risks and opportunities more broadly, to imagine potential futures and different scenarios that might challenge their assumptions, and to spot sources of risk that may otherwise go undetected."[281]

12.5 What Can Go Wrong

The complexity of the cloud exacerbates risks (i.e., known-knowns), introduces new risks (unknown-knowns), and creates unforeseeable risks (unknown-

unknowns). Deloitte published a cloud risk map presenting their perspective on possible risks associated with cloud computing. Table 12.4 highlights examples of cloud risks by major categories of cloud strategic objectives identified by Deloitte.

Table 12.4: List of cloud computing risks, as adapted from Deloitte's Cloud Computing Risk Intelligence Map.[282]

Cloud Objective	Cloud Risk
Cloud Strategy	– Lack of a coherent cloud strategy or misalignment with other business strategies – Lack of an exit strategy for an organization or CSP – Ineffective organizational change management for cloud adoption – Lack of skills and experience to execute strategy
Cybersecurity	Once launched, the cloud ecosystem immediately exposes the organization to risks. Risks include: – Cloud misconfigurations that result in a data breach (see Box 12.1) – Poor security practices by the organization – Failure to secure network traffic – Unauthorized exposure of data at cloud locations – Lack of proper isolation for sensitive data – Failure to apply security patches – Failure to implement proper access controls
Data Governance	– Failure to appropriately remove data from multiple clouds – Lack of clear ownership of cloud-generated data – Poorly designed practices can lead to poor fiscal performance, compliance, regulatory fines, and penalties, and destruction of reputation and stakeholder trust
Operations	– Failure to control cloud expenses – Inadequate records management, preservation, retention, and – disposal policies – Failure to consider e-discovery issues in contracts – 24/7 availability as an expectation
Compliance	– Noncompliance with data privacy laws due to cross-jurisdictional data transfer and lack of visibility into data location – Inability to demonstrate compliance with regulatory requirements – Difficulty validating continuous compliance with evolving regulations and standards

Table 12.4 (continued)

Cloud Objective	Cloud Risk
Incident Response	– Delay by the CSP in the notification or lack of notification of a data breach – Ineffective incident investigation – Lack of ability to develop an effective incident response program when the organization does not have control or access to the cloud infrastructure assets
Vendor Selection	These risks take on significant importance in both scope and scale. These risks are in direct proportion to the migration from legacy technology to the cloud. Risks include: – Inadequate due diligence to select CSP – Failure to plan for cloud portability and interoperability
Performance Management	– Lack of performance monitoring mechanisms – Interruption of cloud services due to critical subcontractor failure – Loss of direct control over and access to the cloud infrastructure – Reliance upon contracts with terms and conditions to manage outcomes – New skills needed to manage and oversee CSP performance
Employee Learning	– Inadequate IT skills to manage cloud technologies – Insufficient staff expertise in auditing the cloud

12.6 Assessing Cloud Risk

A risk assessment follows the risk identification process. NIST suggests that management would assess cloud risk by "estimating the likelihood that each risk event will occur, and the potential impact of the consequences."[283] Qualitative (e.g., high, medium, or low risk) or quantitative techniques may be used to assess the impact and likelihood of each risk. For example, on a scale of 1–5, 5 is the highest risk.

Next, the organization prioritizes those risks in the order that deserve the most attention and sets the stage for responding to those risks (e.g., risk mitigation). The goal of prioritizing the list of risks is to focus management's attention and resources on a select few with the greatest potential likelihood and severity impact.

12.7 Responding to Cloud Risk

Following the risk identification and risk assessment processes, the risk response process takes place. Table 12.5 presents example definitions of risk mitigation.

Table 12.5: Risk mitigation definitions – selected examples.

Source	Risk Mitigation Definitions
NIST[284]	Prioritizing, evaluating, and implementing the appropriate risk-reducing controls/countermeasures recommended by the risk management process.
The Mitre Organization[285]	Developing options and actions to enhance opportunities and reduce threats (risks).

To reduce risk to an acceptable level, management designs and implements risk mitigation activities.

Risk mitigation activities often include a combination of accepting a risk, avoiding a risk, transferring a risk (e.g., insurance policy), and controlling the risk (i.e., control activities). Control activities are an integral and substantial component of risk mitigation. COSO defines the term *control activities* as:

> Control activities are actions (generally described in policies, procedures, and standards) that help management mitigate risks in order to ensure the achievement of objectives. Control activities may be preventive or detective in nature and may be performed at all levels of the organization.[286]

In the context of the cloud, control activities play an essential role in cloud risk mitigation strategies designed to reduce cloud risk to an acceptable level.

The Cloud Security Alliance (CSA) Cloud Controls Matrix (CCM) is an example of a framework for cloud control activities. According to the CSA, "the CCM is a cybersecurity control framework for cloud computing."[287] Table 12.6 presents the CSA CCM domains.

Effective cloud control activities linked to cloud control objectives help prevent or reduce the likelihood of cloud risks occurring, or reduce the impact of cloud risks should they occur.

Table 12.6: CSA CCM – Cloud control domains, as adapted from the Cloud Security Alliance's Cloud Controls Matrix.[288]

Domain #	Domain of the CSA's Cloud Control Matrix	Description
1	Audit and Assurance	Includes independent audits, assurance assessments, and regulatory compliance
2	Application and Interface Security	Governs application security, as well as data integrity/access/security
3	Business Continuity Management and Operational Resilience	Relates to developing strategies for recovery from business disruptions, backing up data stored in the cloud, and preparing for disasters
4	Change Control and Configuration Management	Relates to the management of risks associated with changes to applications and systems, and the quality change control, approval, and testing process
5	Cryptography, Encryption and Key Management	Relates to defining and implementing cryptographic, encryption, and key management to protect, store, and access sensitive data
6	Datacenter Security	Deals with the physical security of data centers and servers
7	Data Security and Privacy Lifecycle Management	Includes the classification, protection, and handling of data throughout its lifecycle
8	Governance, Risk and Compliance	Relates to overall cloud governance, overall cloud policy exceptions, and enterprise risk management
9	Human Resources	Includes employee termination, remote work policies, and IT security training
10	Identity and Access Management	Governs separation of duties, strong authentication, user access restriction, and strong passwords
11	Interoperability and Portability	Interoperability relates to communications between applications or providers Portability relates to the ability to move data/services from one provider to another
12	Infrastructure and Virtualization Security	Includes network security, secure migration to cloud environments

Table 12.6 (continued)

Domain #	Domain of the CSA's Cloud Control Matrix	Description
13	Logging and Monitoring	Deals with the security and retention of audit logs, restriction of access to audit logs, and encryption monitoring and reporting
14	Security Incident Management, E-Discovery, and Cloud Forensics	Deals with security breach notifications and incident response metrics/testing/plans
15	Cloud Supply Chain Management, Transparency, and Accountability	Includes compliance testing, applying the shared responsibility model to cloud security, data quality and integrity, supply chain relationships, and contractual agreements
16	Threat and Vulnerability Management	Relates to preventive controls to protect the organization against cloud breaches such as breach detection tools, compromise assessments, and penetration testing
17	Universal Endpoint Management	Governs the proper security of third-party endpoints with access to the organization's assets and manage endpoints to prevent data loss

12.8 Conclusion

The cloud provides unique and compelling opportunities that range from realized cost savings, innovation, efficiency, and improved decision-making. At the same time, the cloud creates unintended consequences, exacerbates existing risks, and creates new risks. It is important for management to engage in risk management practices to identify, assess, and mitigate the myriad of risks associated with cloud computing.

Key Questions
1. What risks are created by the cloud?
2. What is risk management?
3. What are common control activities that help an organization respond to cloud risk?

Box 12.1: Risk of Cloud Misconfiguration

Both the SANS Cloud Security Survey (2022)[289] and IBM Security's Cost of a Data Breach Report (2021)[290], ranked cloud *misconfigurations* as one of the top cloud risks and top reasons for security breaches of the cloud. A simple example of a misconfiguration is the failure to change the manufacturer's predefined default password setting in a new system installation. Table 12.7 presents survey results from the Fugue and Sonatype State of the Cloud Security Report (2021) on the frequency of categories of misconfiguration root causes.

Table 12.7: Root causes of cloud misconfigurations, as adapted from the 2021 Fugue and Sonatype Report.[291]

Root Causes	Percent
Too many cloud APIs and interfaces to adequately govern	32
Lack of adequate controls and oversight	31
Lack of team awareness of security and policies	27
Inappropriate insider behavior	23
Lack of cloud expertise on team	23
Lack of validation of infrastructure as code	21
Ineffective monitoring of cloud environment	20

As a result, management must continuously monitor and manage security configurations to detect and correct potentially harmful cloud configuration errors. According to NIST,

> The management of configurations has traditionally been viewed as an IT management best practice. Using Security Configuration Management to gain greater control over and ensure the integrity of IT resources facilitates asset management, improves incident response, help desk, disaster recovery and problem solving, aids in software development and release management, enables greater automation of processes, and supports compliance with policies and preparation for audits.[292]

Once management detects such cloud misconfiguration errors, management should take steps to identify, fix, and verify the error. According to Deloitte,

> Many organizations are using cloud access security brokers (CASBs) to monitor activity across cloud services and applications for accidental configuration risks, as well as intentional policy deviations. Organizations can address security loopholes through Zero Trust thinking and restricted user access that configures storage, database, and search access through process (e.g., credentials) or with restrictions in the infrastructure itself (e.g., containers).[293]

If management fails to prevent and remediate the root causes of cloud misconfigurations, then management could be unwittingly putting their organizations at risk.

Box 12.2: Definitions of Selected Technology Terms
Table 12.8 presents a list of selected technology terms and definitions that are mentioned in this chapter.

Table 12.8: Definitions of select technology terms.

Term	Definition
1. Application Portability	"The ability to move executable software from one cloud system to another, and be able to run it correctly in the destination system."[294]
2. Application Programming Interface (API)	"An interface that provides programmatic access to service functionality and data within an application or a database. It can be used as a building block for the development of new interactions with humans, other applications or smart devices."[295]
3. Audit Log	"A chronological record of system activities. Includes records of system accesses and operations performed in a given period."[296]
4. Cloud Supply Chain	"is two or more parties linked by the provision of cloud services, related information and funds."[297]
5. Cloud Forensics	"A blend of digital forensics and cloud computing. It is directly responsible for investigating crimes that are committed using the cloud. Traditional computer forensics is a process by which media is collected at the crime scene, or where the media was obtained; it includes the practice of persevering the data, the validation of said data, and the interpretation, analysis, documentation, and presentation of the results in the courtroom."[298]
6. Cloud Interoperability	"The ability of the systems to work efficiently and collaborate effectively across different cloud platforms."[299]
7. Cloud Misconfiguration	"A setting within a computer program [the cloud] that violates a configuration policy or that permits or causes unintended behavior that impacts the security posture of a system."[300]

Table 12.8 (continued)

Term	Definition
8. Configuration Management	"A collection of activities focused on establishing and maintaining the integrity of information technology products and information systems, through control of processes for initializing, changing, and monitoring the configurations of those products and systems throughout the system development life cycle."[301]
9. Containers	"Executable units of software in which application code is packaged, along with its libraries and dependencies, in common ways so that it can be run anywhere, whether it be on desktop, traditional IT, or the cloud."[302]
10. Cryptography	"The discipline that embodies the principles, means, and methods for the transformation of data in order to hide their semantic content, prevent their unauthorized use, or prevent their undetected modification."[303]
11. Data Portability	"The ability to move data (files, documents, database tables, etc.) from one cloud system to another, and have that data usable in the other system."[304]
12. E-Discovery	"The identification, collection, preservation, processing, review, analysis and production of electronically stored information to meet the mandates imposed by common-law requirements for discovery. These demands may be due to civil or criminal litigation, regulatory oversight or administrative proceedings."[305]
13. Encryption	"The process of a confidentiality mode that transforms usable data into an unreadable form. The translation of data into a form that is unintelligible without a deciphering mechanism."[306]
14. Endpoint	"A remote computing device that communicates back and forth with a network to which it is connected. Examples of endpoints include desktops, laptops, smartphones, tablets, servers, workstations, and Internet-of-things (IoT) devices. Endpoints represent key vulnerable points of entry for cybercriminals."[307]

Table 12.8 (continued)

Term	Definition
15. Infrastructure as Code	"The process of managing and provisioning an organization's IT infrastructure using machine-readable configuration files, rather than employing physical hardware configuration or interactive configuration tools."[308]
16. Key Management	"The activities involving the handling of cryptographic keys and other related security parameters (e.g. passwords) during the entire life cycle of the keys, including their generation, storage, establishment, entry and output, and destruction."[309]
17. Zero Trust Thinking	"A collection of concepts and ideas designed to minimize uncertainty in enforcing accurate, least privilege per-request access decisions in information systems and services in the face of a network viewed as compromised."[310]

Chapter 13
Enterprise Risk Management and the Cloud

> Good risk management fosters vigilance in times of calm and
> instills discipline in times of crisis.[311]
> – Dr. Michael Ong, author

Learning Objectives
– Understand the definition and components of the Committee of Sponsoring Organizations of the Treadway Commission's (COSO) enterprise risk management (ERM) framework
– Understand the value of integrating cloud computing activities into an organization's ERM framework to help manage cloud risks

 Key Terms

1. Cyber Resiliency – "The ability to anticipate, withstand, recover from, and adapt to adverse conditions, stresses, attacks, or compromises on systems that use or are enabled by cyber resources."[312]
2. Enterprise Risk Management – An enterprise-wide approach "to addressing the full spectrum of the organization's significant risks by understanding the combined impact of risks as an interrelated portfolio, rather than addressing risks only within silos."[313]
3. Risk Appetite – "The types and amount of risk, on a broach level, an organization is willing to accept in pursuit of its value."[314]
4. Risk Heat Map – A two-dimensional visualization of the list of risks prioritized by potential likelihood and impact for management to help decide what risks to respond to.
5. Risk Portfolio – List of prioritized risks identified by management.
6. Risk Response – Management's determination about how to respond to a risk (e.g., reduce, accept, transfer).

Chapter Outline
13.1   Introduction
13.2   Defining ERM
13.3   ERM and Cloud Risk

https://doi.org/10.1515/9783110755374-013

13.1 Introduction

Cloud computing exacerbates risks and creates new and unexpected risks. An enterprise risk management (ERM) framework helps management understand the full spectrum of risks – including cloud risks – across the entire organization. ERM also facilitates an approach for management to integrate, communicate, and share a strategically aligned portfolio view of risk. This chapter discusses the value and approach of integrating cloud computing into an organization's ERM process, including an illustrative example of a cloud ERM assessment.

13.2 Defining ERM

A risk management process is designed to identify the population of risks an organization faces, analyze the likelihood of those risks occurring, assess the impact of those risks on strategic goals, and establish risk response strategies to manage these risks. A risk management process may apply to many levels in an organization. For example, at a strategic level, functional level, process level, and technology level (e.g., cloud deployment).

When the risk management process is applied as one integrated process across the entire organization, it is commonly referred to as *enterprise risk management* (ERM). Organizations that leverage ERM take a holistic approach to managing risk. Employing ERM practices allows management to view risk – including cloud risk – across all organizational silos.

The COSO ERM Framework titled, "Enterprise Risk Management Integrating Strategy with Performance," is an example of an internationally recognized ERM framework. COSO defines ERM as "the culture, capabilities, and practices, integrated with strategy-setting and performance that organizations rely on to manage risk in creating, preserving, and realizing value."[315]

13.3 ERM and Cloud Risk

An ERM process can contribute to holistically managing cloud risk. *Why?* ERM can contribute to enhanced cyber resiliency for an organization. Cyber resiliency is an organization's ability to fully recover from cloud failures and cloud security breaches rapidly. ERM and cyber resilience can also help an organization plan for potential cloud risk events, pivot to address actual cloud risk events, and build capacity to respond and continue to thrive during and after a crisis (i.e., significant cloud breach).

The COSO ERM Framework consists of the following five components.

1) Governance and Culture
2) Strategy and Objective Setting
3) Performance (Risk Assessment)
4) Review and Revision
5) Information, Communication and Reporting

Table 13.1 defines the five components of the COSO ERM framework and presents an example of how it may be applied to cloud computing.

Table 13.1: Overview of the COSO ERM framework,[317] with an example of how it may be applied to cloud computing.

COSO ERM Component	Definition	Cloud Example
1. Governance and Culture	"Governance is the organization's tone, reinforcing the importance of, and establishing oversight responsibilities for, ERM. Culture pertains to ethical values, desired behaviors, and understanding of risk in the entity."[318]	Governance and Culture Considerations, Include the Following – Obtain insights into how the organization compares to peers in terms of cloud breaches and best practices in managing cloud risk. – Gain real-time knowledge of the location of stored cloud data. – Obtain assurances concerning cloud governance (e.g., compliance with privacy laws and regulations). – Confirm the relevance, redundancy, and adequacy of the internal IT staff and CSPs with respect to cloud computing.
2. Strategy and Objective Setting	"Business objectives put a strategy into practice while serving as a basis for identifying, assessing, and responding to risk."[319]	Strategy and Objectives Setting Considerations, Including the Following – Ensure that the cloud strategy aligns with the organization's overall strategy. – Ensure the cloud strategy is the basis for applying ERM to assess the risk of failing to achieve cloud-related objectives. Cloud-related objectives may include data privacy, system availability, productivity, reliability, compliance with regulations, and cost savings.

	Risk Identification	Risk Identification and Risk Assessment Considerations Include the Following
3. Performance Three of the underlying principles within this COSO component are: – risk identification – risk assessment – risk response	**Risk Identification** ISO states that "the purpose of risk identification is to find, recognize and describe risks that might help or prevent an organization from achieving its objectives."[320] **Risk Assessment** Risk assessment includes determining the likelihood of risks occurring and their potential impact on strategic objectives. Typically, organizations can use qualitative (e.g., high, medium, or low risk) and/or quantitative techniques (e.g., on a scale of 1–5, 5 is the highest risk) to assess risk. Risk assessment leads to a prioritization of a select few with the greatest potential likelihood and severity impact. The organization prioritizes those risks that deserve attention and sets the stage for responding to those risks (e.g., risk mitigation).	– During the risk identification and assessment steps, management would document the likelihood of the risk and the impact if the problem occurs. – Communicate expectations associated with employee responsibilities for cloud risk identification and risk assessment. – Establish policies and training associated with cloud risk identification and assessment. Box 13.1 presents an illustrative example of a cloud-related ERM risk portfolio.

(continued)

Table 13.1 (continued)

COSO ERM Component	Definition	Cloud Example
	Risk Response There are three common responses for management to select as a risk response: – Reduce: A "reduce" response means risk mitigation. Management would take action to lessen the likelihood of a risk occurring or lessen the Impact if the risk should occur. – Accept: An "accept" response indicates that existing policy, procedures, and controls are effectively managing the risk. No additional activities are underway or planned. An "accept risk" response means management is comfortable with the impact and likelihood and the risk is within the organization's risk appetite. – Transfer: Management leverages this type of risk response when activities are outside the risk appetite of the organization. Management would transfer the risk to a third party to lessen the severity of impact.	Risk Response Considerations, Include the Following – Define clear roles and responsibilities for cloud risk response. – Communicate expectations associated with employee responsibilities for cloud risk response. – Establish policies and training associated with cloud risk response. – Document and monitor the shared responsibilities between the CSP and the organization and hold CSPs accountable for such responsibilities. – Box 13.2 highlights an example of a well-known form of risk transfer: insurance.

4.	Review and Revision	Management's continuous review of enterprise risk is essential to ensure changing business objectives are aligned with law, operations, and performance.	Review and Revision Considerations, Including the Following – Obtain internal audit and external audit reports to review and validate CSP cloud governance. Third-party cloud service assurance providers contribute to greater transparency into CSP processes. This creates an additional layer of defense against cloud enterprise-wide risks.
5.	Information, Communication, and Reporting	Management would share risk information with internal and external stakeholders to manage risk and make informed decisions. Management can report the risks they identify into categories such as: strategic, reputational, financial, operational, and compliance. If an organization shares a list of prioritized enterprise risks, then management will have increased awareness and broader visibility across the enterprise to make informed decisions.	Information, Communication and Reporting Considerations, Including the Following – The Chief Risk Officer, or equivalent senior executive, could present the prioritized enterprise – wide cloud risks and report significant changes and risk response plans to the board of directors. – Use reports such as an ERM risk portfolio and a risk heat map to manage risk and make informed decisions.

A risk heat map is a two-dimensional visualization of the list of risks prioritized by potential likelihood and impact. The map is divided into quadrants. In the top right quadrant are the risks that scored the highest in terms of likelihood and impact that demand management's immediate or greatest attention. James Lam, a globally recognized risk expert, suggests "it's not just about risk monitoring and reporting; it's about using risk insights and analytics to drive better business decisions. [The board needs to] understand what drives earnings, what drives cash flows, and what drives value"[316]

Table 13.2: Examples of ERM responsibilities.

Role	Description of Cloud ERM Responsibilities
Governance Bodies (e.g., Board of Directors, Risk Committee)	– Gain an overall understanding about cloud computing. – Proactively engage management on cloud governance. For example, McKinsey recommends four ways for the board to engage on the topic of cloud: – "Link cloud to overall strategy discussion – Incorporate cloud into risk and compliance discussion – Support development of cloud capabilities – Oversee and communicate cloud financial impact"[321]
Chief Executive Officer (CEO)	– Gain an awareness of how the industry and its competitors are using the cloud. – Understand the lessons learned from high-profile cloud breaches. – Define the company's risk appetite as it relates to outsourcing cloud functions to a CSP.
Chief Financial Officer (CFO)	– Account for implementation costs incurred in cloud computing service agreements in compliance with financial accounting standards. – Calculate cloud return on investment. – Monitor and manage cloud cost management (e.g., cost overruns to stay within budget).

Table 13.2 (continued)

Role	Description of Cloud ERM Responsibilities
Chief Information Officer (CIO)	– Lead the development and implementation of the organization's cloud strategy, cloud security posture, and cloud security controls. – Monitor the performance of CSPs related to ERM. For example, compliance with cloud laws and regulations, cybersecurity attacks, incident response and availability outages. – Analyze external audit reports to validate CSP cloud governance. – Mature incident response capabilities to prevent, detect, and correct cloud breaches.
Chief Audit Executive (CAE)	– Evaluate the organization's approach to managing cloud risk. – Report cloud-related internal audit results to the board of directors (e.g., audit committee of the board). – Conduct due diligence to help management in CSP vendor selection. – Assess the maturity of the organization's vendor risk management program.
Chief Risk Officer (CRO)	– Collaborate with business units to facilitate the assessment of enterprise risks, including cloud risks. – Provide the board of directors, CEO, and the CAE with regular updates on the status of critical cloud risks. – The CRO function may not exist at some organizations. Sometimes, the CFO has the collateral responsibility to communicate risk to management. Some organizations, with or without a CRO, assemble a risk management council to oversee ERM. The council members are typically division heads who own the risks for their respective business units.

13.4 Who is Responsible for Cloud ERM?

Cloud computing differs substantially from traditional on-premises computing. One of the primary differences is data, applications, and technology infrastructure is no longer entirely managed and governed within the protective boundaries of the organization. While the organization's *responsibilities* for managing IT risks do not change with outsourcing services to vendors, *the manner in which organizations manage cloud risks* in an ERM context will change because of the unique characteristics of the cloud.

The cloud will create new responsibilities for the board of directors and senior executive positions. In addition, these executives play an important role in the identification of enterprise risks. Table 13.2 provides examples of ERM responsibilities of internal executives in the context of the cloud. The list of responsibilities is not an all-inclusive, comprehensive representation for every organization.

The organization is responsible and accountable for ERM and overall cloud governance.

It is crucial to clearly define roles, responsibilities, and accountability for cloud governance (e.g., ERM) between the organization and every third-party service provider. For example, the shared responsibilities between the organization, the CSP, and their third-party assurance provider. These shared responsibilities should be included in service contracts between the organization and the third-party service provider.

13.5 Conclusion

The cloud provides compelling opportunities, while at the same time introducing new, and in some cases unfamiliar and unknown risks across the organization. Organizations that leverage ERM take a holistic approach to managing risk. Integrating a cloud perspective into an organization's ERM process facilitates management's understanding of the cloud risks across the entire organization. Sharing this ERM portfolio provides broader visibility into cloud risks across the enterprise and increases awareness among senior executives. ERM also contributes to enhanced cloud resiliency.

Box 13.1: Illustration of a Cloud ERM Portfolio.

Table 13.3: Example cloud ERM portfolio.

Identify Risk	Risk Category	Assess Risk		Risk Responses	Owner
		Likelihood	Impact		
Strategic Objective: Shared-Responsibility Model					
If an organization does not invest in, adequately implement, and maintain cloud computing to meets its business needs, then innovations and efficiencies in operations may not be achieved.	Strategic	Medium	High	Reduce Risk Response: – Formalize terms of cloud services with a service-level agreement (SLA) to document roles and shared responsibilities between the organization and CSP vendor. – Perform due diligence before entering into an agreement with a third-party CSP.	CEO CIO

(continued)

Table 13.3 (continued)

Identify Risk	Risk Category	Assess Risk		Risk Responses	Owner
		Likelihood	Impact		
Organizational Culture Objective: Advance the Use of Cloud					
If stakeholders subvert the initiative to use cloud computing, then the change may not be adopted.	Strategic	Medium	Medium	Accept Risk Response: – Understand how to engage stakeholders and manage their expectations. – Assess the change readiness of stakeholders. – Communicate the importance of the change, timeframes, and responsibilities of stakeholders. Reduce Risk Response: Develop training for stakeholders.	CEO CIO

If management does not consider the relevance, redundancy, and adequacy of the internal IT staff competencies and roles because of the cloud, then the organization will lack experienced personnel, impacting cloud performance on business objectives.	Strategic	Medium	Medium	Reduce Risk Response: – Retain and upskill current staff on cloud. – Hire cloud experts. – Define roles to set clear expectations about staff responsibilities because of cloud adoption.	CIO
Cybersecurity Objective: Safeguard Data					
If there is a failure to safeguard personally identifiable information that results in a breach/incident, then there will be an adverse impact on the business and the individuals whose information was compromised.	Operational	Low	High	Reduce Risk Response: Establish cybersecurity policies and procedures, conduct annual IT audits, and require employees to complete security awareness training. Transfer Risk Response: Invest in cyber insurance policy to cover loss and expenses arising out of a security breach.	CIO

(continued)

Table 13.3 (continued)

Identify Risk	Risk Category	Assess Risk		Risk Responses	Owner
		Likelihood	Impact		
Compliance Objective: Regulatory Requirements					
If the organization does not monitor cloud data transfers across jurisdictions, then it will not be in compliance with data privacy laws.	Compliance	Medium	Medium	Reduce Risk Response: – Create and continuously update a cloud asset inventory, including locations (jurisdictions, regions, countries, states) of cloud servers. – Demonstrate compliance with regulatory requirements to auditors and stakeholders.	CEO CIO

Financial Objective: Concentration of one CSP				
If the organization is unaware of a concentration of one CSP, then cost overruns may harm revenue and financial results.	Financial	Medium	Medium	Accept Risk Response: Cloud administrator actively monitors cloud usage and cost reports. Reduce Risk Response: Adjust risk appetite to consider expanding to a multi-cloud strategy.	CEO CFO CIO

Operations Objective: Increase Business Resilience				
If the organization is unaware of the full inventory of cloud services being used, then critical weaknesses may go undetected, and data may be subject to theft, exploitation, and manipulation.	Operational	High	High	Reduce Risk Response: Create and continuously update a cloud asset inventory.	CEO CIO
If an SLA with CSP does not exist or does not specify terms related to data rights, data usage, or vendor lock-in, then an organization may be at risk of not efficiently managing cloud services and performance.	Operational	Medium	Medium	Reduce Risk Response: – Require the CSP to provide cost calculation tools and data usage monitoring services. – Document data ownership rights and the ability to retrieve data from CSP upon term end.	CIO

(continued)

Table 13.3 (continued)

Identify Risk	Risk Category	Assess Risk		Risk Responses	Owner
		Likelihood	Impact		
If an SLA with CSP does not specify terms related to oversight, accountability, and monitoring, then the organization is unaware of the adequacy of a third-party CSP's risk management practices.	Operational	High	High	Accept Risk Response: – Describe role of CSP to monitor subcontractors providing fourth-party cloud services. – Define whether data stored on CSP servers must be located in the home country. – Document roles, responsibilities, nature, timing, scope, and frequency of internal audit and third-party assurance.	CIO

Key Questions

1. What is an ERM framework?
2. How does an ERM framework apply to managing cloud enterprise risk?
3. How does the cloud expose the organization to enterprise risk?

Box 13.2: Transfer Risk Response: Cyber Insurance
Management could decide to procure a cyber insurance policy as a way to transfer part of the organization's cloud risk. A cyber insurance policy could offer an organization coverage for business interruptions, crisis management costs, and cyber extortion. A cyber insurance policy may also offer coverage for liabilities such as regulatory fines, penalties, and privacy breaches. Table 13.4 provides examples of cyber insurance offered by CSPs.

Table 13.4: Cyber insurance offered by CSPs – selected examples.

CSP	Cyber Insurance
Amazon AWS	In September 2021, Amazon announced it will offer cyber insurance to small and medium-sized businesses in the United Kingdom.[322] For example, the insurance broker Superscript covers risks such as accidental privacy breaches, extortion, and ransomware.
Google Cloud Platform	In March 2021, Google announced that it is partnering with Munich Re and Allianz to provide a cyber insurance product to its Google Cloud customers.[323] The insurance covers risks such as "third-party liability coverage for loss and expenses arising out of a programming error or omission, loss and defense expenses arising out of a security breach or an intellectual property infringement, costs of a public relations firms to respond to negative publicity resulting from a cyber incident."[324]
Microsoft Azure	In September 2021, Microsoft announced that it is partnering with At-Bay to offer data-driven cyber insurance coverage.[325] The insurance covers risks such as cyber extortion, technology errors and omissions, reputational harm, costs of breach notification, and fines.[326]

Chapter 14
Security, Trust and the Cloud

> Cloud computing is a challenge to security, but one that can be overcome.[327]
> – Whitfield Diffie, pioneer in computer security

Learning Objectives
- Understand the basic concepts of cloud security
- Understand cloud security challenges
- Recognize the role of integrating a Zero Trust approach in a cloud security strategy

Key Terms

1. Application Program Interfaces (API) – "An interface that provides programmatic access to service functionality and data within an application or a database."[328]
2. Non-repudiation – "Assurance that the sender of information is provided with proof of delivery and the recipient is provided with proof of the sender's identity, so neither can later deny having processed the information."[329]
3. Security as Code – "The constant implementation of systematic and widely communicated security practices throughout the entire software development life cycle. The goal of this strategy is to streamline the rollout of new software and avoid last-minute vulnerability fixes."[330]
4. Virtualization – "The simulation of the software and/or hardware upon which other software runs; this simulated environment is called a virtual machine."[331]

https://doi.org/10.1515/9783110755374-014

14.1 Introduction

A diverse range of potential benefits are driving the international proliferation of cloud computing. At the same time, the cloud inherently creates cybersecurity threats. In this context, cloud security plays a crucial role in overall cloud governance. This chapter discusses basic concepts and critical elements of cloud security.

14.2 Defining Cloud Security

Cloud security is part of the broader domain of IT security, also referred to as cybersecurity. NIST defines cybersecurity as,

> Prevention of damage to, protection of, and restoration of computers, electronic communications systems, electronic communications services, wire communication, and electronic communication, including information contained therein, to ensure its availability, integrity, authentication, confidentiality, and nonrepudiation.[332]

A range of definitions of *cloud security* have been advanced in the public domain. Examples of such definitions are presented in Table 14.1.

Table 14.1: Definitions of cloud security – selected examples.

Source	Definition
Gartner	"Cloud security refers to the processes, mechanisms and services used to control the security, compliance, and other usage risks of cloud computing. Although all forms of cloud computing have unique security needs, this term primarily refers to public cloud computing. It specifically addresses the security of the cloud service and security within the cloud service, but the term does not encompass security services delivered from the cloud (security as a service) that are intended to be used outside the cloud."[333]
Checkpoint Software Technologies	"Cloud security refers to the technologies, policies, controls and services that protect cloud data, applications and infrastructure from threats."[334]
Red Hat	"Cloud security is the protection of data, applications, and infrastructures involved in cloud computing." "Many aspects of security for cloud environments (whether it's a public, private, or hybrid cloud) are the same as for any on-premise IT architecture." "High-level security concerns – like unauthorized data exposure and leaks, weak access controls, susceptibility to attacks, and availability disruptions – affect traditional IT and cloud systems alike."[335]

While these definitions differ, they do share many of the security objectives reflected in the NIST definition of cybersecurity. Namely, protective measures associated with prevention, detection, recovery, and correction to ensure system availability, integrity, authentication, confidentiality, and nonrepudiation.

14.3 IT Security Frameworks and the Cloud

IT Security frameworks foster and facilitate the design of best practice cybersecurity strategies and plans. A number of cybersecurity frameworks are available in the public domain to use as a guide for preparing cybersecurity strategies, plans, and processes customized to an organization. Such IT frameworks are designed to function as blueprints for building a comprehensive security program to manage cybersecurity threats.

For instance, NIST published a popular cybersecurity framework designed to help organizations of all sizes with understanding and managing cybersecurity threats. While not designed specifically for the cloud, the NIST framework is used by U.S. government agencies and is popular with organizations in other industries. Table 14.2 presents the components of the NIST cybersecurity framework.

Table 14.2: Components of the U.S. NIST cybersecurity framework.[336]

NIST Security Objective	Description
Identify	Develop the organizational understanding to manage cybersecurity risk to systems, assets, data, and capabilities.
Protect	Develop and implement the appropriate safeguards to ensure delivery of critical infrastructure services.
Detect	Develop and implement the appropriate activities to identify the occurrence of a cybersecurity event.
Respond	Develop and implement the appropriate activities to take action regarding a detected cybersecurity event.
Recover	Develop and implement the appropriate activities to maintain plans for resilience and to restore any capabilities of services that were impaired due to a cybersecurity event.

Cybersecurity frameworks vary in degree of complexity and scope. Table 14.3 contains an overview of some of the additional cybersecurity frameworks available in the public domain.

Table 14.3: Summary of additional cybersecurity frameworks available in the public domain IT security frameworks include guidance on risks, controls, and governance.

Framework	Description of Cybersecurity Frameworks
Information Systems Audit and Control Association (ISACA) Control Objectives for Information Security and Related Technology (COBIT)[337]	Provides guidelines, objectives, and practices related to IT governance to align business goals with IT.
International Standards Organization (ISO) 27000[338]	Provides requirements for an information security management system to manage the security of assets such as financial information, intellectual property, employee details, or information entrusted by third parties.
European Union Agency for Cybersecurity (ENISA): Cloud Security Guide for Small and Medium Size Enterprises (SMEs)[339]	Identifies cloud security risks and opportunities. Provides organizations a set of questions to understand the CSP's level of security.
NIST Special Publication 800-53: Security and Privacy Controls for Information Systems and Organizations[340]	Catalogs security and privacy controls for information systems and organizations. Offers public and private organizations a systemic approach to developing a set of safeguarding measures for all types of computing platforms, including general purpose computing systems, cyber-physical systems, cloud-based systems, mobile devices, and Internet of Things (IoT) devices.
NIST Cybersecurity Framework[341]	Focuses on the cybersecurity aspects of defined critical infrastructure industries in the United States.
Center for Internet Security Controls[342]	Prioritizes a set of safeguards to mitigate against system and network cyber-attacks.
HITRUST Common Security Framework[343]	Provides organizations with an approach to regulatory compliance and risk management.
The Cloud Security Alliance (CSA) Cloud Controls Matrix[344]	Provides a tool for assessing the adequacy of security and related controls when deploying cloud computing services.

14.4 Security Implications Unique to the Cloud

Cloud security is a challenge. *Why is that?* The cloud is unique in several respects when compared with most other technologies. The impact of such differences influences cloud cybersecurity threats and associated cloud security protocols. For instance, Table 14.4 presents examples adapted from IBM of unique security threats created by the cloud and associated cloud security implications.

Table 14.4: Examples of security threats unique to the cloud, as adapted from IBM.[345]

Cloud Threat	Cloud Security Implications
Lack of Visibility	"It's easy to lose track of how your data is being accessed and by whom, since many cloud services are accessed outside of corporate networks and through third parties."
Multi-tenancy	"Public cloud environments house multiple client infrastructures under the same umbrella, so it's possible your hosted services can get compromised by malicious attackers as collateral damage when targeting other businesses."
Access Management and Shadow IT	"While enterprises may be able to successfully manage and restrict access points across on-premises systems, administering these same levels of restrictions can be challenging in cloud environments." "This can be dangerous for organizations that don't deploy bring-your-own device (BYOD) policies and allow unfiltered access to cloud services from any device or geolocation."
Compliance	"Regulatory compliance management is oftentimes a source of confusion for enterprises using public or hybrid cloud deployments." "Overall accountability for data privacy and security still rests with the enterprise, and heavy reliance on third-party solutions to manage this component can lead to costly compliance issues."
Misconfigurations	"Misconfigured assets accounted for 86% of breached records in 2019, making the inadvertent insider a key issue for cloud computing environments." "Misconfigurations can include leaving default administrative passwords in place, or not creating appropriate privacy settings."

According to TechTarget, "Cloud security frameworks help CSPs and customers alike, providing easy-to-understand security baselines, validations and certifications."[346] The CSA has created guidance designed to assist with addressing the major conceptual and structural elements of cloud computing that have security, trust and assurance implications. Table 14.5 summarizes this CSA guidance titled Security Guidance for Critical Areas of Focus in Cloud Computing.

Table 14.5: Cloud security domains, as defined in CSA's Security Guidance.[347]

Domain #	Domain Title	Description of CSA's Cloud Security Domains
1	Cloud Computing Concepts	Defines and describes cloud computing, including terminology and architectural frameworks.
2	Governance and Enterprise Risk Management	"The ability of an organization to govern and measure enterprise risk introduced by cloud computing. Items such as legal precedence for agreement breaches, ability of user organizations to adequately assess risk of a cloud provider, responsibility to protect sensitive data when both user and provider may be at fault, and how international boundaries may affect these issues."
3	Legal Issues: Contracts and Electronic Discovery	"Potential legal issues when using cloud computing. Issues touched on in this section include protection requirements for information and computer systems, security breach disclosure laws, regulatory requirements, privacy requirements, international laws, etc."
4	Compliance and Audit Management	"Maintaining and proving compliance when using cloud computing. Issues dealing with evaluating how cloud computing affects compliance with internal security policies, as well as various compliance requirements."
5	Information Governance	"Governing data that is placed in the cloud. Items surrounding the identification and control of data in the cloud, as well as compensating controls that can be used to deal with the loss of physical control when moving data to the cloud."
6	Management Plan and Business Continuity	"Securing the management plane and administrative interfaces used when accessing the cloud, including both web consoles and APIs. Ensuring business continuity for cloud deployments."
7	Infrastructure Security	"Core cloud infrastructure security, including networking, workload security, and hybrid cloud considerations."

Table 14.5 (continued)

Domain #	Domain Title	Description of CSA's Cloud Security Domains
8	Virtualization and Containers	"Virtualization security in cloud computing still follows the shared responsibility model. The cloud provider will always be responsible for securing the physical infrastructure and the virtualization platform itself. Meanwhile, the cloud customer is responsible for properly implementing the available virtualized security controls and understanding the underlying risks, based on what is implemented and managed by the cloud provider."
9	Incident Response (IR)	"Proper and adequate incident detection, response, notification, and remediation. This attempts to address items that should be in place at both provider and user levels to enable proper incident handling and forensics."
10	Application Security	"Securing application software that is running on or being developed in the cloud. This includes items such as whether it's appropriate to migrate or design an application to run in the cloud, and if so, what type of cloud platform is most appropriate (SaaS, PaaS, or IaaS)."
11	Data Security and Encryption	"Implementing data security and encryption, and ensuring scalable key management."
12	Identity, Entitlement, Access Management	"Managing identities and leveraging directory services to provide access control. The focus is on issues encountered when extending an organization's identity into the cloud."
13	Security as a Service	"Providing third-party-facilitated security assurance, incident management, compliance attestation, and identity and access oversight."
14	Related Technologies	"Established and emerging technologies with a close relationship to cloud computing, including Big Data, Internet of Things, and mobile computing."

Selecting a security framework will depend on the unique characteristics of an organization. For instance, laws and regulations, business needs, size, and appetite for risk. For the cloud, management may begin with selecting one of the IT security frameworks available in the public domain that most closely aligns with the organization's cloud strategy. Once a generic framework is selected, organizations will need to customize the framework to align with their unique cloud environment.

14.5 Security as a Code and Cloud Security

According to McKinsey, "Existing cybersecurity architectures and operating models break down as companies adopt public-cloud platforms. *Why?* Many breaches in the cloud stem from misconfiguration."[348] *Security as a code* has emerged as an effective approach to reducing such misconfigurations. Security as code is defined as follows.

> When you're developing software, you keep the purpose of the software in mind. You design and build the software making sure that it works as expected. While doing this, if you also consider the security of the software, that's security as code.[349]

That is, during the software development process, cybersecurity policies and standards are programmed into the new software's configurations.

Once the software is implemented, configuration instructions (i.e., configuration scripts) automatically deploy the embedded security policies. McKinsey provides the following example of security as code in action.

> If the business, for example, sets up a policy that all personally identifiable information (PII) must be encrypted when it's stored, that policy is translated into a process that is automatically launched whenever a developer submits code. Code that violates the PII policy is automatically rejected.[350]

Security as code can reduce or eliminate the need for manual configuration of security controls.

14.6 Integrating a Zero Trust Mindset into a Cloud Security Strategy

Managing cybersecurity risk involves complex decisions concerning cyber-*risk appetite*. Risk appetite is the amount of risk an organization is willing to accept in achieving objectives after controls are implemented.

Trust plays a role in cybersecurity and management's determination of whether the risk is within the organization's risk appetite. Camp (2003) advanced the following enduring definition of designing for trust, "Designing for trust requires identification of the sometimes subtle manner in which trust can be embedded in a system. Defining trust as the intersection of privacy, security, and reliability can enable or simplify the identification of trust as embedded in a technical design."[351]

Defining Zero Trust in the Context of IT and Cloud Security

In the context of cloud security, embedding trust involves management implementing operational security controls (e.g., safeguarding personally identifiable information) and stakeholders' expectations of trust to secure the cloud. For instance, to prevent cyber threats, organizations are adopting a Zero Trust approach to cloud security. A range of definitions of Zero Trust appears in the public domain. Table 14.6 presents examples of these definitions.

Table 14.6: Definitions of Zero Trust – selected examples.

Source	Definition of Zero Trust
NIST[352]	"An evolving set of cybersecurity paradigms that move defenses from status, network-based perimeters to focus on users, assets, and resources. Zero Trust assumes there is no implicit trust granted to assets or user accounts based solely on their physical or network location (i.e., local area networks versus the Internet) or based on asset ownership (enterprise or personally owned)."
Centrify[353]	"Mandates a 'never trust, always verify, enforce least privilege' approach to privileged access, from inside or outside the network."
IBM[354]	"A framework that assumes a complex network's security is always at risk to external and internal threats. It helps organize and strategize a thorough approach to counter those threats."
PaloAlto Networks[355]	"An IT security model that eliminates the notion of trust to protect networks, applications, and data. This is in stark contrast to the traditional perimeter security model, which presumes that bad actors are always on the untrusted side of the network, and trustworthy users are always on the trusted side."

Benefits of Adopting a Zero Trust to Cloud Security

Adopting a Zero Trust approach to cloud security creates a range of benefits for an organization. Table 14.7 presents perspectives on possible opportunities afforded by Zero Trust.

Table 14.7: Perspectives on the benefits of Zero Trust – selected examples.

Adapted from AT&T[356]	Adapted from IBM[357]	Adapted from Palo Alto Networks[358]
1. Reduced threat surface.	1. Enhanced network performance due to reduced traffic on subnets.	1. Better visibility into data, assets, and risks.
2. Maximized use and authority of authentication.		2. Consistent and comprehensive security.
3. Increased visibility into all user activity.	2. Improved ability to address network errors.	3. Speed and agility to stay ahead of evolving technologies.
4. The ability to dynamically provide access based on the current use case.	3. More simplified logging and monitoring process due to the granularity.	4. Reduced operational cost and complexity.
5. Reduce an attacker's ability to move laterally within your organization.	4. Quicker breach detection times.	
6. Limit the possibility for data exfiltration.		
7. Protection against both internal and external threats.		
8. Lowered reliance on point solutions designed to detect/stop specific types of threat activity.		
9. Improved overall security posture both on-premises and in the cloud.		

A reduction in the cost of a security breach appears to be another important benefit of adopting a Zero Trust approach to cloud security. According to IBM's 2021 Cost of a Data Breach Report, on average, the cost of a breach without Zero Trust deployed is $5.04 million, which is $1.76 million more than the cost of a breach where mature Zero Trust was deployed.[359]

14.7 Conclusion

Cloud cybersecurity threats emerge with the deployment of cloud computing. Organizations must therefore protect their data, networks, infrastructure, and applications from such security threats. A comprehensive cloud security strategy, framework, plan, and processes are essential elements to secure the cloud.

Key Questions
1. What is the definition of cloud security?
2. What are the security implications unique to the cloud?
3. What is Zero Trust in the context of the cloud?

Chapter 15
Incident Response and the Cloud

> Not responding is a response – we are equally responsible for what we don't do.[360]
> – Jonathan Safran Foer, American novelist

Learning Objectives
- Understand the basic concepts underlying information technology (IT) incident response
- Understand how cloud computing uniquely impacts incident response

---

Key Terms

1. Cloud Architecture – "Cloud architecture is the way technology components combine to build a cloud, in which resources are pooled through virtualization technology and shared across a network. Cloud computing architecture enables organizations to reduce or eliminate their reliance on on-premises server, storage, and networking infrastructure."[361]
2. DevOps – "A combination of the terms development and operations, meant to represent a collaborative or shared approach to the tasks performed by a company's application development and IT operations teams."[362]
3. Mean Time To Detect – The amount of time it takes to discover the incident.
4. Mean Time to Remediate – The sum of downtime for a given period divided by the number of incidents.

Chapter Outline

15.1 Introduction

Cloud incident response is an essential element of cloud governance. Cloud incident response relates to the organization's deployment of strategies, plans,

https://doi.org/10.1515/9783110755374-015

and activities to respond to cybersecurity breaches. Incident response plays a crucial role in how organizations respond to and recover from cloud cybersecurity attacks.

A range of unique characteristics associated with cloud computing further complicates an organization's incident response to a cybersecurity attack. For instance, shared responsibility for cybersecurity between the organization and their third-party CSPs and the lack of transparency into cloud activities in the extended enterprise.

Existing IT incident response frameworks are useful in a cloud environment. However, addressing cloud incidents is different as compared to addressing incidents within traditional IT environments. Generic IT incident responses strategies, frameworks, and planning considerations can serve as a foundation for customizing a cloud incident response program.

15.2 Defining an IT Incident, Incident Response and Incident Response Planning

A range of definitions of the term *incident response* exist. Table 15.1 presents two examples advanced by government agencies.

Table 15.1: Definitions of incident – selected examples.

Source	Definition
NIST	An occurrence that actually or potentially jeopardizes the confidentiality, integrity, or availability of an information system or the information the system processes, stores, or transmits or that constitutes a violation or imminent threat of violation of security policies, security procedures, or acceptable use policies.[363]
ENISA	A breach of security or a loss of integrity that has impact on the operation of network and information system core services, which public administrations and market operators provide. The "reportable incident" is the one that has deemed significant impact.[364]

An *incident* may include a data breach, a compromised record, a denial of service attack, insider threat, malware attack or network intrusion. Table 15.2 presents definitions of example security incidents.

Table 15.2: Definitions of example security incidents.

Types of Incidents	Definition
Data Breach and Data Theft	"An event in which an individual's name and a medical record and/or a financial record or debit card is potentially put at risk – either in electronic or paper format."[365] "The act of stealing information stored on computers, servers, or other devices from an unknowing victim with the intent to compromise privacy or obtain confidential information."[366]
Compromised Record	"A record is information that identifies the natural person (individual) whose information has been lost or stolen in a data breach. Examples include a database with an individual's name, credit card information and other personally identifiable information (PII) or a health record with the policyholder's name and payment information."[367]
Denial of Service Attack	"Occurs when legitimate users are unable to access information systems, devices, or other network resources due to the actions of a malicious cyber threat actor. Services affected may include email, websites, online accounts (e.g., banking), or other services that rely on the affected computer or network. A denial-of-service condition is accomplished by flooding the targeted host or network with traffic until the target cannot respond or simply crashes, preventing access for legitimate users."[368]
Insider Threat	"An insider threat to a company comes from its own people – employees, vendors, suppliers, consultants, business partners, etc. – the people on the 'inside' of the organization."[369]
Malware Attack	"When cybercriminals create malicious software that's installed on someone else's device without their knowledge to gain access to personal information or to damage the device, usually for financial gain. Different types of malware include viruses, spyware, ransomware, and Trojan horses."[370]
Network Intrusion	"Refers to any unauthorized activity on a digital network. Network intrusions often involve stealing valuable network resources and almost always jeopardize the security of networks and/or their data."[371]

In an information technology context, the term *incident response* is defined by VMware as "the effort to quickly identify an attack, minimize its effects, contain damage, and remediate the cause to reduce the risk of future incidents."[372] Incident response plans are therefore an essential component of cloud governance. Table 15.3 presents three examples of how incident response plans are defined in practice.

Table 15.3: Examples of definitions of IR plans – selected examples.

Source	Definition of an Incident Response Plan
NIST	"The documentation of a predetermined set of instructions or procedures to detect, respond to, and limit consequences of a malicious cyber-attacks against an organization's information systems(s)."[373]
Cynet	"Incident response is an organizational process that enables timely, effective response to cyberattacks. The incident response process includes identifying an attack, understanding its severity and prioritizing it, investigating and mitigating the attack, restoring operations, and taking action to ensure it won't recur."[374]
Awake Security	"An incident response program defines the detailed steps, including instructions and workflows, for an incident response team to follow in the event of a security incident such as a data breach, denial of service attack, insider threat, malware attack or network intrusion."[375]

In basic terms, an incident response plan represents a game plan, or instruction, on how to respond to a cybersecurity incident.

15.3 The Elements of an IT Incident Response Plan

The elements of an incident response plan are often based on an *incident response framework* that defines the sequential phases and planning steps of a response to an incident. TechTarget defines an incident response framework as,

> An incident response framework provides a structure to support incident response operations. A framework typically provides guidance on what needs to be done but not on how it is done. A framework is also loose and flexible enough to allow elements to be added or removed as necessary to satisfy a particular organization or constituency.[376]

An essential step in responding to and correcting a cybersecurity attack is the adoption of a credible incident response framework. An organization can customize an incident response framework to the unique characteristics of their cloud.

Two popular incident response frameworks are the NIST Framework, and the SysAdmin, Audit, Network, and Security (SANS) Framework. NIST is a U.S. Federal Governmental agency, and the SANS Institute is an information security services company. Table 15.4 presents a summary comparison of the high-level phases of each of these incident response frameworks.

Table 15.4: IR frameworks – selected examples.

NIST IT Incident Response Framework[377]		SANS IT Incident Response Framework[378]	
1)	Preparation	1)	Preparation
2)	Detection and Analysis	2)	Identification
3)	Containment, Eradication, and Recovery	3)	Containment
4)	Post-Incident Activity	4)	Eradication
		5)	Recovery
		6)	Lessons Learned

Tables 15.5 and 15.6 present the details of each phase of the NIST and SANS frameworks, respectively.

Table 15.5: Phases of the NIST Incident Response Framework, as adapted from NIST[379] and Security Metrics.[380]

NIST Incident Response Framework	
Phase	**Phase Overview**
1) Preparation: Initial Planning	**Preparation** – establishes the ability to operate and staff an incident management program, including: – Design and automation of process – Obtain communication capabilities and facilities (cloud based) – Define documentation needs and repositories – Define training needs (cloud specific) – Establish required security and analytical tools – Establish and operate relevant threat intelligence needs – Create operating strategy, goals and objectives, key metrics
2) Detection and Analysis	**Detection and Analysis includes:** – Design, create, and test organizational alerts – Inventory cloud versus organization alerts and responsibility – Create validation process and criteria – Establish scope and size parameters – Assignment criteria for incident managers – Create organizational structure for incident teams – Create communications model and staff ownership – Design timeline capability and implement service – Develop sizing tools to estimate potential nature and type of loss – Design notification and coordination activities (internal and external)

Table 15.5 (continued)

NIST Incident Response Framework	
Phase	**Phase Overview**
3) Containment, Eradication and Recovery	**Containment, Eradication and Recovery includes:** – Develop criteria for remediation, backup, disabling, restoration actions – Develop quality control requirements for restoration – Develop criteria for documentation, chain of custody, insurance claims
4) Post-Incident Activity	**Post-Incident Activity includes:** – Complete process improvement assessment – Complete root cause analysis

Table 15.6: Phases of the SANS Incident Response Framework, as adapted from Cynet.[381]

SANS Incident Response Framework	
Phase	**Phase Overview**
1) Preparation Ensure that the organization can comprehensively respond to an incident at a moment's notice.	– Review and codify an organizational security policy, perform a risk assessment, identify sensitive assets, define which are critical security incidents the team should focus on, and build a computer security incident response team.
2) Identification Detect deviations from normal operations in the organization, understanding if a deviation represents a security incident, and determining how important the incident is.	– Monitor IT systems and detect deviations from normal operations, and see if they represent actual security incidents. – When an incident is discovered, collect additional evidence, establish its type and severity, and document everything.
3) Containment Limit damage from the current security incident and prevent any further damage. Several steps are necessary to completely mitigate the incident, while also preventing destruction of evidence that may be needed for prosecution.	– Perform short-term containment, for example by isolating the network segment that is under attack. – Then, focus on long-term containment, which involves temporary fixes to allow systems to be used in production, while rebuilding clean systems.

Table 15.6 (continued)

SANS Incident Response Framework	
Phase	**Phase Overview**
4) Eradication Intended to actually remove malware or other artifacts introduced by the attacks, and fully restore all affected systems.	– Remove malware from all affected systems, identify the root cause of the attack, and take action to prevent similar attacks in the future.
5) Recovery Bring all systems back to full operation, after verifying they are clean, and the threat is removed.	– Bring affected production systems back online carefully, to prevent additional attacks. – Test, verify, monitor affected systems to ensure they are back to normal.
6) Lessons Learned No later than two weeks from the end of the incident, perform a retrospective of the incident.	– Prepare complete documentation of the incident, investigate the incident further, understand what was done to contain it and whether anything in the incident response process could be improved.

While the phases of these two examples of incident response frameworks differ, both capture the essential elements of a prudent framework for planning for and responding to a cybersecurity incident.

15.4 How Cloud Computing Impacts Incident Response

Cyber incidents affect cloud performance and cloud data security. According to Booz Allen Hamilton,

> Similar to traditional information technology environments, adversaries are using cloud environments as entry points to infect, harm, and disrupt business operations. Threat actors know that critical data may be duplicated to poorly protected or unsupervised cloud environments.[382]

As an integral component of cloud governance, it is therefore crucial for an organization to have a comprehensive cloud incident response strategy and an incident response plan. Such strategies and plans should anticipate incidents, immediately raise red flags for possible incidents, and rapidly respond to incidents with the appropriate corrective actions.

Cloud Incident Response Framework

Incident response frameworks are useful in a cloud environment. However, addressing cloud incidents is different as compared to addressing incidents within traditional IT environments. To address such differences, cloud-specific incident response frameworks assist with the unique characteristics of the cloud. For example, Table 15.7 presents a summary of the Cloud Security Alliance's cloud incident response framework.

Table 15.7: Cloud IR framework, as adapted from the Cloud Security Alliance.[383]

Phase	Overview of the Cloud Security Alliance's Cloud IR Framework
1) Preparation Establish an incident response capability so that the organization is ready to respond to incidents	– Solid preparation can improve an incident response team's readiness and efficiency, ensuring they are sufficiently prepared in the face of threats. – A cloud incident response plan should clearly establish everyone's roles and responsibilities, including CSPs. – Organizations should consider vetting additional third-party CSPs to have quick access to resources, should they be needed in an emergency response situation.

2) Detection and Analysis
Detection, confirmation, and analysis of suspected incidents
	– Although detection and analysis may differ from one cloud environment to the other, the monitoring scope must cover the cloud management plan in addition to deployed assets. In-cloud monitoring and alerts can be leveraged to help kick off an automated response workflow.
	– Questions that need to be addressed post incident include:
	  – When did it happen?
	  – Who discovered it and how was it discovered?
	  – Have any other areas been impacted?
	  – What is the confidence level for the non-impacted zones?
	  – Has the source or patient zero been discovered?
	– Incident classification scales may be helpful to gauge the severity of impact of cloud incidents (e.g., services availability).

Table 15.7 (continued)

Phase	Overview of the Cloud Security Alliance's Cloud IR Framework
3) Containment, Eradication, and Recovery Minimize loss, theft of information, or disruption of service, and eliminate the threat, restore services securely and timely	– When an incident is discovered, predefined containment, eradication and recovery should be executed (e.g., taking systems offline, quarantining systems, restricting connectivity). – It is of the utmost importance not to remove the threat by blind deletion as this is equivalent to destroying evidence. – The key is to be meticulous in removing any trace of malware, threats and evaluate the compromise of data loss versus service availability. – To prevent incidents from recurring, systems should be hardened and patched following an immutable infrastructure paradigm.
4) Post-Mortem	– Assess the incident after it occurs to better handle future incidents through the utilization of logs review, "Lessons Learned" and after-action reports, or the mitigation of exploited vulnerabilities to prevent similar incidents in the future.
5) Coordination, Information Sharing (Continuous)	– Communication between CSPs and the organization needs to be properly established, with regular updates for affected users to mitigate losses and strategize business recovery methods. – Coordinating with key partners, IR teams in other departments, law enforcement agencies on their specific roles, responsibilities greatly reinforces cloud incident response capabilities. – This communication should be set up from the start – at the planning phase – and maintained throughout the entire process.

Three Key Aspects of Cloud Incident Response

Existing IT incident response strategies and plans will be useful in a cloud environment. However, cloud incident response plans should be customized to the unique aspects of the cloud. According to the Cloud Security Alliance, "The three key aspects that set cloud incident response apart from traditional incident response processes are governance, visibility, and the shared responsibility of the cloud."[384] Table 15.8 summarizes these aspects.

Table 15.8: Key aspects about cloud IR, as adapted from the Cloud Security Alliance.[385]

Three Aspects of Cloud IR	Overview
1) Governance	– The organization has the primary responsibility for cloud governance, including incident response. Data and applications in the cloud, however, reside in multiple locations, sometimes with different CSPs. Getting the various organizations together to investigate an incident is a major challenge.
	– A cloud incident response governance model therefore must be uniquely customized to integrate the organization's and the CSP's incident response strategies, plans and procedures across all CSP cloud service and deployment models.
	– In turn, governance models need to be supported by relevant service-level agreements, including protocols required to customize and measure the organization's security and incident response expectations including relevant metrics and graphics.
	– Clarity of the shared responsibilities, points of contact, response times and enumerated triggered incidents are critical preparatory steps. For example, incidents associated with privacy laws and regulations in all relevant jurisdictions.
	– Cloud architecture and design should consider incident response in order to design architecture that optimizes detection time; facilitates investigation techniques; and accelerates response time to optimize containment and recoverability capabilities.
	– Organizations should perform periodic testing and assessment of such shared responsibility strategies and plans to ensure continued conformance to expectations, discovery of undocumented changes to processes, and errors in execution.
2) Visibility	– Lack of visibility in the cloud indicates that incidents that could have been resolved quickly are now at risk of escalating.
	– The cloud has the benefit of ensuring an easier, faster, cheaper and more effective incident response when leveraged properly.
	– It is important to take great care when developing IR processes and documentation, taking full advantage of cloud architectures as opposed to traditional data center models.
	– Many tools, services, and capabilities provided by CSPs greatly enhance detection, reaction, recovery and forensic abilities that are curated for, and only possible in the cloud.
	– Cloud IR has to be proactive and architected for failure throughout the process.

Table 15.8 (continued)

Three Aspects of Cloud IR	Overview
3) Shared Responsibility	– When the organization and their CSP share cloud governance responsibilities, conditions precedent to building an effective cloud incident response program and strategy are needed. – For instance, obtaining a baseline understanding of cloud activities that can be continuously monitored to detect suspicious incidents. – This will necessitate a full understanding of the nature and scope of shared responsibilities between the organization and the CSP for incident response strategy, planning and procedures.

Examples of Metrics Measuring Cloud Incident Responses

Management should consider creating a range of key performance indicators (KPIs) associated with cloud incident response. For instance, two of the important incident response KPIs used in practice are mean time to detect (MTTD) and the mean time to remediation (MTTR), also referred to as mean time to response or resolve (MTTR). Table 15.9 presets definitions of MTTD and MTTR.

Table 15.9: Metrics to measure IR – selected examples, as adapted from PlexTrac.[386]

Metric Measuring Incident Responses	Definition
MTTD	Mean time to detect is an extremely common, yet important KPI in the IT incident management space. MTTD can be defined simply as the amount of time passed between the beginning of an IT incident and the discovery of the incident security team. A simple equation to calculate the MTTD on a macro level is: MTTD = (total sum of detection time) / (total number of incidents)
MTTR	Mean time to remediate is another common and important KPI in the IT incident management space. MTTR, in similar fashion to MTTD, can be defined as the average amount of time passed from the discovery of an IT incident to the time the security team remediates said incident. In more simple terms, MTTR is the number of days it takes to close a security vulnerability once it has been discovered. The macro-level equation for MTTR is: MTTR = (total sum of detection to remediation time) / (total number of incidents)

According to survey results from the Fugue and Sonatype State of the Cloud Security Report for 2021, a sophisticated attacker can detect a cloud vulnerability within 10 minutes of deployment, while only 10 percent were matching the speed of the attackers. Table 15.10 presents the MTTR statistics.

Table 15.10: MTTR for cloud incidents, as adapted from the 2021 Fugue and Sonatype Report.[387]

Speed	Ideal MTTR, as a percentage	Real MTTR, as a percentage
Fewer than 15 minutes	14	10
15 minutes to 1 hour	36	39
1 hour to 1 day	30	33
1 day to 1 week	13	12
1 week to 1 month	5	5

According to Booz Allen Hamilton,

> Using the cloud has many benefits, but also increased risks. Without proper configuration, your internal responders might not have proper visibility, tools, or access to dig into the matter and resolve it accordingly. By considering the cloud's unique and complex challenges alongside traditional environments – like proper configuration, visibility and access rights, and alert reporting – companies will benefit from a coordinated incident response effort, saving costly interruptions and data exposure.[388]

Table 15.11 presents a summary of cloud incident response planning considerations reported by Booz Allen Hamilton.

Table 15.11: Cloud IR planning considerations, as adapted from Booz Allen Hamilton.[389]

Cloud IR Planning Considerations	Overview
1) Understand differences between cloud and traditional IT environments	– Focus more on applications, application programming interfaces, and user roles. – Consider all the actions that incident responders need to take to successfully do their job in the cloud. – Ensure incident responders have visibility and proper access, or they will be unable to find, fix, and ultimately eradicate incidents.

Table 15.11 (continued)

Cloud IR Planning Considerations	Overview
2) Make cloud an integral part of incident response	– Keep incident response in mind when building the cloud; reactive incident response does not work in the cloud. – DevOps and cloud architecture teams should consider incident response requirements as they set up cloud environments so that response is automated and coordinated.
3) Do not underestimate the pre-work	– Cloud moves at warp speed, with everything happening much too fast for reactive incident response to start when an alert comes in. – Plan for incident response in the cloud before an event happens.
4) Coordinate with other enterprise teams	– Look at gaps in responsibilities or even geographies, identifying potential hurdles to achieve a more coordinated response effort. – Incident response may not be a priority for the cloud architecture team, yet they may have certain controls the incident responders need to access or understand better. – Breaking down traditional team silos and establishing collaborative relationships between traditionally disparate groups will improve the cloud security posture.
5) Get to know the service providers	– Understand what the CSP is responsible for during an event. – CSPs typically have IR teams. Carefully read the service agreement and know who – your team or the provider's – is available for each aspect of a response.

15.5 Conclusion

Cloud incident response is an essential element of cloud governance. A range of inherent and unique characteristics associated with the cloud complicates an organization's IR strategies and plans. Existing IT incident response frameworks are useful in a cloud environment. However, addressing cloud incidents is different as compared to addressing incidents within traditional IT environments. Cloud-specific IR frameworks assist with addressing the unique characteristics of the cloud.

Key Questions
1. What is incident response, an incident response framework, and an incident response plan?
2. How does the cloud uniquely impact an incident response strategy and plan?

Chapter 16
Compliance and the Cloud

> It takes less time to do things right than to explain why you did it wrong.[390]
> – Henry Wadsworth Longfellow, poet

Learning Objectives
- Understand the definition of cloud compliance.
- Understand the implications of cloud computing on an organization's responsibility and process for complying with cloud policies, laws and regulations.
- Gain an awareness of the role *Security as Code* can play in cloud policy compliance.

 Key Terms

1. Cloud Compliance – "The principle that cloud-delivered systems must be compliant with the standards their customers require. Cloud compliance ensures that cloud computing services meet compliance requirements."[391]
2. Code of Conduct – Rules that guide good and bad behavior. Also known as a code of ethics.
3. Security as Code – "The constant implementation of systematic and widely communicated security practices throughout the entire software development life cycle. The goal of this strategy is to streamline the rollout of new software and avoid last-minute vulnerability fixes."[392]

Chapter Outline

https://doi.org/10.1515/9783110755374-016

16.1 Introduction

Data privacy and technology-related policies, laws, and regulations are growing in number and complexity internationally. In addition, such regulations may differ by region, country, state, and industry sector. Cloud-related policies, laws and regulations are no exception. This chapter discusses the importance of complying with cloud-related policies, laws and regulations, and strategies for establishing and operating cloud compliance programs.

16.2 Defining Cloud Compliance

The Society of Corporate Compliance and Ethics (SCCE) defines compliance as "adherence to the laws and regulations passed by official regulating bodies as well as general principles of ethical conduct."[393] Importantly, cloud compliance encompasses both compliance with cloud-related laws and regulations and compliance with internal organizational policies.

A range of definitions of *cloud compliance* exists in the public domain. Table 16.1 presents two examples.

Table 16.1: Definition of cloud compliance – selected examples.

Source	Definition of Cloud Compliance
AlgoSec[394]	"The principle that cloud-delivered systems must be compliant with the standards their customers require."
Capital One[395]	"Cloud compliance is a set of systematic operations that ensure a business is run in a compliant way, while at the same time protecting an organization's resources, be it a network, compute, or storage."

One of the major challenges with cloud-related compliance requirements is that organizations may be subject to laws and regulations outside of their home country. Reciprocity explains this compliance responsibility as,

> When moving to the cloud it is important to know in which countries your data will be processed, what laws will apply, what impact they will have, and then follow a risk-based approach to comply with them. It can be hard because there are many different kinds of laws, like data protection laws, data localization laws and data sovereignty laws. You also need to consider interception laws or access to information laws, which may enable Governments or others to access your data in the cloud. In addition, the laws of many different countries might apply. It is also important to know what security measures the law requires you to put in place.[396]

Other definitions of cloud compliance address internal policies as well as the responsibilities of third-party CSPs. For instance, cloud security policies. Tech-Target defines cloud security policies as "formal guideline companies adhere to that helps ensure safe and secure operations in the cloud."[397]

16.3 The Impact of the Cloud on Organizational Compliance

Failing to comply with cloud-related laws and regulations can have detrimental financial and brand implications. According to Microsoft,

> With companies around the world shifting from on-premises IT infrastructure to cloud computing, legal and compliance professionals face new questions from their organizations about which industries are moving to the cloud, the compliance requirements and security standards that apply, and what to expect from a cloud services contract.[398]

An example of such a regulation that significantly impacts cloud computing is the General Data Protection Regulation (GDPR). Promulgated by the European Union (the EU), the GDPR was designed to harmonize data privacy laws across the EU. In basic terms, the GDPR requires organizations to protect an individual's personal data. For instance, constraints on where all *personal data* covered by the regulation can be *processed* and *stored* (e.g., cloud data servers). Table 16.2 presents definitions of selected terms in the GDPR.

Table 16.2: Examples of terms used in the GDPR.[399]

GDPR Terminology	Definition
Personal Data	"'personal data' means any information relating to an identified or identifiable natural person ('data subject'); an identifiable natural person is one who can be identified, directly or indirectly, in particular by reference to an identifier such as a name, an identification number, location data, an online identifier or to one or more factors specific to the physical, physiological, genetic, mental, economic, cultural or social identity of that natural person"
Processing and Storing Data	"'processing' means any operation or set of operations which are performed on personal data or on sets of personal data, whether or not by automated means, such as collection, recording, organisation, structuring, storage, adaptation or alteration, retrieval, consultation, use, disclosure by transmission, dissemination or otherwise making available, alignment or combination, restriction, erasure or destruction"

Table 16.2 (continued)

GDPR Terminology	Definition
Third Party	"'third party' means a natural or legal person, public authority, agency or body other than the data subject, controller, processor and persons who, under the direct authority of the controller or processor, are authorised to process personal data"
Personal Data Breach	"'personal data breach' means a breach of security leading to the accidental or unlawful destruction, loss, alteration, unauthorised disclosure of, or access to, personal data transmitted, stored or otherwise processed"

Under the GDPR, the EU's regulator is authorized to issue fines for failure to comply. For example, in 2021, Amazon disclosed a fine of €746 million ($877 million USD) for a GDPR compliance failure.[400] In addition to financial implications, such violations can have a negative impact on market brand and reputation. Therefore, knowing what jurisdiction the data resides in, as well as operating a comprehensive and effective cloud compliance program is an essential component of cloud governance.

16.4 Identifying and Cataloging Cloud Compliance Requirements

Identifying and cataloging cloud-related policy, laws, regulations and compliance requirements are essential foundational steps for effective cloud compliance.
- Identifying, understanding, and communicating the portfolio of compliance requirements.
  This involves engaging appropriately skilled professionals to identify, understand, and communicate the nature and compliance requirements associated with a global portfolio of all applicable external laws and regulations. This portfolio should include internal ethics and governance policies.
- Cataloging and prioritizing the portfolio of compliance requirements.
  Management must answer the questions: *What is the compliance requirement, and where in my operations globally does it apply?* An organization can catalog and prioritize by geographic region, function, external laws, and by internal policies. Management must continuously update this catalog.

With respect to identifying and cataloging external laws, regulations and guidance, an organization must identify all relevant compliance requirements globally.

Table 16.3 presents selected examples of international laws, regulations, and guidelines with cloud implications.

Table 16.3: Examples of laws, regulations and guidelines with cloud implications.

Regulations	Region	Description
General Data Protection Regulation (GDPR)[401]	European Union	GDPR in the EU and UK Regulates the use of personal data of residents within the European Union and the United Kingdom and provides rights to exercise control over resident's data. While not prescriptive, the GDPR does set out measures and principles that organizations must follow to be compliant.
Other Privacy Regulations in the EU	European Union	Within the EU, each member state may have legal requirements beyond GDPR that includes the need for personal data to be processed fairly and lawfully, to be accurate and up-to-date, "to have measures in place against accidental loss or destruction and for personal data only to be transferred to countries with adequate levels of data protection in place."[402]
Organisation for Economic Co-operation and Development (OECD) Anti-Corruption Ethics and Compliance Handbook for Business[403]	International	Developed by companies, for companies, with assistance from the OECD, the United Nations Office on Drugs and Crime, and the World Bank. A source for companies' compliance program guidance.
Personal Information Protection and Electronic Documents Act (PIPED Act)[404]	Canada	Relates to data privacy, governing how private sector organizations collect, use, and disclose personal information in the course of commercial business.
Health Insurance Portability and Accountability Act (HIPAA)[405]	United States	A U.S. Federal regulation designed to ensure the security and privacy of protected healthcare information.
Payment Card Industry Data Security Standard (PCI DSS)[406]	United States	Companies that handle cardholder information (e.g., debit, credit, prepaid, ATM and point of sale card) are required to comply with this standard. Includes 12 major rules to protect cardholder data.

Table 16.3 (continued)

Regulations	Region	Description
Sarbanes-Oxley Act (SOX)[407]	United States	Establishes standards for all U.S. publicly traded companies to protect shareholders and the public from accounting errors and fraud. SOX is not specific to cloud computing, but the regulation does cover IT security controls because data integrity is integral to financial reporting.
Gramm-Leach-Bliley Act (GLBA)[408]	United States	Mandates that all institutions who offer financial products or services to consumers must develop, implement and maintain comprehensive information security programs. The Act protects the confidentiality and integrity of customer records.
Federal Information Security and Management Act (FISMA)[409]	United States	Applies to all U.S. government agencies and affiliated companies that collect and process data on behalf of government agencies. The Act provides guidelines on security controls, user access, identity management, risk assessment, auditing and monitoring.
Department of Justice (DOJ) Evaluation of Corporate Compliance Programs[410]	United States	Provides guidance on how prosecutors should evaluate the effectiveness of compliance and ethics programs in the context of plea and sentencing determinations.
National Association of Securities Dealers Automatic Quotation System (NASDAQ) Exchange Corporate Governance Rules[411]	United States	Requires that listed companies adopt and disclose a code of business conduct and ethics to all directors, officers, and employees. Each company shall adopt a code of conduct applicable to all directors, officers and employees, which shall be publicly available.
New York Stock Exchange (NYSE)[412]	United States	The NYSE rules recommend that codes address: (i) conflicts of interest; (ii) corporate opportunities; (iii) confidentiality; (iv) fair dealing; (v) protection and proper use of company assets; (vi) compliance with laws, rules, and regulations, including insider trading laws; and (vii) reporting illegal or unethical behavior.

Importantly, the process of identifying and cataloging must include both external laws and regulations, as well as internal cloud-related policies and ethical standards.

16.5 Cloud Compliance Policies

Cloud policies are also crucial to managing cloud compliance risks and meeting cloud compliance requirements. Once management creates a portfolio of cloud-related laws, regulations, and internal standards of practice, management must establish associated cloud compliance policies and procedures.

The nature, number, and types of policies and procedures required will depend on a number of factors. For instance, geographic region, industry, and the complexity of the requirement. In addition, important differences exist between policies, standards, procedures, internal controls, and guidelines. Table 16.4 provides definitions of such terms adapted from Compliance Forge.

Table 16.4: Definitions to illustrate the difference between policies, standards, procedures, internal controls, and guidelines, as adapted from Compliance Forge.[413]

Term	Definition
Policy	High-level statement of management's intent that supports the business strategy and satisfies an external law, regulation, or internal standard or practice
Internal Controls	Technical, administrative, or physical compliance requirements
Standard	Organization-specific requirements for cybersecurity and data protection to satisfy controls
Procedure	Defined practices and steps to implement the standards
Guideline	Recommended guidance that is not mandatory

In 2020, the United States Committee of Sponsoring Organizations (COSO) released a framework titled Compliance Risk Management: Applying the COSO Enterprise Risk Management Framework. COSO defined two categories of compliance policies: structural policies and substantive policies. Table 16.5 presents examples of these categories.

Table 16.5: Categories of compliance policies, as adapted from COSO.[414]

Compliance Policy Category	Definition	Example
Structural Policies	Create the framework for how the program operates	Structural policies are those that define the roles and responsibilities of the compliance officer, compliance committee, and the board; methods for reporting suspected wrongdoing; processes used for auditing and monitoring; and investigative responsibilities and procedures.
Substantive Policies	Address the organization's positions on the laws, regulations, and standards that apply to its business activities	Substantive policies focus on preventing and detecting specific compliance violations (e.g., bribery, false claims, antitrust, environmental, record retention) by communicating the organization's expectations for employee behavior in connection with individual risk areas.

The process for creating compliance policies generally begins with a compliance-risk assessment. According to COSO,

> Compliance risks are those risks relating to possible violations of applicable laws, regulations, contractual terms, standards, or internal policies where such violation could result in direct or indirect financial liability, civil or criminal penalties, regulatory sanctions, or other negative effects for the organization or its personnel.[415]

Violations resulting from the manifestation of compliance risks into actual violations are referred to by COSO as "noncompliance with laws, regulations or corporate standards,"[416] or simply "compliance violations."[417]

While the process for creating a policy can vary, most processes include the following steps.

1. Define policy needs
2. Create policy content and establish accountability for compliance
3. Communicate for stakeholder awareness, engagement and buy-in
4. Train stakeholders
5. Deploy, continuously monitor, and revise policies

Such policy creation procedures inform the development of both structural policies associated with roles and responsibilities and substantive policies associated with preventing and detecting specific compliance violations.

Security as a Code

Security as a Code (SaC) is a security architecture used in cloud computing that has policy compliance implications. Among the capabilities of SaC is the ability to automate cloud policy implementation and deployment during the initial coding process. According to McKinsey,

> If a business, for example, sets up a policy that all personally identifiable information (PII) must be encrypted when it is stored, that policy is translated into a process that is automatically launched whenever a developer submits code. Code that violates the PII policy is automatically rejected.[418]

SaC capabilities facilitate the embedding of the design and implementation of cloud security policy controls on a real-time basis during the coding process. Integrating SaC into a cloud implementation and a cloud change management process, however, is complex and disruptive. According to McKinsey,

> Implementing SaC requires a substantial policy, architectural, and cultural departure for almost all companies. For this reason, many have found it helpful to use a SaC framework to classify workloads according to sensitivity and critically, and then apply specific controls based on workload risk and deployment type.[419]

If a SaC approach is used in part for policy implementation and compliance, it should be an integral element of the organization's cloud compliance program. Moreover, the policy development team and the SaC development team should involve representatives from development and software, security, privacy, compliance, and risk functions and CSPs.

16.6 Cloud Compliance Frameworks and Programs

A cloud compliance program is an integral and essential part of the organization's overall cloud governance strategy. Investopedia defines a compliance program as follows.

> A company's set of internal policies and procedures put into place in order to comply with laws, rules, and regulations or to uphold the business's reputation. A compliance team examines the rules set forth by government bodies, creates a compliance program, implements it throughout the company, and enforces adherence to the program.[420]

A range of publicly available compliance frameworks often serves as a helpful guide for creating a cloud compliance program. For example, the U.S. Federal Sentencing Guidelines (USFSG).

The USFSG framework is required to be implemented by all organizations convicted of federal criminal offenses promulgated by the U.S. Sentencing Commission. This compliance framework, however, is also used by many enterprises and government agencies as a best practices benchmark for creating or evaluating a range of compliance and ethics programs.

Importantly, the USFSG acknowledges that there is no standard, or one-size-fits-all, compliance program. Instead, a compliance program must be customized to the unique attributes and compliance requirements of the organization. The USFSG, however, does advance the following two primary elements of all effective compliance programs.

(1) exercising due diligence to prevent and detect criminal activities; and

(2) creating and facilitating a culture that encourages ethical conduct and a commitment to compliance with the law.

The USFSG also defines the eight essential elements of a compliance and ethics program. Table 16.6 presents these essential elements.

Table 16.6: Essential elements of compliance and ethics programs, as adapted from the USFSG.[421]

Essential Elements of an Effective Compliance and Ethics Program
1. Standards and procedures
2. Governance, oversight, and authority
3. Due diligence in delegation of authority
4. Communication and training
5. Monitoring, auditing, and reporting systems
6. Incentives and enforcement
7. Response to wrongdoing
8. Periodically assess the risk of non-compliance and continually look for ways to improve their compliance and ethics programs.

Crucially, a code of ethical conduct should be an integral component of all compliance programs, including cloud compliance programs. For instance, the U.S. NYSE and NASDAQ have rules that mandate that listed companies adopt codes of business conduct and ethics.

16.7 Cloud Compliance and Shared Responsibilities

The shared responsibilities that result from the use of CSPs disrupt and transform existing organizational governance strategies and protocols. With the use of CSPs, organizational management with the primary responsibility for cloud compliance must now share some of these cloud compliance responsibilities with CSPs.

Shared responsibility models are therefore necessary to define shared roles and responsibilities for governing cloud compliance. For instance, service-level agreements (SLAs) would need to include requirements imposed on CSPs for cloud-related compliance policies, data gathering, controls, auditing, monitoring and reporting.

Once shared-responsibility models are operationalized, organizations need to establish a continuous monitoring process to monitor cloud compliance. COSO defines *monitoring* as "the process of evaluating whether internal controls are operating as intended, and timely communicate any deficiencies to those with authority to take corrective action."[422] Such monitoring processes serve to confirm all parties are fulfilling their respective compliance responsibilities and to identify and respond to compliance violations.

In addition, the organization should conduct periodic *compliance audits*. According to the Association of International Certified Professional Accountants a compliance audit is "a program-specific audit or an organization-wide audit of an entity's compliance with applicable compliance requirements."[423]

16.8 Conclusion

Organizations are responsible for conducting risk assessments and establishing policies, processes, and controls to support compliance with cloud laws, regulations, and internal policies. A cloud compliance program is essential to managing cloud risks, including cloud compliance risk, financial risk, and reputational risk.

Key Questions
1. What is cloud compliance and why is it important?
2. What are cloud compliance policies, compliance frameworks, and compliance programs?
3. What role does *Security as Code* play in cloud policy compliance?
4. Why is cloud compliance integral to cloud governance?

Chapter 17
Internal Auditing and Cloud Computing

> We all need people who will give us feedback. That's how we improve.[424]
> – Bill Gates, co-founder of Microsoft and Philanthropist

Learning Objectives
- Define the role of an internal audit function
- Understand the impact of cloud computing on the role of the internal audit function

---

Key Terms

1. Internal Auditors – Represent organizational employees or third-party internal audit services providers that engage in a range of procedures designed to provide the organization with independent, objective assurance, and consulting services.
2. Internal Audit Charter – "A formal document that defines the internal audit activity's purpose, authority, and responsibility."[425]

17.1 Introduction

Internal auditors represent organizational employees or third-party internal audit services providers that engage in a range of procedures designed to provide the organization with independent, objective assurance, and advisory services. As organizations continue to adopt new and increasingly complex technologies, questions emerge as to what role the internal audit function should play in the technology domain of an organization. This chapter explores the role of an organization's internal audit function in cloud computing.

https://doi.org/10.1515/9783110755374-017

17.2 Defining the Role of the Internal Audit Function

The Institute of Internal Auditors (IIA) is an international professional organization that is a recognized and respected leader, advocate, influencer, innovator, and educator in the internal audit profession. The IIA advances the following definition of Internal Auditing.

> Internal auditing is an independent, objective assurance, and consulting activity designed to add value and improve an organization's operations. It helps an organization accomplish its objectives by bringing a systematic, disciplined approach to evaluate and improve the effectiveness of risk management, control, and governance processes.

> Performed by professionals with an in-depth understanding of the business culture, systems, and processes, the internal audit activity provides assurance that internal controls in place are adequate to mitigate the risks, governance processes are effective and efficient, and organizational goals and objectives are met.[426]

The role an internal audit function plays in an organization will vary based on a number of variables. According to the IIA, "internal auditing is conducted in diverse legal and cultural environments; for organizations that vary in purpose, size, complexity, and structure; and by persons within or outside the organization."[427]

Many organizations establish a formal mission or charter articulating the role and responsibilities of their internal audit function. The IIA Auditing Standards define an internal audit charter as follows.

> The internal audit charter is a formal document that defines the internal audit activity's purpose, authority, and responsibility. The internal audit charter establishes the internal audit activity's position within the organization, including the nature of the chief audit executive's functional reporting relationship with the board; authorizes access to records, personnel, and physical properties relevant to the performance of engagements; and defines the scope of internal audit activities. Final approval of the internal audit charter resides with the board [of directors].[428]

In addition to core skills in internal audit, some internal auditors also bring specialized skills in specific domains. For instance, industry specializations (e.g., banking, and healthcare) and functional specializations (e.g., finance and technology). Internal auditors specializing in technology are often referred to as IT auditors. *CIO Digital Magazine* defines an IT Auditor as follows.

> An IT auditor is responsible for analyzing and assessing a company's technological infrastructure to ensure processes and systems run accurately and efficiently, while remaining secure and meeting compliance regulations.

> An IT auditor also identifies any IT issues that fall under the audit, specifically those related to security and risk management. If issues are identified, IT auditors are responsible

for communicating their findings to others in the organization and offering solutions to improve or change processes and systems to ensure security and compliance.[429]

In the context of the cloud, auditors with skills in information systems and technology (i.e., IT auditors) generally and in cloud computing specifically are crucial resources for an organization deploying the cloud at scale.

17.3 Impact of Cloud Computing on the Role of Internal Audit Function

Prior to the current proliferation of cloud computing, internal auditors had a longstanding legacy of responsibilities associated with IT systems and resources owned and operated by the organization. The cloud has dramatically changed this paradigm. *Why is that?* The adoption of the cloud creates a range of organizational changes that are in some cases disrupt and transform the organization. Such disruptions and transformations create risk and require controls. The Internal Audit function plays an important role in assessing such risks and in evaluating the effectiveness of such controls.

One of the biggest changes fueled by the cloud is migrating in-house data, technology, and applications outside of the protective boundaries of the organization to a cloud CSP vendor. Such organizational and technology changes in turn impact the traditional role served by the internal audit function. Table 17.1 presents examples of such impacts.

Table 17.1: Impact of cloud computing on the role of IA.

Organizational and Technology Changes	Impact on the Role of Internal Audit (IA)
Extended Organization: Outsourcing to CSPs Some or all of the organization's technology, applications, software, and data no longer fully reside within the boundaries of the organization.	IA may be tasked with auditing the CSP's cloud risk management process, including risk assessment and risk mitigation (e.g., design and operating effectiveness of cloud controls and security).
Shared Responsibilities for Cloud Governance with CSPs Shared responsibility agreements documented in an SLA will define and describe the assignments of roles and responsibilities of both the organization and the CSP.	IA may be tasked with validating the fulfillment of both the organization's responsibilities and the CSP's responsibilities in cloud governance.

Table 17.1 (continued)

Organizational and Technology Changes	Impact on the Role of Internal Audit (IA)
Need for Cloud-Skills Understanding the technical, audit and governance issues associated with cloud technology, public cloud service models and cloud deployment models is essential. For instance, understanding the risks introduced by cloud computing and the nature and types of controls used to secure and manage these platforms and services.	According to the IIA Standards "Internal auditors must possess the knowledge, skills, and other competencies needed to perform their individual responsibilities. The internal audit activity collectively must possess or obtain the knowledge, skills, and other competencies needed to perform its responsibilities."[430] Proficiency in these cloud technologies and related risks and controls by IA requires a combination of specialized training and experience to upskill existing internal auditors. This change may also require the hiring of new employees with specialized skills and/or contracting with third-party audit services with specialized cloud skills.
The Charter of the Internal Audit Function "A formal document that defines the internal audit activity's purpose, authority, and responsibility."[431]	The nature and scope of IA's role in the cloud will be informed by the IA Charter.

17.4 What Role Should Internal Audit Play in the Cloud?

An internal audit function can play a vital role in the deployment and governance of cloud computing. According to Grant Thornton, "As organizations increasingly migrate to and rely upon cloud-based solutions, internal audit is uniquely positioned to play a critical role in the adoption of a cloud security program."[432]

A big question that emerges for the board of directors and senior management is, *what is the role of internal audit with respect to cloud computing*? The answer to the question will vary by organization and country/jurisdiction.

With a charter supporting cloud responsibilities, the proper cloud competencies, and leadership support, internal audit's role in assisting with cloud governance can span a range of responsibilities. For instance, assessing cloud strategy, CSP selection, design of the CSP level service-level agreement (SLA), identifying key risks, and evaluating controls over cloud operations, security, and compliance. Table 17.2 presents examples of market perspectives on the role of internal audit in the cloud.

Table 17.2: Examples of IA's role in cloud computing, as adapted from Grant Thornton and Protiviti.

Source	IA Role in Cloud Computing
Grant Thornton[433]	– Assessing cloud security strategy and its alignment with risk and compliance. – Understanding cloud security architecture, service types, and associated risks and challenges. – Identifying areas for improvement and communicating them to the board and management. – Collaborating with the cloud service provider, IT, and leadership to translate enterprise risk management objectives.
Protiviti[434]	– Contributing to defining a cloud strategy. For example, assess the business case for adopting the cloud and the strategy for migrating to the cloud. – Evaluating cloud vendors. For example, assesses how assets will be protected by the CSP, shared responsibilities clearly defined and agreed to in an SLA, and how organization's risk and control protocols and expectations align with the CSP. – Evaluating cloud deployment. For example, migration to the cloud, change management, project management, incident response, compliance with laws and regulations, and data governance. – Monitoring the cloud vendor. For example, using a right-to-audit provision in the SLA, evaluate compliance regulatory, security and privacy laws and regulations, and incident response data and events.

17.5 Conclusion

The cloud has had a profound impact on the nature and use of technology resources within an organization. For instance, the movement of technology resources, processing, and related data to an extended off-premise organization will present logistical and accessibility challenges to internal audit. In addition, the technology changes introduced by the cloud will likely require specialized cloud skills for internal auditors. Such cloud-fueled disruptions will often impact the role and responsibilities of the internal audit function.

Key Questions
1. What is the role of an internal audit function?
2. What are some of the major considerations in determining the role and responsibilities of internal audit in cloud computing?

Chapter 18
Third-Party Assurance and the Cloud

> Today, control framework language is catered towards on-premises environments, and
> security IT auditing techniques have not been reshaped for the cloud.[435]
>
> Amazon Web Services (AWS)

Learning Objectives
- Understand the role of third-party assurance services and frameworks in an
  Information Technology (IT) environment
- Explain the role served by third-party assurance providers, and services in the cloud
- Understand the alternatives for third-party assurance providers and assurance frameworks

---

 Key Terms

1. Non-Repudiation – "Assurance that the sender is provided with proof of delivery and that the recipient is provided with proof of the sender's identity so that neither can later deny having processed the data."[436]

2. IT General Controls (ITGC) – "A Control, other than an application control, that relates to the environment within which computer based application systems are developed, maintained and operated, and that is therefore applicable to all applications. The objectives of general controls are to ensure the proper development and implementation of applications and the integrity of program and data files and of computer operations. Like application controls, general controls may be either manual or programmed. Examples of general controls include the development and implementation of an IS strategy and an IS security policy, the organization of IS staff to separate conflicting duties and planning for disaster prevention and recovery."[437]

3. IT Applications Controls (ITAC) – "The policies, procedures and activities designed to provide reasonable assurance that objectives relevant to a given automated solution (application) are achieved."[438]

4. SOC Reports – "SOC for Service Organizations reports are designed to help service organizations that provide services to other entities, build trust and confidence in the service performed and controls related to the services through a report by an independent CPA. Each type of SOC for Service Organizations report is designed to help service organizations meet specific user needs."[439]

https://doi.org/10.1515/9783110755374-018

18.1 Introduction

Engaging CSPs extends the organization and creates shared responsibilities for cloud governance. For instance, data owners no longer physically possess their data storage. As a result, responsibilities for cloud risk management, controls, compliance, and security are shared with CSPs and perhaps other related third-party service providers, including assurance providers (e.g., public accountancy firms).

In such a scenarios, the use of third-party assurance services provides an organization with an additional layer of defense against cloud risks. This chapter discusses the role of third-party assurance providers' in cloud governance.

18.2 Defining Third-Party Assurance

Third-party assurance services rely on third-party specialists, such as a public accountancy firm, to provide professional assessments, opinions, and assurance over a range of governance objectives. Assurance services consist of audits and attestation services, which differ somewhat in purpose and scope. According to the American Institute of Certified Public Accountants (AICPA), assurance services contribute to reducing the risk of incorrect information and increase confidence in the information. Table 18.1 presents a variety of assurance service definitions.

Assurance services may be delivered by a qualified *independent* third-party (e.g., a public accountancy firm) or by an organization's related stakeholders (e.g., an organization's CSP, managed service provider, or internal audit department). Stakeholders perceive the use of an independent, third-party assurance provider as highly-objective and trusted.

Limitations in levels of assurance achieved exist when engaging third-party assurance providers. Some of these inherent limitations may be mitigated.

One limitation is a failure to understand, communicate, and address the findings presented in assurance reports, (i.e., responsive actions) negates any

Table 18.1: Definitions of third-party assurance – selected examples.

Source	Definition of Assurance
AICPA[440]	In an assurance service, an outside professional applies procedures designed to probe the credibility of the information and reports on the results. Uncertainty and risks can be reduced, and market confidence enhanced by hiring an independent assurance services provider.
International Auditing and Assurance Standards Board (IAASB) – Standard IASE 3000[441]	A service or engagement in which a practitioner expresses a conclusion designed to enhance the degree of confidence of the intended users other than the responsible party about the outcome of the evaluation or measurement of a subject matter against criteria. Assurance engagements include both attestation engagements, in which a party other than the practitioner measures or evaluates the underlying subject matter against the criteria, and direct engagements, in which the practitioner measures or evaluates the underlying subject matter against the criteria.
Investopedia[442]	A type of independent professional service usually provided by certified or chartered accountants such as certified public accountants (CPAs). Aimed at improving the quality of information for the individuals' making decisions. Provides assurance that the information on which one makes decisions is reliable, and therefore reduces risks, in this case, information risk.
Corporate Finance Institute[443]	An independent examination of a company's processes and controls. Aims to reduce information risk by improving the quality or context of the information.

value expected from assurance activities. Responsive actions should be conducted by authorized and qualified employees in a timely, comprehensive, and appropriate manner. Such findings should also be communicated to the appropriate levels of management and those responsible for cloud governance (e.g., board of directors, Internal Audit, CIO).

Another limitation is the inherent *point-in-time* nature of assurance activities. That is, most cloud assurance services are not continuously assessing or monitoring cloud activities. The assurance provided is therefore limited to the point-in-time the assurance procedures were conducted. As a consequence, the assurance cannot be projected beyond the point the procedures were conducted. Given the velocity of change in a cloud environment, this point-in time assurance is a limitation in the role of assurance activities.

18.3 Information Technology Assurance

IT assurance plays a crucial role in IT governance. Assurance provides an additional layer of perspectives, opinions, and defense against IT risks. For instance, providing organizations with service organization controls (SOC) assurance reports, as well as additional third-party opinions and feedback on IT-related SLAs, risks, controls, security, and compliance assessments. Third-party assurance providers also contribute to greater transparency into cloud and CSP processes. Table 18.2 presents examples of definitions of IT assurance.

Table 18.2: Definitions of IT assurance – selected examples.

Source	Definition of IT Assurance
The National Institute of Standards and Technology (NIST)[444]	Information technology assurance is often associated with 1. Integrity, 2. Availability, 3. Authentication, 4. Confidentiality, and 5. Nonrepudiation Assurance is typically obtained relative to a set of specific claims. The scope and focus of such claims may vary (e.g., security claims, safety claims) and the claims themselves may be interrelated. Assurance is obtained through techniques and methods that generate credible evidence to substantiate claims.
Information Systems Audit and Control Association (ISACA)[445]	Adequate assurance signifies that specific, predefined security assurance requirements have been satisfied by performing appropriate assurance processes and activities.

A wide range of services are associated with IT Assurance. For instance, assurance over the adequacy, priority, design, and operating effectiveness of *general controls* over the IT operating environment, *application-level controls* over digital applications, and third-party system and organization controls.

General controls include physical hardware controls, data security controls, and computer operations controls. IT assurance may also focus on *technology application-level controls* that attempt to control data risk by mitigating unauthorized applications from executing. Assurance services may focus on completeness and validity controls, identification, authentication, authorization verification controls, and/or data input controls.

In connection with obtaining IT system controls assurance associated with third-party service organizations (e.g., payroll processing services and CSPs), the AICPA offers a suite of System and Organization Controls (SOC). The SOC suite consists of three categories of information system controls and assurance frameworks. One of the categories is the SOC suite for third-party service organization assurance. This suite consists of SOC 1, SOC 2, SOC 3 assurance frameworks. Table 18.3 presents an overview of each of these SOC frameworks.

Table 18.3: Overview of AICPA-SOC for service organization frameworks.[446]

Framework	AICPA-SOCfor Service Organizations	Overview
SOC 1	SOC for Service Organizations: Internal Controls Over Financial Reporting (ICFR)	Report on Controls at a Service Organization Relevant to User ICFR Specifically intended to meet the needs of entities that use service organizations (user entities) and the CPAs that audit the user entities' financial statements, in evaluating the effect of the controls at the service organization on the user financial statements.
SOC 2	SOC for Service Organizations: Trust Services Criteria	Report on Controls at a Service Organization Relevant to Security, Availability, Processing Integrity, Confidentiality or Privacy These reports are intended provide information and assurance about the controls at a service organization relevant to security, availability, and processing integrity of the systems the service organization uses to process users' data and the confidentiality and privacy of the information processed by these systems. These reports can play an important role in: – Oversight of the organization – Vendor management programs – Internal corporate governance and risk management processes – Regulatory oversight

Table 18.3 (continued)

Framework	AICPA-SOCfor Service Organizations	Overview
SOC 3	SOC for Service Organizations: Trust Services Criteria for General Use Report	Trust Services Report for Service Organizations These reports are designed to meet the needs of users who need assurance about the controls at a service organization relevant to security, availability, processing integrity confidentiality, or privacy, but do not have the need for or the knowledge necessary to make effective use of an SOC 2 Report.

These and other available third-party IT-related assurance frameworks, reports, and services provide an organization with an additional layer of defense against IT-related risks. Such third-party assurance frameworks and services also play a crucial role in transparency and governance of cloud-related risks that extend beyond the protective boundaries of the organization.

18.4 Third-Party Assurance Frameworks, Service Providers and Cloud Governance

Engaging CSPs extends the organization and creates shared responsibilities for cloud governance. As a result, data owners no longer physically possess their data storage. The organization shares responsibilities for cloud risk management, controls, compliance, and security with CSPs.

In this context, the use of third-party assurance frameworks and services provide an organization with an additional layer of defense against cloud risks. These risks are the responsibility of the organization that extends beyond the protective boundaries of the organization. A number of factors will inform management's decisions on how best to deploy third-party assurance. Three considerations are the focus of assurance activities, assurance frameworks, and providers of assurance services.

Focus of Cloud Assurance Activities

A strategic decision associated with the deployment of assurance activities is what to focus such activities on. That is, what is the scope and timing of assurance services? In a shared responsibility model, such decisions may be made jointly between the CSP and organization, or independently by the organization.

A wide range of cloud assurance objectives will inform the nature, timing and extents of cloud-assurance activities, such as:
- Verifying cloud service-level agreement by a third-party auditor
- Performing financial statement audits of ICFR
- Complying with international regulatory compliance requirements
- Executing cloud security assurance policies
- Providing SOC reports

Objectives may be created by stakeholders internal to the organization and by stakeholders external to the organization. For instance, regulatory requirements may require periodic assurance activities associated with controls in place for complying with specific regulations. Internal policies may require cloud assurance activities associated with data privacy and cybersecurity. Both internal and external requirements may require the use of an independent third-party assurance provider (e.g., public accountancy firm).

Cloud Assurance Frameworks

In addition to the frameworks discussed in the preceding IT assurance section (e.g., AICPA-SOC for cybersecurity), several frameworks customized to the cloud have grown in popularity internationally. Three such examples are ENISA, CSA, ISACA, and the AICPA.

The European Union (EU) Agency for Cybersecurity (ENISA) is focused on achieving a high level and a common level of cybersecurity across the EU. ENISA was established in 2004 and strengthened by the EU Cybersecurity Act. Table 18.4 presents the ENISA cloud assurance and governance frameworks.

The Cloud Security Alliance (CSA) mission includes defining and increasing awareness of best practices for a secure cloud computing environment. CSA offers a range of cloud security-related research, education, certification, events, and products. Table 18.5 presents two examples of CSA-related assurance frameworks.

Table 18.4: Examples of ENISA cloud assurance frameworks.

ENISA Cloud Assurance Framework	Overview
Cloud Computing Information Assurance Framework[447]	A set of assurance criteria is designed to assess the risk of adopting cloud services, compare different CSP offers, obtain assurance from the selected cloud providers, and reduce the assurance burden on cloud providers.
Cloud Risk Assessment Framework[448]	An IT security guide for potential and existing users of cloud computing to inform an assessment of the security risks and benefits.
Security and Resilience in Government Clouds Framework[449]	A decision-making model that can be used by senior management to determine how operational, legal, and information security requirements, as well as budget and time constraints, can drive the identification of the architectural solution that best suits the needs of their organization. A guide for EU member states on the definition of a national cloud strategy with regard to security and resilience.
Managing Security through SLAs Framework[450]	A framework for managing the security aspects of service contracts to optimize information security. The work of an organization's IT officer has changed from setting up hardware, installing and configuring software, IT officers to managing service contracts with IT service providers.

Table 18.5: Examples of CSA cloud assurance frameworks.

CSA Cloud Assurance Framework	Overview
Security, Trust, Assurance, and Risk (STAR) Registry Framework[451]	A publicly accessible registry that documents the security and privacy controls provided by popular cloud computing offerings. Publishing in the registry allows CSPs to show current and potential customers their security and compliance posture, including the regulations, standards, and frameworks they adhere to. It ultimately reduces complexity and helps alleviate the need to fill out multiple customer questionnaires.

Table 18.5 (continued)

CSA Cloud Assurance Framework	Overview
Cloud Controls Matrix Framework[452]	STAR encompasses the key principles of transparency, rigorous auditing, and harmonization of standards outlined in the Cloud Controls Matrix (CCM). It is composed of 197 control objectives that are structured in 17 domains covering all key aspects of cloud technology. It can be used as a tool for the systematic assessment of a cloud implementation and provides guidance on which security controls should be implemented by which actor within the cloud supply chain. The controls framework is aligned to the CSA Security Guidance for Cloud Computing, a standard for cloud security assurance and compliance.

Information Systems Audit and Control Association (ISACA) is a professional association with a purpose designed to help business technology professionals and their organizations globally realize the positive potential of technology. ISACA offers a range of cloud security-related research, education, certification, events, and products. Table 18.6 presents four examples of ISACA-related assurance frameworks.

Table 18.6: Examples of ISACA cloud assurance frameworks.

ISACACloud Assurance Framework	Overview
Infographics On-Premises Versus Cloud Auditing[453]	A framework of considerations for auditing in a cloud environment, including practices to facilitate the optimization of cloud audit management.
Cloud Computing Management Audit Program[454]	A framework for conducting an assessment of the effectiveness of the cloud computing service provider's internal controls and security; identifying internal control deficiencies within the customer organization and its interface with the service provider; and providing audit stakeholders with an assessment of audit quality and ability to rely upon the service provider's attestations regarding controls. IT audit and assurance professionals are expected to customize this framework to the environment in which they are performing an assurance process.
Control Objectives for IT (COBIT) Framework[455]	A framework for conducting an assessment of the cloud, including its associated security risks, and questions about the governance and management of a cloud computing.

The AICPA also offers controls and assurance frameworks for cybersecurity (i.e., SOC for cybersecurity) and for supply chains (i.e., SOC for supply chain). Table 18.7 presents an overview of each of these SOC frameworks.

Table 18.7: Overview of AICPA-SOC for cybersecurity and supply chain frameworks.[456]

AICPA Cloud Assurance Framework	Overview
SOC for Cybersecurity Framework	A reporting framework through which organizations can communicate relevant useful information about the effectiveness of their cybersecurity risk management program.
	Contributes to demonstrating that third-party service providers (e.g., CSPs) are managing cybersecurity threats, and that they have effective processes and controls in place to detect, respond to, mitigate and recover from breaches and other security events. CPAs can report on such information to meet the cybersecurity information needs.
SOC forSupply Chain Framework	A report on an entity's system and controls for producing, manufacturing or distributing goods to better understand the cybersecurity risks in their supply chains.
	Contributes to identifying, assessing and addressing supply chain risks, and to foster greater transparency in the supply chain. Helps organizations communicate certain information about the supply chain risk management efforts and assess the effectiveness of system controls that mitigate those risks.

Providers of Assurance Services

A wide range of third-party vendors offer cloud assurance services. Such assurance providers are considered independent and objective service providers, such as public accountancy firms. Others may not be perceived as providing highly-independent assurance services, such as an organization's CSP. Table 18.8 presents examples of such assurance services.

Table 18.8: Examples of CSP assurance services.

Provider	Examples of Cloud Assurance Services
CSPs	Certified external assessors work with organizations to achieve, maintain, and automate compliance in the cloud. Scope of assurance services include PCI DSS, HITRUST CSF, NIST, SOC 2, HIPAA, ISO 27001, and GDPR.
Cloud MSPs	Through a CSP, offer a centralized dashboard to manage and automate cloud solutions.

18.5 Conclusion

The use of third-party assurance frameworks and services provides an organization with an additional layer of defense against cloud risks. Such a defense is particularly important in a shared responsibility model.

Key Questions
1. What is third-party assurance in the context of cloud computing?
2. What are the objectives informing cloud assurance?
3. What types of frameworks are available for cloud assurance?
4. What types of third-party service providers provide cloud assurance?

Chapter 19
The Board of Directors: Cloud Governance and Asking the Right Questions

> As organizations increasingly grapple with digital transformations, large technology investments, and shifts to the cloud, these issues regularly appear on board agendas.[457]
>
> – McKinsey

Learning Objectives
- Understand the board's role in cloud governance
- Explore questions the board may have concerning cloud governance

---

 Key Terms

1. Data Literacy – "The ability to read, write and communicate data in context, including an understanding of data sources and constructs, analytical methods and techniques applied, and the ability to describe the use case, application and resulting value."[458]

2. Digital Transformation – "Digital transformation is the process of using digital technologies to create new – or modify existing – business processes, culture, and customer experiences to meet changing business and market requirements. This reimagining of business in the digital age is digital transformation."[459]

3. EMEIA – Europe, Middle East, India and Africa.

4. Fiduciary – "A person or organization that acts on behalf of another person or persons, putting their clients' interests ahead of their own, with a duty to preserve good faith and trust. Being a fiduciary thus requires being bound both legally and ethically to act in the other's best interests."[460]

5. Organizational Learning – An organization's ability to successfully transform itself by unlearning obsolete or outdated modes of operation and behavior, and relearning the new skills and modes necessary to successful adapt to organizational transformations.

https://doi.org/10.1515/9783110755374-019

19.1 Introduction

The board of directors (the board) plays a crucial role in organizational governance, including IT and cloud governance. This chapter explores the board's role in cloud governance. This chapter also presents examples of questions a board member may have for management and other cloud stakeholders concerning cloud governance.

19.2 Defining the Role and Structure of a Board of Directors

The board plays a crucial role in organizational governance, including IT governance generally and cloud governance specifically. According to OnBoard,

> Boards of directors serve as the nuclei of a wide array of organizations across nearly every industry and sector, including public corporations, financial institutions, nonprofit organizations, and professional associations – just to name a few. A board of directors can come in many forms, with varying structures, roles, and responsibilities depending on the needs of the entity it serves. In all cases, however, the board plays a crucial leadership function in shaping an organization's future, ensuring its success, and keeping it on track and focused on its mission and goals.[461]

Table 19.1 presents additional examples of the definition of a board of directors.

The duties and structure of U.S. company boards vary based on a number of factors, including legal structures (e.g., public, private, not-for-profit), size, industry and state jurisdiction. CFI describes the context informing the responsibilities and structure of boards in the U.S. as follows.

> The structure, responsibilities, and powers given to a board of directors are determined by the bylaws of a company or organization. The bylaws generally determine how many board members there are, how the members are elected, and how frequently the board members meet. There's not a set number or structuring for a board of directors; it depends

largely on the company or organization, the industry in which the company or organization operates, and the shareholders.[462]

Table 19.2 presents an overview of the primary roles commonly seen on U.S. boards.

Table 19.1: Definition of board of directors – selected examples.

Source	Definition of Board of Directors
Corporate Governance Institute (CGI) [463]	In a corporation, a board of directors is a group of elected individuals representing the shareholders. A board of directors is a requirement for every public company. Nonprofit and private organizations may also have boards of directors. The board is a governing body that meets at regular intervals to set policies and oversee corporate management.
Corporate Finance Institute (CFI) [464]	A board of directors is essentially a panel of people who are elected to represent shareholders. Every public company is legally required to install a board of directors; nonprofit organizations and many private companies – while not required to – also name a board of directors.

Table 19.2: Board of directors roles in the U.S., as adapted from Investopedia.[465]

Role	Description
Chair of the Board	The CEO may serve as the board chair. If not, the CEO reports to the board chair. In either case, the CEO is responsible for implementing board decisions.
Inside Directors	Inside directors are either shareholders or high-level managers from within the company.
Outside Directors	While having the same responsibilities as the inside directors in determining strategic direction and corporate policy, outside directors are different in that they are not directly part of the management team. The purpose of having outside directors is to provide unbiased perspectives on issues brought to the board.

The roles of boards and their structures for organizations outside of the U.S. differ in some important ways. For instance, CFI suggests that board structures in Europe and Asia are structured as follows.

The structuring of a board of directors tends to be more varied outside of the United States. In certain countries in Asia and the European Union, the structure is often split into two primary boards – executive and supervisory.

The executive board is made up of company insiders that are elected by employees and shareholders. In most cases, the executive board is headed up by the company CEO or a managing officer. The board is typically tasked with overseeing the daily business operations.

The supervisory board concerns itself with a broader spectrum of issues when dealing with the company, and acts much like a typical U.S. board. The chair for the board varies but is always headed up by someone other than the preeminent executive officer.[466]

Another example of such differences is the EU; duties of boards in the EU are often rooted in country-level legal systems. According to the International Finance Corporation of the World Bank Group, "The regulatory approach to directors' duties differs across Europe."[467]

Boards often create board committees. *Diligent* describes the purpose and structure of board committees as,

The idea behind committees of the board is to tap the specific talents, skills and knowledge of individual board directors to inform and educate the full board on particular areas of concern. Committees allow boards to divide the work of the board into manageable sections.[468]

The nature and number of board committees varies. Two common categories of board committees are standing committees and ad hoc committees.

Generally, standing committees are permanent committees of the Board. For example, an Audit Committee of the board. Ad Hoc committees are formed by the board for specific but temporary tasks. For example, a task force of the board charged with evaluating the governance of a pending acquisition. Once the task is completed, the ad hoc committee is usually disbanded.

19.3 Cloud Governance and the Board of Directors

The digital transformation, combined with the global pandemic, has driven the rapid, wide-scale deployment of digital technologies. While the potential benefits are compelling, the accompanying IT risks (e.g., cybersecurity breaches) are a major concern for board members.

For instance, as far back as 2014, the U.S. Securities and Exchange (SEC) Commissioner Luis A. Aguilar asserted the following warning to board members that endures to this day.

> Given the significant cyber-attacks that are occurring with disturbing frequency, and the mounting evidence that companies of all shapes and sizes are increasingly under a constant threat of potentially disastrous cyber-attacks, ensuring the adequacy of a company's cybersecurity measures needs to be a critical part of a board of director's risk oversight responsibilities.
>
> In addition to the threat of significant business disruptions, substantial response costs, negative publicity, and lasting reputational harm, there is also the threat of litigation and potential liability for failing to implement adequate steps to protect the company from cyber-threats. Perhaps unsurprisingly, there has recently been a series of derivative lawsuits brought against companies and their officers and directors relating to data breaches resulting from cyber-attacks.
>
> Thus, boards that choose to ignore, or minimize, the importance of cybersecurity oversight responsibility, do so at their own peril.[469]

This scenario continues to the current state. According to the Big 4 accountancy firm EY, "Cybersecurity risk management should be viewed as an organization-wide risk issue by the board and one that can impact business outcomes."[470]

According to McKinsey, the current continued escalation in large-scale adoption of the cloud is a high-priority topic on board agendas.

> The massive shift to virtual work and the great migration of consumers to digital channels has put digital transformations at the top of the corporate agenda and has increased attention on cloud's role in accelerating that process. That increased attention has tended to gravitate toward risk. Some boards of companies with multinational footprints, for example, harbor concerns around their ability to meet the regulatory requirements of different jurisdictions. This has led to greater board engagement on how cloud transitions may impact compliance and risk management, even as directors remain cautious about encroaching on or hindering management's responsibilities. In general, directors voiced a desire to become more fluent in making cloud a core part of corporate strategy discussion and development.[471]

In this context, the board must address a range of responsibilities concerning cloud governance.

The full spectrum of board responsibilities for governance is beyond the scope of this book. One of the major duties of the board with important cloud implications is the board's *fiduciary* duties.

19.4 Fiduciary Duties, the Board of Directors and the Cloud

The board of an organization has *fiduciary* duties. The term fiduciary derives from the Latin word *fiducia*, which translates to the English word *trust*. *Oxford Reference* defines fiduciary as, "A person, such as a trustee, who holds a position of trust or confidence with respect to someone else and who is therefore obliged to act solely for that person's benefit."[472]

Board of Directors and *Fiduciary Duties*

According to the CFA Institute, "The board of directors has a fiduciary responsibility under U.S. law to the company's shareholders."[473] BoardSource defines fiduciary duty as follows.

> Fiduciary duty requires board members to stay objective, unselfish, responsible, honest, trustworthy, and efficient. Board members, as stewards of public trust, must always act for the good of the organization, rather than for the benefit of themselves. They need to exercise reasonable care in all decision making, without placing the organization under unnecessary risk.[474]

Table 19.3 presents the Cornell Law School Legal Information Institute's perspective on the class of duties that comprise the fiduciary duties of board members.

Table 19.3: Perspectives on fiduciary duties of U.S. boards, as adapted from Cornell Law School.[475]

Fiduciary Duties	Description
Duty of Care	"Directors inform themselves 'prior to making a business decision, of all material information reasonably available to them'. Moreover, a director may not simply accept the information presented. Rather, the director must assess the information with a 'critical eye,' so as to protect the interests of the corporations and its stockholders."
Duty of Loyalty	"All directors and officers of a corporation working in their capacities as corporate fiduciaries must act without personal economic conflict."
Duty of Good Faith	"A corporation's directors and officers must advance interests of the corporation and fulfill their duties without violating the law."
Duty of Confidentiality	"A corporation's directors and officers must keep corporate information confidential and not disclose it for their own benefit."

Table 19.3 (continued)

Fiduciary Duties	Description
Duty of Prudence	"A trustee must administer a trust with a degree of care, skill, and caution that a prudent trustee would exercise."
Duty of Disclosure	"Requires directors to act with 'complete candor.' In certain circumstances, this requires the directors to disclose to the stockholders ' all of the facts and circumstances' relevant to the directors' decision."

Board of Directors and the *Duty of Care*

The *duty of care* is one of the most nuanced duties of a board member, expecting informed and discerning decisions to be made by board members on behalf of organizational stakeholders (e.g., stockholders). Table 19.4 presents On-Board's perspective on the importance of being present, involved, prepared, thorough, informed and alert in meeting the board's duty of care.

Table 19.4: Examples of board duty of care-related responsibilities, as adapted from OnBoard.[476]

Duty of Care Responsibilities	Description
1. Be Present	Attend and actively participate in board and committee meetings.
2. Be Involved	Ask questions, engage in discussions, advocate for progress, and offer ideas or solutions.
3. Be Prepared	Review board agendas and meeting materials in advance and seek expert advice when appropriate.
4. Be Thorough	Research additional information, options, and alternatives before making decisions, such as selecting a vendor or contractor.
5. Be Informed	Know your organization's mission, people, culture, community, budget, processes, policies, and procedures.

Table 19.4 (continued)

Duty of Care Responsibilities	Description
6. Be Alert	Pay attention to your organization's operations, how it is serving its mission, whether it has the resources it needs to effectively act on that mission, and whether it is following appropriate laws and regulations.

19.5 Duties of Inquiry, the Board of Directors and the Cloud

Effective board engagement with management and other stakeholders is crucial to organizational cloud governance. In this context, asking *the right questions* on cloud governance challenges some boards.

Major challenges include cloud literacy and advanced preparation. That is, literacy and fluency in the cloud, as well as adequate preparation, are important elements of the duty of care responsibilities of board members proactively engaging in cloud governance inquiries.

The Board of Directors and the Duty of Reasonable Inquiry

An integral component of the duty of care is the notion of the *duty of reasonable inquiry*. For example, the state of California Corporation Legal Code, Article 3 on Standards of Conduct Code 5231(a) explicitly includes the duty of reasonable inquiry.

> A director shall perform the duties of a director, including duties as a member of any committee of the board upon which the director may serve, in good faith, in a manner that director believes to be in the best interests of the corporation and with such care, including reasonable inquiry, as an ordinarily prudent person in a like position would use under similar circumstances.[477]

Table 19.5 presents examples of a U.S. statutory concept of a board's duty of inquiry.

Table 19.5: Perspectives on duty of reasonable inquiry – selected examples.

Source	U.S. State	Board's Duty of Reasonable Inquiry
Law Firm Carolinas[478]	Carolina	"Directors are also under a 'duty of reasonable inquiry' to inform themselves as to the condition of the corporate entity and the conduct of its affairs."
Stimmel, Stimmel and Roeser[479]	California	"The directors are required to make reasonable inquiry as to the condition and activities of the company. They not only must review the reports delivered (and demand such reports if none are delivered) but must make such inquiry as the reports or conditions of the company seems to require."
Reger, Rizzo, Darnall[480]	Pennsylvania	"Pennsylvania's duty of care rules require officers and directors of corporations to exercise business decisions with adequate information and reasonable diligence when considering all available information. Specifically, the statute requires that officers and directors render their services 'in good faith' and 'with such care, including reasonable inquiry, skill and diligence, as a person of ordinary prudence would use under similar circumstances.'"

What are the Right Questions Board Members Should Ask Concerning Cloud Governance?

It depends on a range of factors and variables that are context-sensitive and organization-specific. Cloud literacy and fluency, and adequate preparation are critical to the board's duty of care responsibilities.

Cloud Literacy and Fluency: Is the Board *Fit-for-Purpose*?

The *Oxford University Press* defines the term *fit-for-purpose* as, "[of an institution, facility, etc.] well equipped or well suited for its designated role or purpose. Quality is inextricably linked with being fit for purpose."[481] Being fit-for-purpose is integral to the board's duty of care responsibilities.

Yet, several market survey results suggest that some boards lack the technical expertise to provide advice and oversight to management about cybersecurity risks and governance. For instance, in a 2021 survey titled Board Effectiveness: A survey of the C-suite, PwC and The Conference Board reported, "Many executives question whether the directors on their boards have the right skills, experience, and background to help steer companies through today's uncertain climate."[482]

In this context, the lack of cloud literacy would challenge the board's ability to fulfill their duty of care-related fiduciary responsibilities for cloud governance. Increasing board fluency through training and other interventions can contribute to mitigating this gap. Table 19.6 presents perspectives on enhancing the board's digital literacy and fluency.

Table 19.6: Perspectives on digital literacy and the board, as adapted from the *HBR* and McKinsey.

Source	Digital Literacy and the Board
The *Harvard Business Review (HBR)* [483]	It becomes management's responsibility to educate the board. *HBR* recommends placing "board members through intensive training programs led by external faculty or top technologists from the company that focus on the business implications of key technologies and methodologies." This continuous training will help ensure that the board is cloud savvy to provide management advice and guidance, creating stronger cloud governance, and cyber resilience.
McKinsey[484]	A cloud strategy doesn't live in isolation; it is a critical enabler of a company's larger technology and digital transformation. Boards therefore need to build their knowledge of cloud and its ability to drive competitive advantage. A critical step in meeting this challenge is onboarding directors who have successfully introduced cloud in another organization and who are able to scrutinize the business implications of cloud and understand cloud's role in accelerating digital transformations. But a key facet of a successful governance model is to ensure, through continuous board education, that cloud doesn't become a topic only for members with prior technology and cloud experience.

Is the Board *Prepared* to Ask Questions about the Cloud?

For those board members that are cloud literate, adequate preparation for cloud-related board agenda items is crucial. Yet, survey results suggest that some board members are not prepared for board agenda items. For instance in a 2021 survey titled, Board Effectiveness: A survey of the C-suite, PwC and The Conference Board reported, "Many executives see directors' preparation and time spent in their role as insufficient. Fewer than one in four executives (23%)

said their board is fully prepared for meetings, and only 27% said directors spend enough time on their duties."[485]

Table 19.7 lists examples of questions presented by *HBR* that may help assess a board member's preparedness.

Table 19.7: Questions the board should ask on cloud governance, as adapted from *Harvard Business Review*.[486]

Cloud Governance Question	Overview
1. Does the board understand the implications of digital and technology well enough to provide valuable guidance?	Building up the board's digital aptitude isn't about turning directors into proficient technologists. Rather, the goal is for the board to understand the implications of technology and digital on the business and sources of revenue.
2. Is the digital transformation fundamentally changing how the business (and sector) creates value?	In the context of a digital transformation, there are three vectors of value: scale (is the new value big enough?), source (where is the value coming from?), and scope (are we thinking long term enough?).
3. How does the board know if the digital transformation is working?	Digital transformations are complex programs with dozens or even hundreds of initiatives. This can generate a soothing level of activity, but it tells you very little about whether your digital transformation is on track. To get past the noise, boards can start with a hard-nosed assessment of the strategy and roadmap.
4. Does the board have a sufficiently expansive view of talent?	The digital-talent discussion at the board level is often limited to expressing the need to hire more executives who are digital natives or people from consumer-facing companies that might be further along on their digital journeys. This is only part of the story. Given the scope of change required across the entire business, boards must develop an expansive view and pressure test the talent roadmap as much as they might the technology or digital-transformation roadmap.

Table 19.7 (continued)

Cloud Governance Question	Overview
5. Does the board have a clear view of emerging threats?	Digital expands companies' competitive footprint by blurring traditional sector boundaries. While this creates new opportunities for companies to participate in emerging ecosystems, it also generates a more complex set of threats to assess. On the risk side, boards generally have a clear understanding of the importance of cybersecurity. Many have a framework, vetted by third parties, to help evaluate cyber risk. Digital, however, opens new and different pools of risk. Regulations about privacy grab headlines, but local compliance or national security laws, for example, have introduced unforeseen risks to businesses when their servers are located in those corresponding locations.

What Language are they Speaking? Confronting Cloud Jargon

Jargon and technical expression in the digital domain generally, and in the cloud specifically, challenge many of us, including some board members. For instance, hybrid cloud, configuration management, and GDPR compliance. According to Security Roundtable, "Cloud computing is mainstream, but a lot of the terminology used in talking about cloud are arcane and confusing."[487] Cloud jargon can derail a cloud-literate and well-prepared board member.

19.6 Cloud Governance, the Board of Directors and Asking the Right Questions

Crafting appropriate questions concerning cloud governance is an integral part of the board's due care responsibilities. Relevant and targeted questions associated with cloud governance also help to facilitate meaningful discussions between board, management and other cloud stakeholders (e.g., third-party assurance providers). Table 19.8 presents Google Cloud's suggested questions the board may ask concerning cloud governance.

Table 19.8: Questions from the board on cloud governance, as adapted from Google Cloud.[488]

Questions the Board Should Consider Concerning Cloud Governance
1. How is the use of cloud technology being governed within the organization? Is clear accountability assigned and is there clarity of responsibility in decision-making structures?
2. How well does the use of cloud technology align with, and support, the technology and data strategy for the organization, and, ideally, the overarching business strategy, in order that the cloud approach can be tailored to achieve those right outcomes?
3. Is there a clear technical and architectural approach for the use of cloud that incorporates the controls necessary to ensure that infrastructure and applications are deployed and maintained in a secure state?
4. Has a skills and capabilities assessment been conducted, in order to determine what investments are needed across the organization?
5. How is the organization structure and operating model evolving to both fully leverage cloud, but also to increase the likelihood of a secure and compliant adoption?
6. How are risk and control frameworks being adjusted, with an emphasis on understanding how the organization's risk profile is changing and how the organization is staying within risk appetite?
7. How are independent risk and audit functions adjusting their approach in light of the organization's adoption of cloud?
8. How are regulators and other authorities being engaged in order to keep them informed and abreast of the organization's strategy and of the plans for the migration of specific business processes and data sets?
9. How is the organization prioritizing resourcing to enable the adoption of cloud, but also to maintain adequate focus on managing existing and legacy technologies?
10. Is the organization consuming and adopting the cloud provider's set of best practices and leveraging the lessons the cloud provider will have learned from their other customers?

The National Audit Office (NAO) advanced three categories of questions an audit committee of a board might consider asking concerning cloud governance. Table 19.9 presents these questions. This is not a complete list of questions. Management should customize the questions to the organization.

Table 19.9: Examples of possible questions the board may ask associated with cloud governance, as adapted from National Audit Office (2021).[489]

Part 1: Assessment of Cloud Services **Considers cloud services as part of organizational and digital strategies, the business case process, and due diligence.**
1. What are the priorities for the digital strategy?
2. Has the cloud strategy had input from an appropriate range of stakeholders?
3. Have technical requirements been articulated?
4. Have any specific features or legislative requirements been considered and identified?
5. Is the complexity of the legacy system issues really understood?
6. Will best practice be followed with respect to security?
7. Have costing models been considered to an appropriate level of detail?
8. How sensitive are planned costs to scenario testing?
9. What extra skills and capacity will be needed?
10. Has the organization addressed technical lock-in considerations?
11. Has the organization considered cloud concentration risk?
12. What time horizon is being considered in the commercial model?
13. Is there an exit strategy?
14. Will there be clear accountability between the organization and the cloud provider?
15. Have the service features being promoted been verified?
16. What are the terms of service?
17. Where is the provider's infrastructure physically situated, and in what jurisdiction(s) is the organization's data being held and accessed?
18. Will the cloud service contract be governed by the law and subject to the jurisdiction in the UK?
19. What security accreditation and protocols does the provider have?
20. Is there an understanding of what assurances are available from the provider?
21. Does the organization understand what security information will be supplied by the provider as part of the service?

Table 19.9 (continued)

Part 2: Implementation of Cloud Services
System configuration, data migration and service risk and security.

---

1. Is there a strong governance and project management plan in place?

2. Have infrastructure, applications and data been prepared for the move?

3. Is the organization following configuration best practice?

4. Is the organization overly reliant on third-party resource?

5. Will people be ready for the new systems?

6. Are technical risks covered with clear responsibilities and mitigating actions?

7. Does the organization have the capacity and capability to analyze security data made available by the cloud provider?

8. Are the required legal and policy agreements in place?

9. Have business continuity plans been updated?

10. Are plans in place to cover the event of data loss?

11. Are financial controls fully tested and compliant with best practice?

12. Have privileged accounts been secured?

13. Have key stakeholders been engaged through a comprehensive change management strategy?

14. Are contingency plans in place to manage implementation issues?

15. Are there sufficient plans for technical and user acceptance testing?

16. Is there sufficient information for a Go/No-Go decision?

Part 3: Management and Optimization of Cloud Services
Operational considerations, the need for assurance from third parties, and the capability required to manage live services.

---

1. Is there effective governance to prioritize the removal of any temporary workarounds?

2. Is there clear oversight over what the cloud providers are planning?

3. Are responsibilities clear for system changes, upgrades, patches?

4. Is there sufficient capability to take advantage of the reporting functionality?

5. Is the monitoring its usage of the cloud to confirm that it is getting the best value?

6. Does management understand the general scope and limitations of different Service Organization Controls reports?

7. Is management clear on the scope of controls tested and the extent of testing?

Table 19.9 (continued)

Part 3: Management and Optimization of Cloud Services
Operational considerations, the need for assurance from third parties, and the capability required to manage live services.

---

8. Do Service Organization Controls reports give assurance on the success of operational controls over time?

---

9. Are Service Organization Controls reports frequent enough to keep pace with continuous improvement?

---

10. Does management carefully scrutinize Service Organization Controls report findings?

---

11. Will the organization retain the necessary technical knowledge post-implementation?

---

12. Does the technical team have the capability to take full advantage of the cloud systems?

---

13. Will there be sufficient capability to manage updates, downtime, and system changes?

---

14. Will there be sufficient commercial and legal capacity to challenge value for money and compliance?

---

15. Is there sufficient base-level stakeholder capability to optimize cloud system usage?

---

16. Does the organization have access to skills and knowledge of a broad range of technical solutions?

19.7 Conclusion

The board plays a crucial role in organizational governance, including cloud governance. The duty of care challenges board member to be literate and fluent in the cloud, and adequately prepared to discuss the cloud. The duty of reasonable inquiry also challenges boards to ask the right questions.

Key Questions
1. What is the class of duties that comprises the fiduciary responsibility of the board?
2. How do contextual factors impact the board's duty of inquiry in cloud governance?
3. What types of questions should the board ask concerning cloud governance?

Box 19.1: Board of Director's Liable for Cloud Data Breaches

In January 2019, the *New York Times* reported that "the former officers and directors of Yahoo agreed to pay $29 million (USD) to settle charges that they breached their fiduciary duties in their handling of customer data during a series of cyberattacks from 2013 until 2016. Three billion Yahoo user accounts were compromised in the attacks."[490]

The law firm of White and Williams LLP stated that the derivative law suit action contained "allegations that Yahoo officials breached their fiduciary duties by failing to protect Yahoo's data, failing to investigate and remediate the breaches after they occurred, by failing to put proper safety mechanisms in place to prevent such attacks (i.e., "the Board's refusal to spend necessary money to improve [Yahoo's] data security infrastructure exposed [Yahoo] to significant hacking incidents") and by issuing false and misleading statements about Yahoo's knowledge of the data breaches."[491] The U.S. SEC charged Yahoo, now named Altaba, a $35 million USD penalty for failing to make a timely disclosure of the data breach.[492]

White and Williams LLP, also warned that the Yahoo settlement "could inspire future civil actions and usher in a new wave of shareholder derivative litigation seeking to hold directors liable for damages to the company resulting from cybersecurity breaches and alleged board oversight duty failures."[493] Shareholders are suing directors and officers from the boards of SolarWinds and Home Depot alleging the boards failed to fulfill their fiduciary duties that resulted in cloud security breaches.[494]

Part V: **Conclusion: Cloud Reflections**

Chapter 20
Reflections on the Utopian Promises of the Cloud, Wicked Problems and the Metaverse-Driven Future

> Utopias have their value – nothing so wonderfully expands the imaginative horizons of human potentialities – but as guides to conduct they can prove literally fatal.[495]
> – Isaiah Berlin, Oxford philosopher, historian, and author

Learning Objectives
- Reflect on whether the cloud delivers on its utopian promises
- Reflect on wicked problems and the potential chaos of the cloud
- Consider what the Metaverse-driven future holds for the cloud

 Key Terms

1. Cloud-Washing – "The purposeful and sometimes deceptive attempt by a vendor to rebrand an old product or service by associating the buzzword cloud with it."[496]
2. Metaverse – Derived from the Greek *meta*, meaning beyond, and *verse*, short for universe. "Metaverse describes a fully realized digital world that exists beyond the one in which we live."[497] "Whether in virtual reality, augmented reality, or simply on a screen, the promise of the Metaverse is to allow a greater overlap of our digital and physical lives in wealth, socialization, productivity, shopping and entertainment."[498]
3. Zettabyte – 1,000,000,000,000,000,000,000 bytes of data (21 zeros)

Chapter Outline

https://doi.org/10.1515/9783110755374-020

20.1 Introduction

Utopian promises of the cloud, combined with the organizational disruption of deploying and scaling the cloud, have profound governance implications. This chapter reflects on the promises and chaos of the cloud, and considers what the Metaverse-driven future holds for the cloud.

20.2 The Promise of the Cloud

> Don't celebrate promises, and don't fear threats.[499]
> – Sicilian proverb

The *Oxford Learner's Dictionary* defines utopia as "an imaginary place or state in which everything is perfect."[500] Ernst Bloch, author of *The Principle of Hope*, suggests that imagining the achievement of utopian conditions is an important catalyst for change. In the context of the cloud, many organizations have embraced the promises of the cloud and are therefore willing to transform to achieve a cloud-driven *utopia* of sorts.

Cloud vendors, academics, influencers, and media have contributed to defining and signaling a wide range of transformational benefits available through the cloud. That is, compelling promises of ideal performance, innovation, productivity, cost savings, and much more. Table 20.1 presents examples of such utopian promises of the cloud.

Table 20.1: Examples of utopian promises of the cloud.

Categories of the Utopian Promises of the Cloud

1. Substantial Cost Reduction | Substantial Return on Investment (ROI)
  – On-demand CSP pay-as-you-go model lowers capital investments, including in-house hardware, software, and IT maintenance
  – Increase in revenue through innovation improved customer engagement

2. Sweeping, Accelerated Gains in Productivity, Efficiency, Innovation, Customer Service
  – Cloud-democratized employees who can collaborate and access data in the cloud from anywhere at anytime
  – Previously unavailable options now enabled by the CSP to transform IT capacity (e.g., data storage and IT scaling opportunities, automated software updates)

3. Reduced Risk | Improved IT Governance
  – Reduces risks associated with data privacy, security, compliance, denial of service
  – Cloud accelerates ESG-driven positive impacts (e.g., reduced carbon footprint)

20.3 Does the Cloud Deliver on its Promise? It Depends . . .

> Don't promise, prove. Your results will speak for themselves.[501]
> – Jim Kwikm, author

As the cloud enters a more mature phase, and the Metaverse looms as the most significant technological disruption in a decade, an essential question emerges, Does the cloud deliver sufficiently on it promises or are some promises utopian in nature? The short answer is, *it depends.*

As with any disruptive and transformational change undertaken by an organization, the level of success attained depends on a range of complex variables. With respect to the cloud, we focus on three major variables that influence the attainment, depth and timing of success. First, whether the promises of the cloud are realistic; Second, whether the organization can navigate and govern the inherent and unavoidable chaos of the cloud; and Third, the context that the organization operates in.

1. The Promises of the Cloud – *Are expected outcomes from the cloud realistic and achievable*?

The first variable influencing cloud success is to what extent are all of the marketed promises expected from the cloud realistic and achievable. The cloud strategic plan and associated cloud performance measures should be based on realistic and achievable cloud objectives, anticipated results, and the timing of such expected results. This spans all aspects of the cloud.

For instance, strategy, including cloud migration planning, cloud change management, developing a cloud-enabled workforce, and transforming the roles and responsibilities of organizational governance functions. As necessary, management should modify the strategy, and associated anticipated performance outcomes as time progresses and learning increases.

2. The Chaos of the Cloud – *Is the organization prepared to navigate and govern the chaos?*

The second variable influencing cloud success is the inherent and inevitable chaos of the cloud. Ernst Bloch stated that, "Utopias are seen as impossible."[502] This perspective seems reasonably relevant to the cloud. Some organizations expect to achieve the promises of the cloud, but fall short because of the inherent *chaos* of the cloud. The *Cambridge Dictionary* defines chaos as "A state of total confusion with no order."[503]

Is chaos a reality of the cloud? At a minimum, some confusion, uncertainty, and gaps in performance have emerged in cloud deployments. For instance,

Gartner reported the following gaps that have commonly emerged during a cloud deployment and operations journey.

- Gap between an organization's aspirations and the ability of in-house staff to execute
- Gap between expected gains from cloud versus the reality of what cloud can deliver
- Gap between an organization's business strategy and its cloud strategy
- Gap between existing and required operating model, or between the existing and required foundational practices such as governance, compliance and security[504]

Table 20.2 presents a random list of the chaotic realities of the cloud.

Table 20.2: Top 25 list of the chaotic realities of the cloud.

Chaos of the Cloud – Top 25 (Random Order)
1. Incoherent cloud strategy
2. Unbridled vendor activities with organization assets
3. Overreliance on one CSP vendor (concentration risk)
4. Haphazard controls over the extended enterprise
5. Lack of accountability for respective cloud-shared responsibilities
6. Shared cloud responsibility stakeholders are not accountable and responsible
7. No one is in charge of the cloud – bifurcated cloud leadership in the organization
8. Cloud unleashes ungoverned workarounds and reengineering needs
9. Cloud-washing and upselling/overselling by vendors
10. Lack of a cloud-enabled workforce (e.g., in-house IT function, employees)
11. Ineffective incident response and investigation of root causes
12. Failure to address configuration settings results in an increase in security risk
13. Unaware of the scope, frequency of cyber-threats, unsuccessful attacks, breaches
14. Poor configuration settings
15. Unsanctioned shadow IT and a lack of a reliable, real-time cloud asset inventory
16. Understatement of cloud costs (e.g., vendor, change management training, insurance, migration, business interruptions costs, crisis management costs, ransomware)
17. Success takes much longer than planned
18. Pressure to rapidly adopt and scale the cloud before prepared to do so
19. Distributed and remote workforce using ad hoc tech creating increased vulnerabilities
20. Rapidly shifting regulatory requirements that differ across geographic jurisdictions
21. Unknown gaps between liability insurance policies and cyber insurance policies
22. Customer loyalty challenged by cloud breaches and service downtime
23. Growing pressure for board members to be more cloud literate
24. CSP security policies and priorities not aligned with organization policies
25. Convoluted and complicated SLA and CSP contracts

Source: Authors.

3. The Context of the Cloud

Another important variable influencing cloud success is the context of the cloud. An organization is highly-sensitive to the context that it operates in. This context substantially influences the success and failure of innovative initiatives that are disruptive and transformational. The cloud is an example of such an innovation initiative.

The Technological, Organizational and Environmental (TOE) framework (DePietro et al., 1990) is used to as a theoretical lens to explore how context influences cloud success. This section presents examples of how the technological, organizational and environmental context influences the cloud innovation adoption process.[505] Table 20.3 presents examples for each of the three TOE framework categories.

Table 20.3: Context variables of TOE framework to consider during cloud adoption to limit chaos.

TOE Framework[506]	Cloud Success Depends On . . .
Technological Context Represents the internal and external technologies related to the firm	1. Maturity of the cloud technology and implementation 2. Infrastructure fit for cloud purpose 3. Integrating cloud into existing IT governance protocols 4. Risk appetite (e.g., Zero Trust) 5. Incident response capabilities 6. Enabling digital transformation (e.g., machine learning) 7. Governing remote technology 8. Data ethics and data governance 9. Legacy system limitations
Organizational Context Related to the resources and the characteristics of the firm	1. Strategies for multi-level deployment (e.g., unit, segment) 2. Oversight of vendor performance 3. Knowledge of the location of cloud assets 4. Compliance with global regulations across geography 5. ESG governance considerations in vendor selection 6. Top-down change management efforts 7. Ability to transform in-house IT function 8. A cloud-enabled workforce 9. Role of the CIO as a business savvy technologist

Table 20.3 (continued)

TOE Framework[506]	Cloud Success Depends On . . .
Environmental Context Refers to the arena in which a firm conducts its business	1. Receptiveness to innovation to explore Edge, AI, Metaverse 2. Due diligence in assessing CSP capabilities 3. Importance of the shared responsibility model 4. High-profile cyber-attacks at other organizations 5. Lessons learned from good practices at other organizations 6. New and emerging global regulations 7. Competition for cloud-enabled talent, including the board 8. Competitive landscape of cloud vendors 9. ESG-regulations and expectations with cloud implications

Source: Authors.

An organization's cloud adoption journey will not be a straight line; the path will be filled with twists and turns – risks and opportunities. Cloud governance plays a crucial role moderating the extremes; striving to achieve the promises of the cloud, on the one hand, and successfully navigating and governing the chaos of the cloud on the other hand. The lessons learned during the journey will contribute to adjusting the sails for the continued journey to cloud success.

20.4 What Does the Metaverse-Driven Future Hold for the Cloud?

The future depends on what you do today.[507]
– Mahatma Gandhi, Indian leader and social activist

According to The World Economic Forum's 2020 Future of Jobs Report, "By 2025, automation and a new division of labor between humans and machines will disrupt 85 million jobs globally in medium and large businesses across 15 industries and 26 economies."[508] The Metaverse is on the verge of joining the cloud at the vanguard of this paradigm shift. According to EY,

> Every so often a new technology paradigm emerges, promising to fundamentally reengineer industries, economies, societies and daily life. Roughly 10 years since the last such shift – social, mobile, cloud – we may be on the cusp of a new one: the Metaverse.

Touted as the successor to the internet, the Metaverse refers to a shared, persistent, three-dimensional virtual realm where people interact with objects, the environment and each other through digital representations of themselves or avatars.[509]

What does this Metaverse-driven future hold for the cloud?

Media reports suggest that the Metaverse will influence the future of the cloud, and at the same time, the cloud will influence the future of Metaverse. For instance, according to InfoWorld, "The truth is that the Metaverse will be a boon for cloud computing, considering the amount of storage and processing required to support a virtual reality universe. As more performance and details will be demanded, remote cloud-based computers will become the only cost-effective way to solve that problem."[510]

Metaverse influencers suggest that organizations and CSPs are already seizing the opportunities to leverage cloud-enabled Metaverse technologies and applications. Such technologies include cloud gaming, Internet of Things (IoT), and artificial intelligence (AI).

Cloud Gaming, the Metaverse and the Cloud

Cloud gaming uses the connectivity of the 5G wireless network to enable the user to stream digital content from a cloud server to mobile phone devices, game consoles, laptops, and tablets. Cloud-based gaming eliminates the requirement for users to buy hardware and upgrade content. A high-definition cloud game requires low latency, large bandwidth, and low response time.

The market for gaming is massive and growing. For instance, Microsoft expects 4.5 billion gaming consumers worldwide by 2030.[511] Based on a 2021 worldwide survey, Statista predicted the games market will generate revenues of 218.8 billion U.S. dollars (USD) and the global cloud gaming market will generate 6.5 billion USD in revenue by 2024."[512]

In January 2022, Microsoft, Sony, and Netflix announced plans to embark on enormous cloud gaming initiatives.

- Microsoft offered 68.8 billion USD to acquire Activision Blizzard,[513] the publisher of *Call of Duty* and *Candy Crush* video games. *The New York Times* reported that "Microsoft cited the Metaverse as a reason for buying Activision Blizzard."[514]
- Sony offered 3.6 billion USD to acquire Bungie,[515] the video game developer of *Halo.*
- Netflix announced that the subscription service would build its cloud gaming unit.[516]

These investments are anecdotal evidence that technology companies are betting big on the Metaverse, which will be in part dependent on the cloud.

IoT, the Metaverse and the Cloud

IoT devices connected to the cloud will use 5G and WiFi-6 networks to share data quickly. According to Intel,

> 5G will be used for connected cars, smart city deployments, and even for large manufacturing operations. Wi-Fi will remain the most efficient way to connect the growing number of devices throughout the home, including PCs, tablets, smartphones, smart speakers, home security cameras, thermostats, and appliances.[517]

Statista projects that there will be 30.9 billion IoT devices in place globally by 2025.[518]

IoT devices create large amounts of data, which creates the need for more storage capacity. This is where the benefits of the cloud are realized. Statista projects that by 2025, worldwide, the digital universe will create 180 zettabytes of data.[519] Large amounts of data will require organizations and their CSPs to mitigate data privacy and security risks. Gartner highlighted that data risks demand extensive governance for things (i.e., IoT).

> The scale and pace of data generated by "things" introduces integrity challenges and obviates traditional approaches that data and analytics leaders have used for data quality assurance. The highly distributed nature of IoT architectures challenges expectations on data availability, requiring data and analytics leaders to accept that purely centralized approaches to governance controls will become less viable.[520]

See Box 20.1 for a further discussion on IoT devices and edge computing.

AI, the Metaverse and the Cloud

IBM defines AI as "a field, which combines computer science and robust datasets, to enable problem-solving. It also encompasses sub-fields of machine learning and deep learning."[521] Organizations can leverage AI datasets stored in the cloud and extract meaningful information to make business decisions. An organization's use of cloud AI datasets also exacerbate risks such as data ethics, cloud security, and data privacy. See Box 20.2 about AI.

In addition, the massive growth in AI applications exacerbates data ethics and privacy risks. As a result, the AI regulatory landscape is shifting, with international governments planning and passing AI regulations. For instance, in April 2021, the European Commission proposed a legal framework to address the risks of using AI.[522] In February 2022, the U.S. Congress introduced a bill titled the Algorithmic Accountability Act of 2022 to require impact assessments of automated decision systems and augmented critical decision processes.[523] Both organizations and cloud vendors will be impacted by such AI advances and regulations.

20.5 Conclusion: Is the Cloud a *Wicked Problem?*

> Come lay your head on my cloud, it won't rain. Unless you make it so.[524]
> "A Wicked Cloud" – poem by Raekwon Jones

The chaos of the cloud is a *problem* that creates confusion, perplexity, and risk at various points during a cloud journey. This raises a question, is the cloud a *wicked* problem?

Camillus (2008) explains how wicked problems differ from ordinary problems as follows.

> Wicked problems often crop up when organizations have to face constant change or unprecedented challenges. They occur in a social context; the greater the disagreement among stakeholders, the more wicked the problem. In fact, it's the social complexity of wicked problems as much as their technical difficulties that make them tough to manage. Not all problems are wicked; confusion, discord, and lack of progress are telltale signs that an issue might be wicked.[525]

Horst Rittel (1973), one of the pioneers of the theory of wicked problems, described a wicked problem as difficult to describe, has many root causes, and has no correct answer.[526]

In a business strategy context, Camillus (2008) identified five common characteristics of a wicked problem in an organizational strategy context.
1. The problem involves many stakeholders with different values and priorities.
2. The issue's roots are complex and tangled.
3. The problem is difficult to come to grips with and changes with every attempt to address it.
4. The challenge has no precedent.
5. There's nothing to indicate the right answer to the problem.[527]

As we conclude this chapter reflecting on the utopian promises and chaos of the cloud, we reflect on whether the strategic deployment of the cloud at scale creates a *wicked problem*. Specifically: Does the cloud create a problem that is difficult to describe? Is it a problem with many root causes? Is it a problem with no precedent? Are the roots of the problem complex and tangled? Does it create confusion? Does it involve many stakeholders with different values and priorities?

Whether or not the cloud strategy creates a wicked problem has cloud governance implications. That is, how an organization goes about governing a wicked problem may differ in some important ways as compared to governing an ordinary or difficult problem. So . . . we ask a final question . . . *Is the cloud a wicked problem*? What do you think?

Box 20.1: IoT Devices and Edge Computing

Implanted medical and wearable health devices are emerging cloud technologies in the healthcare industry. Medical devices and wearable health technology devices are examples of IoT devices. Wearable health technologies are "small electronic devices that, when placed on the body, can help measure temperature, blood pressure, blood oxygen, breathing rate, sound, GPS location, elevation, physical movement, changes in direction, and the electrical activity of the heart, muscles, brain, and skin."[528] Consumers who use cloud-connected medical devices and wear health technology devices are susceptible to cybersecurity attacks. Government agencies such as the U.S. Food and Drug Administration help protect the public by issuing alerts to health care delivery organizations to avoid cybersecurity breaches that could affect the safety and performance of medical devices.[529]

The U.S. Government Accountability Office (GAO) identified "intentional threats" to implantable medical devices. IoT medical devices that transfer unencrypted data using wireless cloud technology are at risk of,

- "Unauthorized access: a malicious person intercepting and altering signals sent wirelessly to the medical device
- Malware: a malicious software program designed to carry out annoying or harmful actions and often masquerading as or embedded in useful programs so that users are induced to activate it
- Denial-of-service attack: computer worms or viruses that overwhelm a device by excessive communication attempts, making the device unusable by either slowing or blocking functionality or draining the device's battery."[530]

Ransomware is a type of cybersecurity attack. Ransomware is an emerging risk area with a velocity that can quickly disrupt an organization. According to the U.S. Cybersecurity & Infrastructure Security Agency, ransomware is "an ever-evolving form of malware designed to encrypt files on a device, rendering any files and the systems that rely on them unusable. Malicious actors then demand ransom in exchange for decryption."[531]

Edge computing supports IoT. Edge makes it possible to send, receive, and analyze data from IoT devices. Instead of sending the data to a centralized cloud data center, computing at the edge can help an organization locally process data in real time because the computing occurs at or near the user or source of data. According to RedHat, one of the benefits of edge includes,

The ability to conduct on-site big data analytics and aggregation, which is what allows for near real-time decision making. Edge computing further reduces the risk of exposing sensitive data by keeping all of that computing power local, thereby allowing companies to enforce security practices or meet regulatory policies.[532]

Organizations and CSPs must have strong cloud data governance policies that document how it stores, secures, and analyzes the large amounts of data collected at the edge from connected devices.

Box 20.2: AI
An autonomous vehicle such as a Tesla, is made up of many IoT devices. All Tesla vehicles send data to the cloud. When one vehicle learns something new, the entire Tesla fleet is instantly improved. Bernard Marr, an IT futurist and business influencer, described how Tesla uses AI and the cloud.

The data is used to generate highly data-dense maps showing everything from the average increase in traffic speed over a stretch of road, to the location of hazards which cause drivers to take action. Machine learning in the cloud takes care of educating the entire fleet, while at an individual car level, edge computing decides what action the car needs to take right now. A third level of decision-making also exists, with cars able to form networks with other Tesla vehicles nearby in order to share local information and insights. In a near future scenario where autonomous cars are widespread, these networks will most likely also interface with cars from other manufacturers as well as other systems such as traffic cameras, road-based sensors or mobile phones.[533]

The COVID-19 pandemic revealed vulnerabilities in the global supply chain. The pandemic created a global semiconductor chip shortage that impacted automotive and communications products. Vehicles need semiconductor chips to operate. In November 2021, the U.S. Secretary of the Department of Commerce remarked that "the average electric vehicle has about 2,000 chips, roughly double the average number of chips in a non-electric car."[534] CSPs like AWS, Microsoft, and Google are designing their chips. These CSP hyperscalers are not manufacturing the chips they design.

Endnotes

1 Martin, G. (n.d.). *Every cloud has a silver lining – the meaning and origin of this phrase.* Phrasefinder. https://www.phrases.org.uk/meanings/every-cloud-has-a-silver-lining.html

2 United States Code. (2021, January 1). *15 U.S. Code § 9401 – Artificial Intelligence Definition.* Cornell Law School. https://www.law.cornell.edu/uscode/text/15/9401#3

3 Sheldon, R. (2022, February). *What is Cloud Washing?* TechTarget. https://www.techtarget.com/searchstorage/definition/cloud-washing.

4 United States National Institute of Standards and Technology (2020, February). *NIST Special Publication 800-171, Revision 2: Protecting Controlled Unclassified Information in Nonfederal Systems and Organizations.* NIST. https://doi.org/10.6028/NIST.SP.800-171r2

5 IBM Cloud Education. (2020, July 15). *What is Machine Learning?* IBM Cloud Learn Hub. https://www.ibm.com/cloud/learn/machine-learning

6 *What is Digital Transformation? Why Is It Important.* (n.d.). Salesforce. https://www.salesforce.com/products/platform/what-is-digital-transformation/

7 Choney, S. (2016, April 4). *Satya Nadella: Why businesses should embrace digital transformation, not only to survive – but also to thrive.* Microsoft News Center. https://news.microsoft.com/features/satya-nadella-why-businesses-should-embrace-digital-transformation-not-only-to-survive-but-also-to-thrive/

8 Grance, T., Mell, P. (2011, September). *SP 800–145, The NIST Definition of Cloud Computing.* National Institute of Standards and Technology. https://csrc.nist.gov/publications/detail/sp/800-145/final

9 Herbst, N., Bauer, A., Kounev, S., Oikonomou, G., Eyk, E. V., Kousiouris, G., . . . & Iosup, A. (Eds.). (2018). *Quantifying Cloud Performance and Dependability: Taxonomy, Metric Design, and Emerging Challenges.* ACM Transactions on Modeling and Performance Evaluation of Computing Systems, Volume 3, Issue 4. https://dl.acm.org/doi/pdf/10.1145/3236332?casa_token=_mDr9B3wLZsAAAAA:i7amQe9PyAT9D744neapHRh_tu8YiqEe4VKr9rWsmB63CijavRoPMLnF4_FK-6Djj67ERrZg2mh-

10 *What is the Cloud – Definition.* (n.d). Microsoft Azure. https://azure.microsoft.com/en-us/overview/what-is-the-cloud/

11 *What is Cloud Computing?* (n.d). Salesforce. https://www.salesforce.com/uk/learning-centre/tech/cloudcomputing/

12 Accenture. (n.d.). *Introduction to Cloud Computing.* https://www.accenture.com/us-en/cloud/insights/cloud-computing-index

13 Regalado, A. (2011, October 31). Who Coined the Term Cloud Computing? MIT Technology Review. https://www.technologyreview.com/2011/10/31/257406/who-coined-cloud-computing/

14 Gartner. (2021, November 10). *Gartner Says Cloud Will Be the Centerpiece of New Digital Experiences.* Gartner. https://www.gartner.com/en/newsroom/press-releases/2021-11-10-gartner-says-cloud-will-be-the-centerpiece-of-new-digital-experiences

15 Forrest, W., Gu, M., Kaplan, J. Liebow, M., Sharma, R., Smaje, K., Van Kuiken, S. (2021, February 26). Cloud's Trillion-Dollar Prize is Up for Grabs. McKinsey Quarterly. https://www.mckinsey.com/business-functions/mckinsey-digital/our-insights/clouds-trillion-dollar-prize-is-up-for-grabs

16 Scammells, J. (2020, March 2). *History of the Internet of Things (IoT).* ITonlinelearning. https://www.itonlinelearning.com/blog-history-iot/

17 Satyanarayanan, M. (2017, January). *The Emergence of Edge Computing.* THE IEEE COMPUTER SOCIETY. https://elijah.cs.cmu.edu/DOCS/satya-edge2016.pdf

https://doi.org/10.1515/9783110755374-021

18 Forrest, W., Gu, M., Kaplan, J. Liebow, M., Sharma, R., Smaje, K., Van Kuiken, S. (2021, February 26). *Cloud's Trillion-Dollar Prize is Up for Grabs.* McKinsey Quarterly. https://www.mckinsey.com/business-functions/mckinsey-digital/our-insights/clouds-trillion-dollar-prize-is-up-for-grabs

19 Keary, T. (2021, April 9). *10 Benefits of Cloud Computing for Businesses in 2021.* ITPRC https://www.itprc.com/cloud-computing-benefits-for-business/

20 Flexera (9 March 2022). *Flexera 2022 State of the Cloud Report.* https://info.flexera.com/CM-REPORT-State-of-the-Cloud

21 Rivner, U. (2009, August 13). *Dark Cloud.* Finextra Research. https://www.finextra.com/blogposting/3179/dark-cloud

22 *What is an Attack Vector?* (n.d.). Techslang. https://www.techslang.com/definition/what-is-an-attack-vector/

23 National Institute of Standards and Technology Computer Security Resource Center. (n.d.). *Cyber-Attack – Glossary.* NIST. https://csrc.nist.gov/glossary/term/cyber_attack

24 Hanna, K. T., Ferguson, K., & Beaver, K. (2021, May). *What is a Data Breach?* TechTarget. https://www.techtarget.com/searchsecurity/definition/data-breach

25 U.S. Cybersecurity & Infrastructure Security Agency. (n.d.). *Stop Ransomware.* CISA.Gov. https://www.cisa.gov/stopransomware

26 *Supply Chain Attacks.* (2022, April 5). Microsoft. https://docs.microsoft.com/en-us/microsoft-365/security/intelligence/supply-chain-malware?view=o365-worldwide

27 National Institute of Standards and Technology Computer Security Resource Center. (n.d.). *Cyber-Attack – Glossary.* NIST. https://csrc.nist.gov/glossary/term/cyber_attack

28 National Institute of Standards and Technology Computer Security Resource Center. (n.d.). *Breach – Glossary.* NIST. https://csrc.nist.gov/glossary/term/breach

29 ITRC. (2021, October 6). *Number of Data Breaches in 2021 Surpasses All of 2020.* Identity Theft Resource Center. https://www.idtheftcenter.org/post/identity-theft-resource-center-to-share-latest-data-breach-analysis-with-u-s-senate-commerce-committee-number-of-data-breaches-in-2021-surpasses-all-of-2020/

30 *Cost of a Data Breach Report 2021.* (2021, July). IBM. https://www.ibm.com/downloads/cas/OJDVQGRY

31 Thomas, B. (2019, August 9). *Cloud Security: Lessons from the Capital One Data Breach.* BitSight Technologies. https://www.bitsight.com/blog/cloud-security-lessons-learned-from-capital-one-data-breach

32 Oladimeji, S., & Kerner, S. M. (2021, June 16). *SolarWinds Hack Explained: Everything You Need to Know.* TechTarget. https://www.techtarget.com/whatis/feature/SolarWinds-hack-explained-Everything-you-need-to-know

33 McGee, M. K. (2020, September 11). *Tally of Those Affected by Blackbaud Hack Soars.* BankInfoSecurity. https://www.bankinfosecurity.com/blackbaud-chart-update-a-14982

34 U.S. Cybersecurity & Infrastructure Security Agency. (n.d.). *Stop Ransomware.* CISA.Gov. https://www.cisa.gov/stopransomware

35 Kaplan, J., Rezek, C., & Sprague, K. (2013, January 1). *Protecting Information in the Cloud.* McKinsey & Company. https://www.mckinsey.com/business-functions/mckinsey-digital/our-insights/protecting-information-in-the-cloud

36 Panetta, K. (2019, October 10). *Is The Cloud Secure?* Gartner. https://www.gartner.com/smarterwithgartner/is-the-cloud-secure

37 *Cost of a Data Breach Report 2021.* (2021, July). IBM. https://www.ibm.com/downloads/cas/OJDVQGRY

38 *"We shape our tools and thereafter our tools shape us."* (2017, September 4). McLuhan Galaxy. https://mcluhangalaxy.wordpress.com/2013/04/01/we-shape-our-tools-and-thereafter-our-tools-shape-us/

39 Grance, T., Mell, P. (2011, September). *Special Publication 800–145, The NIST Definition of Cloud Computing.* National Institute of Standards and Technology. https://csrc.nist.gov/publications/detail/sp/800-145/final

40 Badger, L., Bohn, R. Leaf, D. Liu, F., Mao, J., Messina, J., & Tong, J. (2011, September). *Special Publication 500-292: Cloud Computing Reference Architecture.* NIST. https://tsapps.nist.gov/publication/get_pdf.cfm?pub_id=909505

41 Ibid.

42 Ibid.

43 National Cybersecurity Center of Excellence. (2020, February). *Trusted Cloud Fact Sheet: VMware Hybrid Cloud IaaS Environments.* National Institute of Standards and Technology. https://www.nccoe.nist.gov/sites/default/files/legacy-files/Trusted-Cloud-Fact-Sheet.pdf

44 *Special Publication 800-145: The NIST Definition of Cloud Computing.* (No. 800–145). (2011, September). NIST. https://csrc.nist.gov/publications/detail/sp/800-145/final

45 European Union Agency for Cybersecurity. (2009, November 20). *Cloud Computing Risk Assessment.* ENISA. https://www.enisa.europa.eu/publications/cloud-computing-risk-assessment

46 *Introduction to Cloud Computing.* (n.d.). Accenture. https://www.accenture.com/us-en/cloud/insights/cloud-computing-index

47 Grance, T., Mell, P. (2011, September). *Special Publication 800–145, The NIST Definition of Cloud Computing.* National Institute of Standards and Technology. https://csrc.nist.gov/publications/detail/sp/800-145/final

48 Overby, S. (2017, November 6). *What is Outsourcing? Definitions, Best Practices, Challenges and Advice.* CIO Digital Magazine. https://www.cio.com/article/272355/outsourcing-outsourcing-definition-and-solutions.html

49 Badger, L., Bohn, R. Leaf, D. Liu, F., Mao, J., Messina, J., & Tong, J. (2011, September). *Special Publication 500-292: Cloud Computing Reference Architecture.* NIST. https://tsapps.nist.gov/publication/get_pdf.cfm?pub_id=909505

50 Hon, K., & Millard, C. (2012, October 31). *Cloud Computing vs Traditional Outsourcing – Key Differences.* Society for Computers and Law. https://www.scl.org/articles/2576-cloud-computing-vs-traditional-outsourcing-key-differences

51 Badger, L., Bohn, R. Leaf, D. Liu, F., Mao, J., Messina, J., & Tong, J. (2011, September). Special Publication 500-292: Cloud Computing Reference Architecture. NIST. https://tsapps.nist.gov/publication/get_pdf.cfm?pub_id=909505

52 Gartner Information Technology Glossary. (n.d.-c). *Definition of Desktop as a Service.* Gartner. https://www.gartner.com/en/information-technology/glossary/desktop-as-a-service-daas-

53 Gartner Information Technology Glossary. (n.d.-a). *Definition of Business Process As A Service.* Gartner. https://www.gartner.com/en/information-technology/glossary/business-process-as-a-service-bpaas

54 Gartner Information Technology Glossary. (n.d.). *Definition of Cloud Management Platforms.* Gartner. https://www.gartner.com/en/information-technology/glossary/cloud-management-platforms

55 Grance, T., Mell, P. (2011, September). *Special Publication 800–145, The NIST Definition of Cloud Computing.* National Institute of Standards and Technology. https://csrc.nist.gov/publications/detail/sp/800-145/final

56 Badger, L., Bohn, R. Leaf, D. Liu, F., Mao, J., Messina, J., & Tong, J. (2011, September). *Special Publication 500-292: Cloud Computing Reference Architecture*. NIST. https://tsapps.nist.gov/publication/get_pdf.cfm?pub_id=909505

57 Linthicum, D. (2021, April 2). *Are Industry Clouds an Opportunity or a Distraction?* InfoWorld. https://www.infoworld.com/article/3613714/are-industry-clouds-an-opportunity-or-a-distraction.html

58 Flexera (9 March 2022). *Flexera 2022 State of the Cloud Report*. https://info.flexera.com/CM-REPORT-State-of-the-Cloud

59 Forrest, W., Gu, M., Kaplan, J. Liebow, M., Sharma, R., Smaje, K., Van Kuiken, S. (2021, August 11). *Cloud's trillion-dollar prize is up for grabs*. McKinsey Quarterly. https://www.mckinsey.com/business-functions/mckinsey-digital/our-insights/clouds-trillion-dollar-prize-is-up-for-grabs

60 Keary, T. (2021a, April 9). *10 Benefits of Cloud Computing for Businesses in 2021*. ITPRC. https://www.itprc.com/cloud-computing-benefits-for-business/

61 *12 Benefits of Cloud Computing and Its Advantages*. (n.d.). Salesforce. https://www.salesforce.com/products/platform/best-practices/benefits-of-cloud-computing/

62 *6 Business Challenges of Moving to the Cloud [2021]*. (2020, October 27). Conosco. https://www.conosco.com/blog/6-challenges-of-moving-to-the-cloud/

63 Flexera (9 March 2022). *Flexera 2022 State of the Cloud Report*. https://info.flexera.com/CM-REPORT-State-of-the-Cloud

64 Forbes Technology Council. (2017, June 5). *13 Biggest Challenges When Moving Your Business To The Cloud*. Forbes. https://www.forbes.com/sites/forbestechcouncil/2017/06/05/13-biggest-challenges-when-moving-your-business-to-the-cloud/?sh=2966b6329b0e

65 Mezzio, S., Stein, R., & Stein, S. (2019, December 1). *Robotic Process Automation for Tax*. Journal of Accountancy. https://www.journalofaccountancy.com/issues/2019/dec/robotic-process-automation-for-tax.html

66 Holmes, O. W. (n.d.). *A Quote by Oliver Wendell Holmes Jr*. GoodReads. https://www.goodreads.com/quotes/7613719-greatness-is-not-in-where-we-stand-but-in-what

67 *Root Cause Analysis Explained: Definition, Examples, and Methods*. (n.d.). Tableau. https://www.tableau.com/learn/articles/root-cause-analysis

68 CloudCheckr. (2021, October 22). *How to Build a Cloud Center of Excellence*. https://cloudcheckr.com/white-paper/how-to-build-a-cloud-center-of-excellence

69 Cecci, H. (2020, February 25). *Move from Cloud First to Cloud Smart to Improve Cloud Journey Success*. Gartner. https://www.gartner.com/en/documents/3981333

70 *Cloud Smart Strategy*. (2019, October 29). U.S. Department of the Interior. https://www.doi.gov/cloud/strategy

71 Cecci, H. (2020, February 25). *Move from Cloud First to Cloud Smart to Improve Cloud Journey Success*. Gartner. https://www.gartner.com/en/documents/3981333

72 Berry, D., Emmanuel, P., Justice, C., & Ryan, D. (2020). *Cloud Smart*. KPMG. https://advisory.kpmg.us/content/dam/advisory/en/pdfs/2020/cloud-smart.pdf

73 *Definition of Cloud Strategy* – Gartner Information Technology Glossary. (n.d.). Gartner. https://www.gartner.com/en/information-technology/glossary/cloud-strategy

74 *What is Cloud Migration?*. (n.d.). VMware Glossary. https://www.vmware.com/topics/glossary/content/cloud-migration-strategy.html

75 *Creating Value with the Cloud*. (2018, December). Digital McKinsey: Insights. https://www.mckinsey.com/~/media/McKinsey/Business%20Functions/McKinsey%20Digital/Our%20Insights/Creating%20value%20with%20the%20cloud%20compendium/Creating-value-with-the-cloud.ashx

76 Keary, T. (2021a, April 9). *10 Benefits of Cloud Computing for Businesses in 2021.* ITPRC. https://www.itprc.com/cloud-computing-benefits-for-business/

77 Forrest, W., Gu, M., Kaplan, J. Liebow, M., Sharma, R., Smaje, K., Van Kuiken, S. (2021, August 11). *Cloud's trillion-dollar prize is up for grabs.* McKinsey Quarterly. https://www.mckinsey.com/business-functions/mckinsey-digital/our-insights/clouds-trillion-dollar-prize-is-up-for-grabs

78 Martin, R. (2015, October 12). *The Big Lie of Strategic Planning.* Harvard Business Review. https://hbr.org/2014/01/the-big-lie-of-strategic-planning

79 *The Cloud Strategy Cookbook.* (2019, May). Gartner. https://www.gartner.com/smarterwithgartner/the-cloud-strategy-cookbook

80 Knorr, E. (2020, June 8). *2020 IDG Cloud Computing Survey.* InfoWorld. https://www.infoworld.com/article/3561269/the-2020-idg-cloud-computing-survey.html

81 Bigelow, S. J. (2021, January 8). *How to build a Cloud Center of Excellence.* TechTarget. https://searchcloudcomputing.techtarget.com/tip/How-to-build-a-cloud-center-of-excellence

82 McCafferty, D. (2021, May 12). *9 Cloud Implementation Best Practices.* CIO Insight. https://www.cioinsight.com/cloud-virtualization/cloud-implementation-best-practices/

83 Mehravari, N. (2014, January 23). *Everything You Always Wanted to Know About Maturity Models.* Carnegie Mellon University Software Engineering Institute. https://resources.sei.cmu.edu/asset_files/webinar/2014_018_101_293863.pdf

84 Paulk, M., Curtis, W., Chrissis, M.B., & Weber, C. (1993). *Capability Maturity Model for Software (Version 1.1).* Carnegie Mellon University, Software Engineering Institute. (CMU/SEI-93-TR-024). https://resources.sei.cmu.edu/asset_files/technicalreport/1993_005_001_16211.pdf

85 Chapla, S., Charania, S., Dupley, W., Estes, M., Fichadia, P., Scott, T., Skipp, R., Tong, W., Williams, M., & Wilson, B. (2018). *Cloud Maturity Model Rev. 4.* Open Alliance for Cloud Adoption. https://www.oaca-project.org/wp-content/uploads/2018/10/CloudMaturityModelUMv4-0.pdf

86 Paliwal, S. (2014, March 1). *Performance Challenges in Cloud Computing.* CMG.Org. https://www.cmg.org/wp-content/uploads/2014/03/1-Paliwal-Performance-Challenges-in-Cloud-Computing.pdf

87 *Definition of Performance Management – Gartner Information Technology Glossary.* (2021, December 26). Gartner. https://www.gartner.com/en/information-technology/glossary/performanceperformance-management

88 Otley, D. (1999, December 1). *Performance Management: A Framework for Management Control Systems Research.* ScienceDirect. https://www.sciencedirect.com/science/article/abs/pii/S1044500599901154

89 Ghesquieres, J., Kotzen, J., Nolan, T., Rodt, M., Roos, A., & Tucker, J. (2017, April 30). *The Art of Performance Management.* Boston Consulting Group. https://www.bcg.com/publications/2017/finance-function-excellence-corporate-development-art-performanceperformance-management

90 Carpi, R., Douglas, J., & Gascon, F. (2017, October 4). *Performance Management: Why Keeping Score is so Important, and so Hard.* McKinsey & Company. https://www.mckinsey.com/business-functions/operations/our-insights/performanceperformance-management-why-keeping-score-is-so-important-and-so-hard

91 Poister, T. (2003). *Measuring Performance in Public and Nonprofit Organizations.* San Francisco: Jossey-Bass.

92 KPI.org. (2022). *What is a Key Performance Indicator (KPI)?* KPI.Org. https://kpi.org/KPI-Basics

93 National Institute of Standards and Technology Computer Security Resource Center. (2021, December 26). *Performance Reference Model – Glossary*. NIST https://csrc.nist.gov/glossary/term/performanceperformance_reference_model

94 Allen, A. (2016, May 24). *IT Performance Management*. TechTarget. https://searchitoperations.techtarget.com/definition/IT-performanceperformance-management-information-technology-performance-management

95 Ibid.

96 *Definition of Key Performance Indicator (KPI) – Gartner Information Technology Glossary*. (n.d.). Gartner. https://www.gartner.com/en/information-technology/glossary/kpi-key-performanceperformance-indicator

97 Techopedia. (2017, January 18). *Cloud Performance Management*. Techopedia.Com. https://www.techopedia.com/definition/30563/cloud-performanceperformance-management

98 Twin, A., Jackson, A., & James, M. (2022, June 12). Understanding Key Performance Indicators (KPIs). Investopedia. https://www.investopedia.com/terms/k/kpi.asp

99 Cornfield, G. (2020, May 2). *The Most Important Metrics You're Not Tracking (Yet)*. Harvard Business Review. https://hbr.org/2020/04/the-most-important-metrics-youre-not-tracking-yet

100 Raza, M. (2022a, January 1). *Introduction To IT Metrics & KPIs*. BMC Blogs. https://www.bmc.com/blogs/it-metrics-kpis/#

101 Herbst, N., Bauer, A., Kounev, S., Oikonomou, G., Eyk, E. V., Kousiouris, G., . . . & Iosup, A. (Eds.). (2018). *Quantifying Cloud Performance and Dependability: Taxonomy, Metric Design, and Emerging Challenges*. ACM Transactions on Modeling and Performance Evaluation of Computing Systems, Volume 3, Issue 4. https://dl.acm.org/doi/pdf/10.1145/3236332?casa_token=_mDr9B3wLZsAAAAA:i7amQe9PyAT9D744neapHRh_tu8YiqEe4VKr9rWsmB63CijavRoPMLnF4_FK-6Djj67ERrZg2mh-

102 Flexera (9 March 2022). *Flexera 2022 State of the Cloud Report*. https://info.flexera.com/CM-REPORT-State-of-the-Cloud

103 Whitaker, J., Cloud Data Services. (2021, January 19). *What is Cloud Performance and How to Implement it in Your Organization*. NetApp. https://cloud.netapp.com/blog/azure-anf-blg-what-is-cloud-performanceperformance

104 Altarawneh, M., Al-Qaisi, A., & Salamah, J. (2019). *Evaluation of Cloud Computing Platform for Image Processing Algorithms*. J. Eng. Sci. Technol, 14, 2345–2358.

105 Flexera. (2021, March 9). *2021 State of the Cloud Report*. https://www.flexera.com/about-us/press-center/flexera-releases-2021-state-of-the-cloud-report

106 Techopedia. (2016, December 15). *Availability*. Techopedia.Com. https://www.techopedia.com/definition/990/availabilityavailability

107 Techopedia. (2014, October 28). *Application Performance*. Techopedia.Com. https://www.techopedia.com/definition/30457/application-performanceperformance

108 Techopedia. (2011, December 31). *Capacity*. Techopedia.Com. https://www.techopedia.com/definition/18179/capacity-network

109 Lucidchart. (2020, November 9). *Cloud Computing 101: Scalability, Reliability, and Availability*. https://www.lucidchart.com/blog/reliability-availabilityavailability-in-cloud-computing

110 Techopedia. (2017, January 27). *Scalability*. Techopedia.Com. https://www.techopedia.com/definition/9269/scalabilityscalability

111 Neenan, S. (2020, May 29). *Five Ways to Reduce Cloud Costs*. TechTarget. https://www.techtarget.com/searchcloudcomputing/feature/5-ways-to-reduce-cloud-costs

112 Haley, K. (2019, June 24). *Symantec's Cloud Security Threat Report Shines a Light on the Cloud's Real Risks. Symantec Blogs.* https://symantec-enterprise-blogs.security.com/blogs/feature-stories/symantecs-cloud-security-threat-report-shines-light-clouds-real-risks

113 Dalrymple, M., Pickover, S., & Sheppard, B. (2021, March 23). *Made to Measure: Getting Design Leadership Metrics Right.* McKinsey & Company. https://www.mckinsey.com/business-functions/mckinsey-design/our-insights/made-to-measure-getting-design-leadership-metrics-right

114 Bisson, D. (2021, January 15). *Misconfigurations: A Hidden but Preventable Threat to Cloud Data. Security Intelligence.* Security Intelligence. https://securityintelligence.com/articles/misconfigurations-hidden-threat-to-cloud-data/

115 Capra, F. (n.d.). *Fritjof Capra Quote.* QuoteFancy. https://quotefancy.com/quote/1494676/Fritjof-Capra-The-more-we-study-the-major-problems-of-our-time-the-more-we-come-to

116 Vidgen, R., & Wang, X. (2006). *From Business Process Management to Business Process Ecosystem.* Journal of Information Technology, 21(4), 262–271.

117 Oxford University Press. (n.d.). *Governance - Definition.* Oxford Advanced Learner's Dictionary. https://www.oxfordlearnersdictionaries.com/us/definition/english/governance?q=governance

118 Merriam-Webster. (n.d.). *Governance – Definition.* Merriam-Webster Dictionary. https://www.merriam-webster.com/dictionary/governance

119 Tricker, B. (2022, February). *The Future of Corporate Governance: A Personal Odyssey,* in McRitchie, J. (2022, April 23). *Corporate Governance Defined.* Corporate Governance. https://www.corpgov.net/library/corporate-governance-defined/

120 OECD. (2015). *G20/OECD Principles of Corporate Governance.* OECD Publishing, Paris. https://doi.org/10.1787/9789264236882-en

121 International Finance Corporation. (2015). *A Guide to Corporate Governance Practices in the European Union.* IFC. https://www.ifc.org/wps/wcm/connect/506d49a2-3763-4fe4-a783-5d58e37b8906/CG_Practices_in_EU_Guide.pdf?MOD=AJPERES&CVID=kNmxTtG

122 *What is Corporate Governance?* (n.d.). Institute of Chartered Accountants in England and Wales. https://www.icaew.com/technical/corporate-governance/principles/principles-articles/does-corporate-governance-matter

123 Chen, J., James, M., & Bellucco-Chatham, A. (2021, July 4). *What Corporate Governance Means for the Bottom Line.* Investopedia. https://www.investopedia.com/terms/c/corporategovernance.asp

124 Grembergen, W. V. *Introduction to the Minitrack: IT Governance and Its Mechanisms.* 40th Annual Hawaii International Conference on System Sciences (2007). pp. 233–233, doi:10.1109/HICSS.2007.292

125 *IT Governance.* (n.d.). The MITRE Corporation. https://www.mitre.org/publications/systems-engineering-guide/enterprise-engineering/enterprise-planning-and-management/it-governance

126 International Organization for Standardization. (2015, February). *ISO/IEC 38500:2015, Information Technology – Governance of IT for the Organization.* ISO. https://www.iso.org/standard/62816.html

127 Ibid.

128 OECD. (2015). *G20/OECD Principles of Corporate Governance.* OECD Publishing, Paris. https://doi.org/10.1787/9789264236882-en

129 Capasso, Arturo & Dagnino, Giovanni Battista. (2012). *Beyond the 'Silo View' of Corporate Governance and Strategic Management:* Evidence from Fiat, Telecom Italia and Unicredit. Journal of Management and Governance. 10.1007/s10997-012-9247-0

130 Committee of Sponsoring Organizations of the Treadway Commission. (2017). *Enterprise Risk Management: Integrating Strategy with Performance.* https://www.coso.org/Documents/2017-COSO-ERM-Integrating-with-Strategy-and-Performance-Executive-Summary.pdf

131 Thuraisingham, B. (2020, October). *Cloud Governance.* In 2020 IEEE 13th International Conference on Cloud Computing. (pp. 86–90). Institute of Electrical and Electronics Engineers. https://ieeexplore.ieee.org/document/9284234

132 Vidgen, R., & Wang, X. (2006). *From Business Process Management to Business Process Ecosystem.* Journal of Information Technology, 21(4), 262–271.

133 Baker, J. (2011). *The Technological-Organization-Environment Framework.* In Dwivedi, Y., Wade, M. and Schneberger, S. (Eds). *Information Systems Theory: Explaining and Predicting Our Digital Society.* Springer, New York, NY, pp. 231–246.

134 Paine, L. S., & Srinivasan, S. (2019, October 14). *A Guide to the Big Ideas and Debates in Corporate Governance.* Harvard Business Review. https://hbr.org/2019/10/a-guide-to-the-big-ideas-and-debates-in-corporate-governance

135 Thuraisingham, B. (2020, October). *Cloud Governance.* In 2020 IEEE 13th International Conference on Cloud Computing. (pp. 86–90). Institute of Electrical and Electronics Engineers. https://ieeexplore.ieee.org/document/9284234

136 Baker, J. (2011). *The Technological-Organization-Environment Framework.* In Dwivedi, Y., Wade, M. and Schneberger, S. (Eds). *Information Systems Theory: Explaining and Predicting Our Digital Society.* Springer, New York, NY, pp. 231–246.

137 Ibid.

138 Ibid.

139 Churchill, W. (1993). *The Price of Greatness.* International Churchill Society. https://winstonchurchill.org/old-site/learn/speeches-learn/the-price-of-greatness/

140 International Organization for Standardization. (2015, February). *Information Technology – Governance of IT for the Organization.* (ISO Standard No. 38500:2015). https://www.iso.org/standard/62816.html

141 Casey, K., & Bigelow, S. J. (2022, April). *Shared Responsibility Model.* TechTarget. https://www.techtarget.com/searchcloudcomputing/definition/shared-responsibility-model

142 *Shared Responsibility Model | Cloud Security Defined.* (n.d.). Threatscape. https://www.threatscape.com/what-is-the-shared-responsibility-model-your-cloud-security-responsibilities-defined/

143 Cloud Passage. (2020, August 26). *Shared Responsibility Model Explained.* Cloud Security Alliance. https://cloudsecurityalliance.org/blog/2020/08/26/shared-responsibility-model-explained/

144 Cornelissen, J. (2018, July 27). *The Democratization of Data Science.* Harvard Business Review. https://hbr.org/2018/07/the-democratization-of-data-science

145 Buchanan, S., Heiser, J., & Lowans, B. (2016, March 31). *Unsanctioned Business Unit IT Cloud Adoption Will Increase Financial Liabilities.* Gartner. https://www.gartner.com/en/documents/3269523

146 Kinsella, D. (2019, January 15). *Extended Enterprise Risk Management to be a Focus in 2019.* Deloitte. https://www2.deloitte.com/us/en/pages/about-deloitte/articles/press-releases/deloitte-poll-extended-enterprise-risk-management-to-be-2019-focus.html

147 Lane, M., Shrestha, A., & Ali, O. (2017). *Managing the Risks of Data Security and Privacy in the Cloud: A Shared Responsibility Between the Cloud Service Provider and the Client Organisation.* The Bright Internet Global Summit 2017, Seoul, Korea. https://eprints.usq.edu.au/33510/

1/B5.%20Managing%20the%20Risks%20of%20Data%20Security%20and%20Privacy%20in%20the%20Cloud.pdf

148 Campitelli, V., Mezzio, S., & Stein, M. (2020, July 12). *Managing the Impact of Cloud Computing*. The CPA Journal. https://www.cpajournal.com/2020/07/13/managing-the-impact-of-cloud-computing/

149 Nollkaemper, A. (2018). *The Duality of Shared Responsibility*. Contemporary Politics, 24:5, 524–544, DOI: 10.1080/13569775.2018.1452107

150 Cloud Passage. (2020, August 26). *Shared Responsibility Model Explained*. Cloud Security Alliance. https://cloudsecurityalliance.org/blog/2020/08/26/shared-responsibility-model-explained/

151 Watson, E. *Fast Fashion*. (n.d.). Fast Fashion. https://www.cleanup.org.au/fastfashion

152 Raza, M. (2020, May 13). *Reliability vs Availability: What's The Difference?* BMC Blogs. https://www.bmc.com/blogs/reliability-vs-availability/

153 *What is cloud management?* (2018, March 7). Red Hat. https://www.redhat.com/en/topics/cloud-computing/what-is-cloud-management

154 *What is Cloud Native?* (2022, March 11). Microsoft. https://docs.microsoft.com/en-us/dotnet/architecture/cloud-native/definition

155 *Proposed Interagency Guidance on Third-Party Relationships: Risk Management*. (2021, September 10). U.S. Office of the Comptroller of the Currency. https://www.occ.gov/news-issuances/bulletins/2021/bulletin-2021-42.html

156 *Definition of At Scale*. (n.d.). PC Magazine. https://www.pcmag.com/encyclopedia/term/at-scale

157 Hosken, M. (2021, March 11). *It's Time to Develop a Cloud Exit Strategy*. VMware. https://octo.vmware.com/its-time-to-develop-a-cloud-exit-strategy/

158 Synergy Research Group. (n.d.) *Definition of Hyperscaler*. https://www.srgresearch.com/research/hyperscale-cloud-market

159 Raza, M. (2020, May 13). *Reliability vs Availability: What's The Difference?* BMC Blogs. https://www.bmc.com/blogs/reliability-vs-availability/

160 National Institute of Standards and Technology Computer Security Resource Center. (n.d.). *Scalability – Glossary*. NIST. https://csrc.nist.gov/glossary/term/scalability

161 Fuzes, P. (2018, November). *The Impact of Cloud Computing on Business – IT Strategic Alignment*. Corvinus University Budapest. http://kgk.uni-obuda.hu/sites/default/files/FIKUSZ2018_11.pdf

162 Choudhary, V., & Vithayathil, J. (2013). *The Impact of Cloud Computing: Should the IT Department be Organized as a Cost Center or a Profit Center?* Journal of Management Information Systems, 30(2), 67–100.

163 Kavis, M., Kearns-Manolatos, D., Linthicum, D., & Miller, M. (2020, September 23). *The Future of Cloud-Enabled Work Infrastructure*. Deloitte Insights. https://www2.deloitte.com/us/en/insights/topics/digital-transformation/cloud-infrastructure-strategy.html

164 Choudhary, V., & Vithayathil, J. (2013). *The Impact of Cloud Computing: Should the IT Department be Organized as a Cost Center or a Profit Center?* Journal of Management Information Systems, 30(2), 67–100.

165 Cramm, S. (2008, July 22). *IT Centralization or Decentralization?*. Harvard Business Review. https://hbr.org/2008/07/it-centralization-or-decentral

166 Wood, O. (2020, August 24). *How is Cloud Computing Changing the CIO's Role?* K2 Partnering Solutions. https://k2partnering.com/cloud/how-is-cloud-computing-changing-the-cios-role/

167 Dogan, C. (2018). From the Basement to the Cloud | *The Role of the CIO over Four Decades.* Deloitte. https://www2.deloitte.com/content/dam/Deloitte/ar/Documents/technology/THE-ROLE-OF-THE-CIO-OVERF-OUR-DECADES.pdf

168 Kark, K., Nann, E., Nguyen Phillips, A., & Perton, M. (2020, April 10). *The New CIO: Business-Savvy Technologist.* Deloitte. https://www2.deloitte.com/us/en/insights/focus/cio-insider-business-insights/the-new-cio.html

169 Gillin, P. (2015, July 1). *How Cloud Is Changing the IT Workforce?* CIO. https://www.cio.com/article/244408/how-cloud-is-changing-the-it-workforce.html

170 Red Hat. (2018, April 6). *What are cloud service providers?* https://www.redhat.com/en/topics/cloud-computing/what-are-cloud-providers

171 *Definition of Managed Security Service Provider – Gartner Information Technology Glossary.* (n.d.). Gartner. https://www.gartner.com/en/information-technology/glossary/mssp-managed-security-service-provider

172 *8 Criteria to Ensure you Select the Right Cloud Service Provider.* (n.d.). Cloud Industry Forum. https://www.cloudindustryforum.org/content/8-criteria-ensure-you-select-right-cloud-service-provider

173 *Service Roadmap.* (n.d.). Service Design Tools. https://servicedesigntools.org/tools/service-roadmap#:%7E:text=The%20service%20roadmap%20is%20the,evolution%20of%20a%20service%20solution

174 Witkowski, W. (2021, October 5). *Facebook Outage, by the Numbers: Largest Outage Ever Tracked Could Cost Millions.* MarketWatch. https://www.marketwatch.com/story/facebook-outage-by-the-numbers-largest-outage-ever-tracked-could-cost-millions-11633387093

175 Ikram, K. (2020, October 19). *Your Journey to Cloud: How to Select Your Provider(s).* Accenture Banking Blog. https://bankingblog.accenture.com/journey-cloud-select-provider

176 Trappler, T.J. (2010, December). *If It's in the Cloud, Get It on Paper: Cloud Computing Contract Issues. Educause Quarterly, 33.* https://www.educause.edu/ir/library/pdf/LIVE1034b.pdf

177 Badger, L., Bohn, R. Leaf, D. Liu, F., Mao, J., Messina, J., & Tong, J. (2011, September). *Special Publication 500-292: Cloud Computing Reference Architecture.* NIST. https://tsapps.nist.gov/publication/get_pdf.cfm?pub_id=909505

178 *Cloud Computing: Shared Responsibility Security Models.* (2019, July). New Zealand Government Communications Security Bureau, National Cyber Security Centre. https://www.ncsc.govt.nz/assets/NCSC-Documents/July-2019-Cloud-Computing-Shared-Security-Models.pdf

179 European Commission Joinup. (2021, April 20). Service Level Agreement. ICT Standards for Procurement. https://joinup.ec.europa.eu/collection/ict-standards-procurement/service-level-agreement

180 *Definition of Service-Level Agreement (SLA) – Gartner Information Technology Glossary.* (n.d.). Gartner. https://www.gartner.com/en/information-technology/glossary/sla-service-level-agreement

181 Bhardwaj, A., & Goundar, S. (2016). *Designing a Framework for Cloud Service Agreement for Cloud Environments.* International Journal of Cloud Applications and Computing (IJCAC), 6 (4), 83–96.

182 Flexera (2022, March 9). *Flexera 2022 State of the Cloud Report.* https://info.flexera.com/CM-REPORT-State-of-the-Cloud

183 Efrati, A. and McLaughlin, K. (2019, February 25). *As AWS Use Soars, Companies Surprised by Cloud Bills.* The Information. https://www.theinformation.com/articles/as-aws-use-soars-companies-surprised-by-cloud-bills

184 Flexera (2022, March 9). *Flexera 2022 State of the Cloud Report*. https://info.flexera.com/CM-REPORT-State-of-the-Cloud

185 Gartner. (2020, March 23). *How to Manage and Optimize Costs of Public Cloud IaaS and PaaS*. https://www.gartner.com/en/documents/3982411/how-to-manage-and-optimize-costs-of-public-cloud-iaas-an

186 *What is Cloud ROI?* (n.d.). VMware. https://www.vmware.com/topics/glossary/content/cloud-roi.html

187 *Procurement of Public Cloud: Not Just Blue Sky Thinking*. (January 2018). Deloitte. https://www2.deloitte.com/content/dam/Deloitte/uk/Documents/consultancy/deloitte-uk-procurement-of-public-cloud.pdf

188 *Pinterest SEC Form 10-K*. (2021, February 2). United States Securities and Exchange Commission. https://d18rn0p25nwr6d.cloudfront.net/CIK-0001506293/0c811ec8-0109-4e9a-8f81-974b15595671.pdf

189 *Pinterest SEC Form S-1*. (2019, March 22). United States Securities and Exchange Commission https://www.sec.gov/Archives/edgar/data/1506293/000119312519083544/d674330ds1.htm

190 Bhatnagar, A., Kadyan, A., Lala, W., & Saleme, A. (2020, April 6). *CIOs are Redefining what a Successful Relationship with Their IT Providers Looks Like*. McKinsey & Company, pg. 49 https://www.mckinsey.com/business-functions/mckinsey-digital/our-insights/cios-are-redefining-what-a-successful-relationship-with-their-it-providers-looks-like

191 Baig, A. (2021, November 1). *The CIO Agenda for the Next 12 months: Six Make-or-Break Priorities*. McKinsey & Company. https://www.mckinsey.com/business-functions/mckinsey-digital/our-insights/the-cio-agenda-for-the-next-12-months-six-make-or-break-priorities

192 Ibid.

193 Judy Garland Quotes. (n.d.). BrainyQuote.com. https://www.brainyquote.com/quotes/judy_garland_38024

194 Gartner Research. (n.d.). *Define Cloud Access Security Broker*. https://www.gartner.com/en/information-technology/glossary/cloud-access-security-brokers-casbs

195 Bigelow, S. J. (2021, October). *What is Cloud Sprawl?* TechTarget. https://www.techtarget.com/searchcloudcomputing/definition/cloud-sprawl

196 Gartner Research. (n.d.). *Define Shadow IT*. https://www.gartner.com/en/information-technology/glossary/shadow

197 Pettey, C. (2016, May). *Don't Let Shadow IT Put Your Business At Risk*. Gartner. https://www.gartner.com/smarterwithgartner/dont-let-shadow-it-put-your-business-at-risk

198 *What is Shadow IT and How it Appears?* (2021, February 1). Binadox. https://www.binadox.com/blog/shadow-it-what-is-it-and-how-it-appears/

199 Amazon.com. (2021, June 30). *United States Security and Exchange Commission Form 10-Q*. Page 13. https://ir.aboutamazon.com/sec-filings/default.aspx

200 The CRO Forum. (2018, December 20). *Understanding and managing the IT risk landscape: A practitioner's guide*. KPMG Advisory N.V. https://www.thecroforum.org/2018/12/20/understanding-and-managing-the-it-risk-landscape-a-practitioners-guide/

201 Jerzewski, M. (2021, July 7). *What is Asset Discovery? A Look Beneath the Surface*. Tripwire.com. https://www.tripwire.com/state-of-security/security-data-protection/security-controls/what-is-asset-discovery/

202 Gartner Research. (n.d.). *Define Cloud Access Security Broker*. https://www.gartner.com/en/information-technology/glossary/cloud-access-security-brokers-casbs

203 Press, D. (2018, July 16). *What is a CASB?* Cloud Security Alliance. https://cloudsecurityalliance.org/blog/2018/07/16/what-is-a-casb/

204 *What is cloud management?* (2018, March 7). Red Hat. https://www.redhat.com/en/topics/cloud-computing/what-is-cloud-management

205 Flexera (2022, March 9). *Flexera 2022 State of the Cloud Report.* https://info.flexera.com/CM-REPORT-State-of-the-Cloud

206 Accenture. (2020, September). *The Green Behind the Cloud.* https://www.accenture.com/us-en/insights/strategy/green-behind-cloud

207 Natural Capital Partners. *CarbonNeutral Protocol* (2021, January). https://carbonneutral.com/pdfs/The_CarbonNeutral_Protocol_Jan_2021.pdf

208 Ibid.

209 Institute of Internal Auditors. (2020, May). *Fraud and Emerging Tech: Data Ethics and Governance with COVID-19 Considerations.* https://dl.theiia.org/Documents/Fraud-and-Emerging-Tech-COVID-19-Considerations.pdf

210 United Nations (1987). *Report of the Word Commission on Environment and Development: Our Common Future.* http://www.un-documents.net/our-common-future.pdf

211 Global Reporting Initiative. (n.d.) https://www.globalreporting.org/information/sustainability-reporting/Pages/default.aspx

212 United Nations (1987). *Report of the Word Commission on Environment and Development: Our Common Future.* http://www.un-documents.net/our-common-future.pdf

213 Accenture. (2020, September). *The Green Behind the Cloud.* https://www.accenture.com/us-en/insights/strategystrategy/green-behind-cloud

214 *Global Risks Report 2021.* (2021, January 19). World Economic Forum. https://www.weforum.org/reports/the-global-risks-report-2021

215 Kahn, A., Koehler, J., Jayaraman, V., Subramanian, S. (2021, June 15). *U.S. Cloud Business Survey.* PwC. https://www.pwc.com/us/en/tech-effect/cloud/cloud-business-survey.html

216 Salesforce. (2021, September). *Climate Action Plan.* https://www.salesforce.com/content/dam/web/en_us/www/assets/pdf/reports/salesforce-climate-action-plan-2021.pdf

217 Google. *Cloud Sustainability.* (n.d.). https://cloud.google.com/sustainability

218 Amazon Web Service (n.d.). *Sustainability in the Cloud.* https://sustainability.aboutamazon.com/environment/the-cloud#section-nav-id-5

219 Microsoft. *Azure Sustainability.* (n.d.). https://azure.microsoft.com/en-us/global-infrastructure/sustainability/#environmental-impact

220 Oracle. (2021, June 23). *Oracle Commits to Powering Its Global Operations with Renewable Energy by 2025.* https://www.oracle.com/news/announcement/oracle-2025-renewable-energy-goal-2021-06-23/

221 IBM. (2021, February 16). *IBM Commits To Net Zero Greenhouse Gas Emissions By 2030.* https://newsroom.ibm.com/2021-02-16-IBM-Commits-To-Net-Zero-Greenhouse-Gas-Emissions-By-2030

222 Natural Capital Partners. *CarbonNeutral Protocol* (2020, January). https://www.carbonneutral.com/pdfs/The_CarbonNeutral_Protocol_Jan_2020.pdf

223 *Global Risks Report 2020.* (2020, January 15). World Economic Forum. https://www.weforum.org/reports/the-global-risks-report-2020

224 Ascierto, R., Lawrence, A. (2020, July 20). *Global Data Center Survey 2020.* Uptime Institute. https://drift-lp-66680075.drift.click/UptimeInstituteGlobalDataCenterSurvey2020

225 Institute of Internal Auditors. (2020, May). *Fraud and Emerging Tech: Data Ethics and Governance with COVID-19 Considerations.* https://dl.theiia.org/Documents/Fraud-and-Emerging-Tech-COVID-19-Considerations.pdf

226 European Parliament. (2019, September 19). *Sustainable Finance Disclosure Regulation*. Official Journal of the European Union. https://eur-lex.europa.eu/legal-content/EN/TXT/PDF/?uri= CELEX:32019R2088&rid=1

227 World Business Council for Sustainable Development & World Resources Institute. (n.d.). Greenhouse Gas Protocol Frequently Asked Questions. Greenhouse Grass Protocol. https:// ghgprotocol.org/sites/default/files/standards_supporting/FAQ.pdf

228 *Carbon free energy for Google Cloud regions*. (2021, November 19). Google Cloud. https:// cloud.google.com/sustainability/region-carbon

229 Althoff, J. (2021, July 14). *Microsoft Cloud for Sustainability: Empowering organizations on their path to net zero*. Microsoft Blog. https://blogs.microsoft.com/blog/2021/07/14/microsoft-cloud-for-sustainability-empowering-organizations-on-their-path-to-net-zero/

230 *Learn about ESG data on AWS Data Exchange*. (n.d.). Amazon Web Services. https://aws. amazon.com/data-exchange/sustainability/

231 *Moody's ESG Solutions*. (n.d.). Moody's. https://esg.moodys.io/solutions

232 Salesforce. (2021, September). *Climate Action Plan*. https://www.salesforce.com/content/ dam/web/en_us/www/assets/pdf/reports/salesforce-climate-action-plan-2021.pdf

233 Ibid.

234 Sutton, D. (2017, October 12). *20 Transformational Quotes on Change Management*. TopRight Partners. https://www.toprightpartners.com/insights/20-transformational-quotes-on-change-management/

235 *What is ITSM? A Guide to IT Service Management*. (n.d.). Atlassian. https://www.atlas sian.com/itsm

236 Stobierski, T. (2020, January 21). *What Is Organizational Change Management?* Harvard Business School. https://online.hbs.edu/blog/post/organizational-change-management

237 Harvard Business School Online's Business Insights Blog. (2020, March 20). *Types of Organizational Change & How to Manage Them*. Harvard Business School. https://online.hbs. edu/blog/post/types-of-organizational-change

238 *How Cloud is Disrupting IT Operations*. (2022, March 9). CIO Digital Magazine. https:// www.cio.com/article/306076/how-cloud-is-disrupting-it-operations.html

239 Choudhary, V., & Vithayathil, J. (2013). *The Impact of Cloud Computing: Should the IT Department be Organized as a Cost Center or a Profit Center?* Journal of Management Information Systems, 30(2), 67–100.

240 Allen, J., Clark, P., Delgoshaie, N., & Monahan, R. (2021, June 9). *I, Technologist | Placing the Power of Tech in Everyone's Hands*. Accenture. https://www.accenture.com/us-en/insights/ utilities/i-technologist

241 Lucid Content Team. (n.d.). *All About Cloud Change Management*. Lucidchart. https://www. lucidchart.com/blog/cloud-change-management

242 *What is cloud management?* (2018, March 7). Red Hat. https://www.redhat.com/en/ topics/cloud-computing/what-is-cloud-management

243 *2021–2023 Emerging Technology Roadmap*. (2021, October 29). Gartner. https://www.gart ner.com/en/information-technology/trends/2023-emerging-technology-roadmap

244 Lucid Content Team. (n.d.). *All About Cloud Change Management*. Lucidchart. https://www. lucidchart.com/blog/cloud-change-management

245 *What is Change Management?* (n.d.). American Society for Quality. https://asq.org/qual ity-resources/change-management

246 *Definition of Change Management*. (n.d.). Prosci. https://www.prosci.com/resources/ar ticles/definition-of-change-management

247 Lawton, G., & Pratt, M. K. (n.d.). *What is Change Management?* TechTarget. https://www.techtarget.com/searchcio/definition/change-management

248 Gianni, J. (2021, June 9). *Change Management: 6 Reasons it Fails.* The Enterprisers Project. https://enterprisersproject.com/article/2021/6/change-management-6-reasons-fails

249 *What is Change Management?* (n.d.). American Society for Quality. https://asq.org/quality-resources/change-management

250 IBM Cloud Education. (2019, May 22). *IT Infrastructure Library (ITIL).* IBM. https://www.ibm.com/cloud/learn/it-infrastructure-library

251 Kotter, J. (n.d.). *The 8-Step Process for Leading Change.* Kotter. https://www.kotterinc.com/8-step-process-for-leading-change/

252 Nyhius, M. (2020, October 21). *What is the ITIL Framework?* Diligent. https://www.diligent.com/insights/compliance/what-is-the-itil-framework/

253 Linthicum, D. (n.d.). *Dealing with the Cloud Computing Skills Gap.* Deloitte. https://www2.deloitte.com/lu/en/pages/risk/articles/cloud-skills-gap.html

254 *2021–2023 Emerging Technology Roadmap.* (2021, October 29). Gartner. https://www.gartner.com/en/information-technology/trends/2023-emerging-technology-roadmap

255 AWS. (n.d.). *AWS Skills Centers.* Amazon Web Services, Inc. https://aws.amazon.com/training/skills-centers/

256 Protiviti & North Carolina State University. (2021, December 9). *2022 and 2031 Executive Perspectives on Top Risks.* Protiviti. https://www.protiviti.com/US-en/insights/protiviti-top-risks-survey

257 Brisse, M., Cole, S., Delory, P., Dukes, M., Iams, T., Leong, L., Meinardi, M., Quinn, F., Toombs, D., & Troy, A. (2022, March 16). *2022 Planning Guide for Cloud and Edge Computing.* Gartner. https://www.gartner.com/en/doc/753853-2022-planning-guide-for-cloud-and-edge-computing

258 Jones, R., Kamen, M., & Kearns-Manolatos, D. (2021, October 21). *Cloud Enabled Workforce.* Deloitte. https://www2.deloitte.com/us/en/blog/deloitte-on-cloud-blog/2021/putting-the-power-of-a-cloud-enabled-workforce-to-work.html

259 *Definition of Change Management.* (n.d.). Prosci. https://www.prosci.com/resources/articles/definition-of-change-management

260 Lucid Content Team. (n.d.). *All About Cloud Change Management.* Lucidchart. https://www.lucidchart.com/blog/cloud-change-management

261 Boleman, J., Lakshminarayanan, M., Panagakis, M., Schalk, K., Schenkewitz, L., & van Order, B. (2018, May). *Best Practices for Developing and Growing a Cloud-Enabled Workforce.* Cloud Standards Customer Council. https://www.omg.org/cloud/deliverables/CSCC-Best-Practices-for-Developing-and-Growing-a-Cloud-Enabled-Workforce.pdf

262 *What is Learning and Development?* (n.d.). Association for Talent Development. https://www.td.org/talent-development-glossary-terms/what-is-learning-and-development

263 van Vulpen, E. (n.d.). *Learning and Development: A Comprehensive Guide.* Academy to Innovate HR. https://www.aihr.com/blog/learning-and-development/

264 *What is Learning and Development?* (n.d.). Association for Talent Development. https://www.td.org/talent-development-glossary-terms/what-is-learning-and-development

265 Brassey, J., Christensen, L., & van Dam, N. (2019, February 13). *The Essential Components of a Successful L&D Strategy.* McKinsey & Company. https://www.mckinsey.com/business-functions/people-and-organizational-performanceperformance/our-insights/the-essential-components-of-a-successful-l-and-d-strategystrategy

266 van Vulpen, E. (n.d.). *Learning and Development: A Comprehensive Guide.* Academy to Innovate HR. https://www.aihr.com/blog/learning-and-development/

267 *2022 Arcitura Course Catalog Certification Programs.* (n.d.). Arcitura. https://www.arcitura.com/wp-content/uploads/2022/04/Arcitura-Course-Catalog-Certification-Programs-2022.pdf

268 Benjamin Franklin Quotes. (n.d.). BrainyQuote.com. https://www.brainyquote.com/quotes/benjamin_franklin_138217

269 Committee of Sponsoring Organizations of the Treadway Commission. *Internal Control – Integrated Framework.* (2013, May 20). COSO. https://www.coso.org/Documents/990025P-Executive-Summary-final-may20.pdf

270 International Organization for Standardization. (2016). *Guide 73:2009, Risk Management – Vocabulary.* https://www.iso.org/standard/44651.html

271 Gardner, R.K., Quinn, S., Stine, K., Witte, G. (2020, October). *NISTIR 8286: Integrating Cybersecurity and Enterprise Risk Management.* NIST. https://doi.org/10.6028/NIST.IR.8286

272 Eckmaier, R., Fumy, W., Mouille, S., Quemard, J.P., Polemi, N. Rumpel, R. (2022, March 16). *Risk Management Standards.* European Union Agency for Cybersecurity. https://www.enisa.europa.eu/publications/risk-management-standards

273 National Institute of Standards and Technology Computer Security Resource Center. (n.d.). *Risk Mitigation – Glossary.* NIST. https://csrc.nist.gov/glossary/term/risk_mitigation

274 National Institute of Standards and Technology Computer Security Resource Center. (n.d.). *Risk Management – Glossary.* NIST. https://csrc.nist.gov/glossary/term/risk_management

275 Eckmaier, R., Fumy, W., Mouille, S., Quemard, J.P., Polemi, N. Rumpel, R. (2022, March 16). *Risk Management Standards.* European Union Agency for Cybersecurity. https://www.enisa.europa.eu/publications/risk-management-standards

276 *BSI-Standard 200-3: Risk Analysis based on IT-Grundschutz.* (2017). Germany's Federal Office for Information Security (BSI). www.bsi.bund.de/grundschutz

277 International Organization for Standardization. (2018, February). *ISO 31000:2018, Risk Management Guidelines.* ISO. https://www.iso.org/standard/65694.html

278 International Organization for Standardization. (2016). *Guide 73:2009, Risk Management – Vocabulary.* https://www.iso.org/standard/44651.html

279 European Network and Information Security Agency. (2006, June). *Risk Management – Principles and Inventories for Risk Management.* ENISA. https://www.enisa.europa.eu/publications/risk-management-principles-and-inventories-for-risk-management-risk-assessment-methods-and-tools

280 Piney, C. (2003). *Risk Identification: Combining the Tools to Deliver the Goods.* Paper presented at PMI® Global Congress 2003 – EMEA, The Hague, South Holland, The Netherlands. Newtown Square, PA: Project Management Institute.

281 Deloitte. (2019, April 15). *Scenario Planning and Wargaming for the Risk Management Toolkit.* WSJ. https://deloitte.wsj.com/articles/scenario-planning-and-wargaming-for-the-risk-management-toolkit-01555376533

282 Deloitte. (2019). *Cloud Computing Risk Intelligence Map.* https://www2.deloitte.com/content/dam/Deloitte/in/Documents/risk/in-ra-roap-map-noexp.pdf

283 Gardner, R.K., Quinn, S., Stine, K., Witte, G. (2020, October). *NISTIR 8286: Integrating Cybersecurity and Enterprise Risk Management.* NIST. https://doi.org/10.6028/NIST.IR.8286

284 National Institute of Standards and Technology Computer Security Resource Center. (n.d.). *Risk Mitigation – Glossary.* NIST. https://csrc.nist.gov/glossary/term/risk_mitigation

285 *Risk Mitigation Planning, Implementation, and Progress Monitoring.* (2015, April 10). The MITRE Corporation. https://www.mitre.org/publications/systems-engineering-guide/acquisi

tion-systems-engineering/risk-management/risk-mitigation-planning-implementation-and-progress-monitoring

286 Schandl, A., & Foster, P. L. (2019, January). *COSO Internal Control – Integrated Framework: An Implementation Guide for the Healthcare Provider Industry.* Committee of Sponsoring Organizations of the Treadway Commission. https://www.coso.org/documents/coso-crowe-coso-internal-control-integrated-framework.pdf

287 Cloud Controls Matrix Working Group. (2021, December 8). *Cloud Controls Matrix (Version 4).* Cloud Security Alliance. https://cloudsecurityalliance.org/research/cloud-controls-matrix/

288 Ibid.

289 Shackleford, D. (2022, March). SANS 2022 Cloud Security Survey Highlights. Vulcan. https://vulcan.io/blog/sans-cloud-security-survey-2022-highlights/

290 *Cost of a Data Breach Report 2021.* (2021, July). IBM. https://www.ibm.com/downloads/cas/OJDVQGRY

291 *The State of Cloud Security 2021.* (2021, July). Fugue & Sonatype. https://f.hubspotusercontent20.net/hubfs/4846674/Resources%20Content/State_of_Cloud_Security_2021.pdf

292 Bailey, D., Dempsey, K., Gupta, S., Johnson, A., Ross, R. (2011, August). *Special Publication 800-128: Guide for Security-Focused Configuration Management of Information Systems.* NIST. https://doi.org/10.6028/NIST.SP.800-128

293 Barot, B., Bagayat, R., Kearns-Manolatos, D., Bavare, A., & Parekh, J. (2021, April 15). *Cloud Misconfiguration.* Deloitte. https://www2.deloitte.com/us/en/blog/deloitte-on-cloud-blog/2021/cloud-misconfiguration.html

294 Jeffrey, M. (2017, December 15). *Interoperability and Portability in Cloud Computing.* Microsoft EU Policy Blog. https://blogs.microsoft.com/eupolicy/2017/12/15/interoperability-portability-cloud-computing/

295 Gartner Information Technology Glossary (n.d.). *Definition of Application Programming Interface.* Gartner. https://www.gartner.com/en/information-technology/glossary/application-programming-interface

296 National Institute of Standards and Technology Computer Security Resource Center. (n.d.). *Audit Log – Glossary.* NIST. https://csrc.nist.gov/glossary/term/audit_log

297 Chapman, C., Clayman, C., Elmroth, E., Galan, F., Henriksson, S., & Lindner, M. (2010). *The Cloud Supply Chain: A Framework for Information, Monitoring, Accounting and Billing.* University College London, Department of Electronic and Electrical Engineering. https://www.ee.ucl.ac.uk/~sclayman/docs/CloudComp2010.pdf

298 Rembert, L. (2020, February 28). *How the Cloud Complicates the Digital Crime Scene.* Infosecurity Magazine. https://www.infosecurity-magazine.com/opinions/cloud-complicates-digital-crime/

299 Durg, K. (2019, July 3). *Navigating the Interoperability Challenge in Multi-Cloud Environments.* Accenture. https://www.accenture.com/us-en/blogs/cloud-computing/kishore-durg-cloud-interoperability-challenges

300 National Institute of Standards and Technology Computer Security Resource Center. (n.d.). *Misconfiguration – Glossary.* NIST. https://csrc.nist.gov/glossary/term/misconfiguration

301 National Institute of Standards and Technology Computer Security Resource Center. (n.d.). *Configuration Management – Glossary.* NIST. https://csrc.nist.gov/glossary/term/configuration_management

302 *What are Containers?* (2021, June 23). IBM Cloud Education. https://www.ibm.com/cloud/learn/containers

303 National Institute of Standards and Technology Computer Security Resource Center. (n.d.). *Cryptography – Glossary*. NIST. https://csrc.nist.gov/glossary/term/cryptography

304 Jeffrey, M. (2017, December 15). *Interoperability and Portability in Cloud Computing*. Microsoft EU Policy Blog. https://blogs.microsoft.com/eupolicy/2017/12/15/interoperability-portability-cloud-computing/

305 Gartner Information Technology Glossary. (n.d.). *Definition of E-Discovery Software*. Gartner. https://www.gartner.com/en/information-technology/glossary/e-discovery-software

306 National Institute of Standards and Technology Computer Security Resource Center. (n.d.). *Encryption – Glossary*. NIST. https://csrc.nist.gov/glossary/term/encryption

307 *What is an Endpoint?* (n.d.). Palo Alto Networks. https://www.paloaltonetworks.com/cyberpedia/what-is-an-endpoint

308 National Institute of Standards and Technology Computer Security Resource Center. (n.d.). *Infrastructure as a Code – Glossary*. NIST. https://csrc.nist.gov/glossary/term/infrastructure_as_code

309 National Institute of Standards and Technology Computer Security Resource Center. (n.d.). *Key Management – Glossary*. NIST. https://csrc.nist.gov/glossary/term/key_management

310 National Institute of Standards and Technology Computer Security Resource Center. (n.d.). *Zero Trust – Glossary*. NIST. https://csrc.nist.gov/glossary/term/zero_trust

311 Ong, Michael K., (2005, December). *Risk Management, A Modern Perspective*. Emerald Group Publishing Limited.

312 National Institute of Standards and Technology Computer Security Resource Center. (n.d.). *Cyber Resiliency – Glossary*. NIST. https://csrc.nist.gov/glossary/term/cyber_resiliency

313 U.S. Office of Management and Budget. (2019, Decmeber 18). Circular No. A-11, Preparation, Submission, and Execution of the Budget. OMB. https://www.whitehouse.gov/wpcontent/uploads/2018/06/a11.pdf

314 National Institute of Standards and Technology Computer Security Resource Center. (n.d.). *Risk Appetite – Glossary*. NIST. https://csrc.nist.gov/glossary/term/risk_appetite

315 Committee of Sponsoring Organizations of the Treadway Commission. (2017). *Enterprise Risk Management: Integrating Strategy with Performance*. https://www.coso.org/Documents/2017-COSOCOSO-ERMERM-Integrating-with-Strategy-and-Performance-Executive-Summary.pdf

316 Moorcraft, B. (2020, October 26). *A Risk Manager's Rise to the C-Suite and the Boardroom*. Insurance Business Magazine. https://www.insurancebusinessmag.com/us/risk-management/news/a-risk-managers-rise-to-the-csuite-and-the-boardroomboardroom-237239.aspx

317 Committee of Sponsoring Organizations of the Treadway Commission. (2017). *Enterprise Risk Management: Integrating Strategy with Performance*. https://www.coso.org/Documents/2017-COSOCOSO-ERMERM-Integrating-with-Strategy-and-Performance-Executive-Summary.pdf

318 Ibid.

319 Ibid.

320 International Organization for Standardization. (2018, February). *ISO 31000:2018, Risk Management Guidelines*. ISO. https://www.iso.org/standard/65694.html

321 Forrest, W., Li, S., Tamburro, I., & van Kuiken, S. (2021, April 30). *Four Ways Boards Can Shape the Cloud Agenda*. McKinsey & Company. https://www.mckinsey.com/business-functions/mckinsey-digital/our-insights/four-ways-boards-can-shape-the-cloud-agenda

322 Todd, D. (2021, September 28). *Amazon to offer cyber insurance to UK SMBs*. IT PRO. https://www.itpro.com/security/cyber-security/361039/amazon-to-offer-cyber-insurance-to-uk -smbs

323 CB Insights. (2021, March 4). *Google Is Partnering With Cyber Insurance Giants. Here's What It Means For The Future Of Cloud Security & Insurance*. CB Insights Research. https://www.cbin sights.com/research/google-cloud-cyber-insurance/

324 Munich RE. *Cyber crime is increasing – make sure your business is protected*. (2021, July). https://www.munichre.com/content/dam/munichre/mram/content-pieces/pdfs/reinsurance-solutions/Cyber-Product_BRO-FINAL-WEB.pdf/_jcr_content/renditions/original./Cyber-Product_ BRO-FINAL-WEB.pdf

325 Microsoft. *Microsoft and At-Bay partner to offer data-driven cyber insurance coverage*. (2021, September 29). https://news.microsoft.com/2021/09/29/microsoft-and-at-bay-partner-to-offer-data-driven-cyber-insurance-coverage/

326 At-Bay Insurance. *Cyber Insurance*. (n.d.) https://www.at-bay.com/insurance/cyber/

327 Diffie, W. (n.d.). *Quotemaster*. https://www.quotemaster.org/q39d0d450f73c57 e5af97fc8077168135

328 Gartner Information Technology Glossary (n.d.). *Definition of Application Programming Interface (API)*. Gartner. https://www.gartner.com/en/information-technology/glossary/applica tion-programming-interface

329 National Institute of Standards and Technology Computer Security Resource Center. (n.d.). *Non-repudiation – Glossary*. NIST. https://csrc.nist.gov/glossary/term/non_repudiation

330 Ford, C. (2021, May 3). *'Security as code' Demands Proactive DevSecOps*. Dynatrace. https://www.dynatrace.com/news/blog/security-as-code-demands-proactive-devsecops/

331 National Institute of Standards and Technology Computer Security Resource Center. (n.d.). *Virtualization – Glossary*. NIST. https://csrc.nist.gov/glossary/term/Virtualization

332 National Institute of Standards and Technology Computer Security Resource Center. (n.d.). *Cybersecurity – Glossary*. NIST. https://csrc.nist.gov/glossary/term/cybersecurity

333 Gartner Information Technology Glossary (n.d.). *Definition of Cloud Security*. Gartner. https://www.gartner.com/en/information-technology/glossary/cloud-security

334 *What is Cloud Security?* (n.d.). Check Point. https://www.checkpoint.com/cyber-hub/ cloud-security/what-is-cloud-security/

335 Red Hat. (2019, March 18). *What is different about cloud security?* https://www.redhat. com/en/topics/security/cloud-security

336 *Framework for Improving Critical Infrastructure Cybersecurity*. (2018, April 16). NIST https://nvlpubs.nist.gov/nistpubs/CSWP/NIST.CSWP.04162018.pdf

337 Brook, C. (2020, September 29). *What is COBIT?* Digital Guardian. https://digitalguardian. com/blog/what-cobit

338 *ISO/IEC 27001 – Information security management*. (2021, February 16). International Standards Organization. https://www.iso.org/isoiec-27001-information-security.html

339 *Cloud Security Guide for SMEs*. (2015, April 10). European Union Agency for Cybersecurity. https://www.enisa.europa.eu/publications/cloud-security-guide-for-smes

340 Joint Task Force Interagency Working Group. (2020, September). *Special Publication: Security and Privacy Controls for Information Systems and Organizations*. (No. 800–53, Revision 5). NIST. https://nvlpubs.nist.gov/nistpubs/SpecialPublications/NIST.SP.800-53r5.pdf

341 *Framework for Improving Critical Infrastructure Cybersecurity*. (2018, April 16). NIST https://nvlpubs.nist.gov/nistpubs/CSWP/NIST.CSWP.04162018.pdf

342 *Critical Security Controls Version 8.* (2021, May 18). Center for Internet Security. https://www.cisecurity.org/controls/v8/

343 *HITRUST Alliance Common Security Framework: Information Risk Management.* (2021, October 20). HITRUST Alliance. https://hitrustalliance.net/product-tool/hitrust-csf/

344 Cloud Controls Matrix Working Group. (2021, December 8). *Cloud Controls Matrix (Version 4).* Cloud Security Alliance. https://cloudsecurityalliance.org/research/cloud-controls-matrix/

345 *What is Cloud Security? Cloud Security Defined.* (n.d.). IBM. https://www.ibm.com/topics/cloud-security

346 Moyle, E. (2021, June 15). *What are Cloud Security Frameworks and How are they Useful?* TechTarget. https://searchcloudsecurity.techtarget.com/tip/What-are-cloud-security-frameworks-and-how-are-they-useful

347 *Security Guidance for Critical Areas of Focus in Cloud Computing.* (2017, July 26.). Cloud Security Alliance. https://cloudsecurityalliance.org/artifacts/security-guidance-v4/

348 Adtani, C., Bawcom, A., Brown, J. S., Cracknell, R., Isenberg, R., Kazmier, K., Prieto-Munoz, P., & Weinstein, D. (2021, July 22). *Security as Code: The Best (and Maybe Only) Path to Securing Cloud Applications and Systems.* McKinsey & Company. https://www.mckinsey.com/business-functions/mckinsey-digital/our-insights/security-as-code-the-best-and-maybe-only-path-to-securing-cloud-applications-and-systems

349 Hiremath, O. (2021, February 9). *What is "Security as Code" and How Can it Help You?* Sqreen Blog. https://blog.sqreen.com/security-as-code/

350 Adtani, C., Bawcom, A., Brown, J. S., Cracknell, R., Isenberg, R., Kazmier, K., Prieto-Munoz, P., & Weinstein, D. (2021, July 22). *Security as Code: The Best (and Maybe Only) Path to Securing Cloud Applications and Systems.* McKinsey & Company. https://www.mckinsey.com/business-functions/mckinsey-digital/our-insights/security-as-code-the-best-and-maybe-only-path-to-securing-cloud-applications-and-systems

351 Camp, L.J. (2003). Design for Trust. Trust, Reputation and Security: Theories and Practice. Rino Falcone, ed., Springer-Verlang (Berlin).https://ssrn.com/abstract=627610

352 Borchert, O., Connelly, S. Mitchell, S. & Rose, S. (2020, August). *Special Publication 800-207: Zero Trust Architecture.* NIST. https://doi.org/10.6028/NIST.SP.800-207

353 *What is Zero Trust Privilege?* (n.d.). Centrify. https://www.centrify.com/education/what-is-zero-trust-privilege/

354 *What is Zero Trust?* (n.d.). IBM. https://www.ibm.com/topics/zero-trust

355 *What Is Zero Trust for the Cloud?* (n.d.). Palo Alto Networks. https://www.paloaltonetworks.com/cyberpedia/what-is-a-zero-trust-for-the-cloud

356 Cavalancia, N. (2022, September 29). *Zero Trust Architecture Explained.* AT&T. https://cybersecurity.att.com/blogs/security-essentials/what-is-a-zero-trust-architecture

357 *What is Zero Trust?* (n.d.). IBM. https://www.ibm.com/topics/zero-trust

358 *What Is Zero Trust for the Cloud?* (n.d.). Palo Alto Networks. https://www.paloaltonetworks.com/cyberpedia/what-is-a-zero-trust-for-the-cloud

359 *Cost of a Data Breach Report 2021.* (2021, July). IBM. https://www.ibm.com/downloads/cas/OJDVQGRY

360 Worsley, A. (n.d.). Jonathan Safran Foer Quote. The Art of Living. https://theartofliving.com/quote/jonathan-safran-foer-not-responding-is-a-response/

361 *What is Cloud Architecture?* (n.d.). VMware. https://www.vmware.com/topics/glossary/content/cloud-architecture.html

362 Courtemanche, M., Mell, E., Gillis, A. S., & C. (2021, December). *What is DevOps?* TechTarget. https://www.techtarget.com/searchitoperations/definition/DevOps

363 National Institute of Standards and Technology Computer Security Resource Center. (2021, December 26). *Incident – Glossary*. NIST. https://csrc.nist.gov/glossary/term/incident

364 Dekker, M., Lakka, M., & Liveri, D. (2013, December). *Cloud Security Incident Reporting Framework for Reporting about Major Cloud Security Incidents*. European Union Agency for Network and Information Security. https://www.enisa.europa.eu/publications/incident-reporting-for-cloud-computing/at_download/fullReport

365 *Cost of a Data Breach Report 2021*. (2021, July). IBM. https://www.ibm.com/downloads/cas/OJDVQGRY

366 *What is Insider Data Theft?* (n.d.) Data Theft Definition, Statistics and Prevention Tips. Digital Guardian. https://digitalguardian.com/dskb/insider-data-theft

367 *Cost of a Data Breach Report 2021*. (2021, July). IBM. https://www.ibm.com/downloads/cas/OJDVQGRY

368 U.S. Cybersecurity & Infrastructure Security Agency. (2019, November 20). *Understanding Denial-of-Service Attacks*. CISA. https://www.cisa.gov/uscert/ncas/tips/ST04-015

369 Brook, C. (2021, December 28). *Insider Threat: Definition & Examples*. Digital Guardian. https://digitalguardian.com/blog/insider-threat-definition-examples

370 Johansen, A. G. (2019, July 17). *Malware Attacks: What You Need to Know*. Norton. https://us.norton.com/internetsecurity-malware-malware-101-how-do-i-get-malware-complex-attacks.html

371 Awake Security. (n.d.). *Network Intrusion Definition & Examples*. https://awakesecurity.com/glossary/network-intrusion/

372 *What is Incident Response?* (n.d.). VMware. https://www.vmware.com/topics/glossary/content/incident-response.html

373 National Institute of Standards and Technology Computer Security Resource Center. (2021, December 26). *Incident Response Plan – Glossary*. NIST. https://csrc.nist.gov/glossary/term/incident_response_plan

374 *NIST Incident Response Plan: Building Your Own IR Process Based on NIST Guidelines*. (2022, March 29). Cynet. https://www.cynet.com/incident-response/nist-incident-response/

375 Awake Security. (n.d.). *Incident Response Program & Management*. https://awakesecurity.com/glossary/incident-response-program-management/

376 Geer, D. (n.d.). *Building an Incident Response Framework for Your Enterprise*. TechTarget. https://www.techtarget.com/searchsecurity/tip/Incident-response-frameworks-for-enterprise-security-teams

377 Cichonski, P., Millar, T., Grance, T., & Scarfone, K. (2012, August). *Special Publication 800-61 – Computer Security Incident Handling Guide, Revision 2*. NIST. http://dx.doi.org/10.6028/NIST.SP.800-61r2

378 SysAdmin, Audit, Network, and Security (SANS) Institute. (n.d.). *Advanced Persistent Threat Incident Handling Checklist*. SANS. https://www.sans.org/media/score/checklists/APT-IncidentHandling-Checklist.pdf

379 Cichonski, P., Millar, T., Grance, T., & Scarfone, K. (2012, August). *Special Publication 800-61 – Computer Security Incident Handling Guide, Revision 2*. NIST. http://dx.doi.org/10.6028/NIST.SP.800-61r2

380 Ellis, D. (n.d.). *6 Phases in the Incident Response Plan*. SecurityMetrics. https://www.securitymetrics.com/blog/6-phases-incident-response-plan

381 Cynet. (2022, February 1). *Incident Response SANS: The 6 Steps in Depth*. https://www.cynet.com/incident-response/incident-response-sans-the-6-steps-in-depth/

382 Bessette, J., & Christou, C. (n.d.). *5 Tips to Build a Cloud Incident Response Plan*. Booz Allen Hamilton. https://www.boozallen.com/c/insight/blog/5-tips-to-build-a-cloud-incident-response-plan.html

383 Lim, S. T., & Siow, A. (n.d.). Cloud Incident Response. Cloud Security Alliance. https://cloudsecurityalliance.org/research/working-groups/cloud-incident-response/

384 Ibid.

385 Ibid.

386 *MTTD and MTTR in Cybersecurity*. (n.d.). PlexTrac. https://plextrac.com/mttd-and-mttr-in-cybersecurity/

387 *The State of Cloud Security 2021*. (2021, July). Fugue & Sonatype. https://f.hubspotusercontent20.net/hubfs/4846674/Resources%20Content/State_of_Cloud_Security_2021.pdf

388 Bessette, J., & Christou, C. (n.d.). *5 Tips to Build a Cloud Incident Response Plan*. Booz Allen Hamilton. https://www.boozallen.com/c/insight/blog/5-tips-to-build-a-cloud-incident-response-plan.html

389 Ibid.

390 Wadsworth Longfellow, H. (n.d.). *"It takes less time to do things right than to explain why you did it wrong."* PassItOn. https://www.passiton.com/inspirational-quotes/3760-it-takes-less-time-to-do-things-right-than-to

391 AlgoSec. (2021, March 21). *What is Cloud Compliance?*. https://www.algosec.com/cloud-compliance/

392 Ford, C. (2021, May 3). *'Security as code' Demands Proactive DevSecOps*. Dynatrace. https://www.dynatrace.com/news/blog/security-as-code-demands-proactive-devsecops/

393 Society of Corporate Compliance and Ethics (n.d.). *Definition of Compliance*. https://www.corporatecompliance.org/publications/compliance-dictionary

394 AlgoSec. (2021, March 21). *What is Cloud Compliance?* https://www.algosec.com/cloud-compliance/

395 Kadhaba, G. (2021, August 2). *Elements of Effective Cloud Compliance*. Capital One. https://www.capitalone.com/tech/cloud/effective-cloud-compliance/

396 *What is Cloud Compliance?* (2020, January 7). Reciprocity. https://reciprocity.com/resources/what-is-cloud-compliance/

397 Kirvan, P. (2021, January). *How to Create a Cloud Security Policy, Step by Step*. TechTarget. https://www.techtarget.com/searchsecurity/tip/How-to-create-a-cloud-security-policy-step-by-step

398 Microsoft. (n.d.). *Navigating your Way to the Cloud: Region and Country-specific Information for Legal and Compliance Professionals*. https://www.microsoft.com/en-us/trust-center/compliance/regional-country-compliance

399 General Data Protection Regulation. (2016). https://gdpr-info.eu/

400 Amazon.com. (2021, June 30). *United States Security and Exchange Commission Form 10-Q*. Page 13. https://ir.aboutamazon.com/sec-filings/default.aspx

401 *General Data Protection Regulation*. (2016). https://gdpr-info.eu/

402 Ibid.

403 Organisation for Economic Co-Operation and Development. (2013, November 28). *Anti-Corruption Ethics and Compliance Handbook for Business*. https://www.oecd.org/corruption/anti-corruption-ethics-and-compliance-handbook-for-business.htm

404 Government of Canada. (2015, June 23). *Personal Information Protection and Electronic Documents Act*. https://laws-lois.justice.gc.ca/eng/acts/P-8.6/page-1.html

405 U.S. Congress. (1996, August 21). *Health Insurance Portability and Accountability Act.* https://www.govinfo.gov/content/pkg/PLAW-104publ191/pdf/PLAW-104publ191.pdf

406 Payment Card Industry (PCI) Security Standards Council. (2018, May). *PCI Data Security Standard.* https://www.pcisecuritystandards.org/documents/PCI_DSS_v3-2-1.pdf?agreement=true&time=1631301601091

407 U.S. Congress. (2002, July 30). *Sarbanes-Oxley Act of 2002.* https://www.congress.gov/107/plaws/publ204/PLAW-107publ204.pdf

408 U.S. Congress. (1999, November 12). *Gramm-Leach-Bliley Act.* https://www.govinfo.gov/content/pkg/PLAW-106publ102/pdf/PLAW-106publ102.pdf

409 U.S. Congress. (2018, December 18). *Federal Information Security and Management Act.* https://www.govinfo.gov/content/pkg/PLAW-113publ283/pdf/PLAW-113publ283.pdf

410 U.S. Department of Justice, Criminal Division (2020, June). *Evaluation of Corporate Compliance Programs* https://www.justice.gov/criminal-fraud/page/file/937501/download.

411 *NASDAQ Stock Market LLC Rules, Section 5600: Corporate Governance Requirements, Part 5610: Code of Conduct.* (2009, March 12). NASDAQ. https://listingcenter.nasdaq.com/rulebook/nasdaq/rules/Nasdaq%205600%20Series

412 Cain, K. L., Niles, S. V., Rosenblum, S. A., & Wachtell, Lipton, Rosen & Katz. (2014, December). *NYSE Corporate Governance Guide.* New York Stock Exchange. https://www.nyse.com/publicdocs/nyse/listing/NYSE_Corporate_Governance_Guide.pdf

413 Compliance Forge (n.d.). *Policy vs Standard vs Control vs Procedure.* https://www.complianceforge.com/word-crimes/policy-vs-standard-vs-control-vs-procedure

414 Committee of Sponsoring Organizations (2020, November). *Compliance Risk Management: Applying the COSO ERM Framework.* https://www.coso.org/Documents/Compliance-Risk-Management-Applying-the-COSO-ERM-Framework.pdf

415 Ibid.

416 Ibid.

417 Ibid.

418 Adtani, C., Bawcom, A., Brown, J.S., Cracknell, R., Isenberg, R., Kazmier, K., Prieto-Munoz, P., & Weinstein, D. (2021, July 22). *Security as Code: The Best (and maybe only) Path to Securing Cloud Applications and Systems.* McKinsey & Company. https://www.mckinsey.com/business-functions/mckinsey-digital/our-insights/security-as-code-the-best-and-maybe-only-path-to-securing-cloud-applications-and-systems

419 Ibid.

420 Kenton, W. (2021, July 16). *Compliance Program.* Investopedia. https://www.investopedia.com/terms/c/compliance-program.asp

421 *2013 Guidelines Manual, Chapter Eight – Sentencing of Organizations, Part B – Remedying Harm from Criminal Conduct, And Effective Compliance and Ethics Program.* (2013, November 1). United States Sentencing Commission. https://www.ussc.gov/guidelines/2015-guidelines-manual/archive/2013-8b21

422 Committee of Sponsoring Organizations (2020, November). *Compliance Risk Management: Applying the COSO ERM Framework.* https://www.coso.org/Documents/Compliance-Risk-Management-Applying-the-COSO-ERM-Framework.pdf

423 Auditing Standards Board, "Compliance audits; Statement on Auditing Standards, 117" (2009). *Statements on Auditing Standards, Definitions.* American Institute of Certified Public Accountants. https://us.aicpa.org/content/dam/aicpa/research/standards/auditattest/downloadabledocuments/au-00801.pdf

424 Bill Gates Quotes. (n.d.). BrainyQuote.com. https://www.brainyquote.com/quotes/bill_gates_626252

425 *IIA Attribute Standard 1010 – Recognizing Mandatory Guidance in the Internal Audit Charter.* (n.d.). Institute of Internal Auditors. https://www.theiia.org/en/standards/what-are-the-standards/mandatory-guidance/standards/attribute-standards/

426 *Definition of Internal Auditing.* (n.d.). Institute of Internal Auditors. https://www.theiia.org/en/standards/what-are-the-standards/mandatory-guidance/definition-of-internal-audit/

427 *Introduction to the International Standards for the Professional Practice of Internal Auditing.* (n.d.). Institute of Internal Auditors. https://www.theiia.org/en/standards/what-are-the-standards/mandatory-guidance/standards/introduction/

428 *IIA Attribute Standard 1010 – Recognizing Mandatory Guidance in the Internal Audit Charter.* (n.d.). Institute of Internal Auditors. https://www.theiia.org/en/standards/what-are-the-standards/mandatory-guidance/standards/attribute-standards/

429 White, S. (2019, March 5). *What is an IT Auditor? A Vital Role for Risk Assessment.* CIO Digital Magazine. https://www.cio.com/article/219805/it-auditor-role-defined.html

430 *IIA Attribute Standard 1210 – Proficiency.* (n.d.). Institute of Internal Auditors. https://www.theiia.org/en/standards/what-are-the-standards/mandatory-guidance/standards/attribute-standards/

431 *IIA Attribute Standard 1010 – Recognizing Mandatory Guidance in the Internal Audit Charter.* (n.d.). Institute of Internal Auditors. https://www.theiia.org/en/standards/what-are-the-standards/mandatory-guidance/standards/attribute-standards/

432 Peyton, S., & Rai, V. (2021, August 3). *Internal Audit in the Cloud.* Grant Thornton. https://www.grantthornton.com/library/articles/advisory/2021/internal-audit-in-the-cloud.aspx

433 Ibid.

434 *Internal Audit's Role in Cloud Computing.* (2012). Protiviti. https://www.protiviti.com/sites/default/files/united_states/insights/ia-role-cloud-computing-protiviti.pdf

435 *AWS Cloud Audit Academy.* (n.d.). Amazon Web Services. https://aws.amazon.com/compliance/auditor-learning-path/

436 National Institute of Standards and Technology. (n.d.). *Non-Repudiation – Glossary.* Computer Security Resource Center. https://csrc.nist.gov/glossary/term/non__repudiation

437 *Interactive Glossary & Term Translations.* (n.d.). ISACA. https://www.isaca.org/resources/glossary

438 Ibid.

439 American Institute of CPAs. (n.d.). *SOC for Service Organizations:* Information for Service Organizations. AICPA. https://us.aicpa.org/interestareas/frc/assuranceadvisoryservices/serviceorganization-smanagement

440 *Assurance Services: A White Paper for Providers and Users of Business Information.* (2013). AICPA Assurance Services Executive Committee. https://us.aicpa.org/content/dam/aicpa/interestareas/frc/assuranceadvisoryservices/downloadabledocuments/asec_wp_providers_users_bi.pdf

441 International Standard on Assurance Engagements. (2013, December). *ISAE 3000 (Revised), Assurance Engagements Other than Audits or Reviews of Historical Financial Information.* International Auditing and Assurance Standards Board. https://www.ifac.org/system/files/publications/files/ISAE%203000%20Revised%20-%20for%20IAASB.pdf

442 Hayes, A. (2020, December 3). *How Assurance Services Work.* Investopedia. https://www.investopedia.com/terms/a/assurance-services.asp

443 Corporate Finance Institute. (2020, November 2). *Assurance Services.* https://corporate financeinstitute.com/resources/knowledge/accounting/assurance-services/

444 National Institute of Standards and Technology. (n.d.). *Assurance – Glossary.* Computer Security Resource Center. https://csrc.nist.gov/glossary/term/assurance

445 Hamidovic, H. (2012, March 1). *Fundamental Concepts of IT Security Assurance | ISACA Journal.* ISACA. https://www.isaca.org/resources/isaca-journal/past-issues/2012/fundamental-concepts-of-it-security-assurance

446 AICPA. (n.d.). *System and Organization Controls: SOC Suite of Services.* https://us.aicpa.org/interestareas/frc/assuranceadvisoryservices/sorhome

447 *Cloud Computing Information Assurance Framework.* (2009, November 20). ENISA. https://www.enisa.europa.eu/publications/cloud-computing-information-assurance-framework

448 *Risk Assessment.* (2009). ENISA. https://www.enisa.europa.eu/topics/cloud-and-big-data/cloud-security/risk-assessment

449 *Security and Resilience in Governmental Clouds.* (2011, January 17). ENISA. https://www.enisa.europa.eu/publications/security-and-resilience-in-governmental-clouds

450 *Survey and analysis of security parameters in cloud SLAs across the European public sector.* (2011, December 21). ENISA. https://www.enisa.europa.eu/publications/survey-and-analysis-of-security-parameters-in-cloud-slas-across-the-european-public-sector

451 *STAR.* (n.d.). CSA. https://cloudsecurityalliance.org/star/

452 *Cloud Controls Matrix.* (2021, January). Cloud Security Alliance. https://cloudsecurityalliance.org/research/cloud-controls-matrix/

453 *On-Premise vs. Cloud Auditing.* (2021, September 23). ISACA. https://www.isaca.org/resources/infographics/on-premise-vs-cloud-auditing

454 *Cloud Computing Management Audit Program.* (2010). ISACA. https://store.isaca.org/s/store#/store/browse/detail/a2S4w000004KoH1EAK

455 *COBIT Framework: Control Objectives for Information Technologies.* (2019). ISACA. https://www.isaca.org/resources/cobit

456 *System and Organization Controls: SOC Suite of Services.* (n.d.). AICPA. https://us.aicpa.org/interestareas/frc/assuranceadvisoryservices/sorhome

457 van Kuiken, S. (2021, November 18). *Boards and the Cloud.* McKinsey & Company. https://www.mckinsey.com/business-functions/strategy-and-corporate-finance/our-insights/boards-and-the-cloud

458 Panetta, K. (2021, August 26). *A Data and Analytics Leader's Guide to Data Literacy.* Gartner. https://www.gartner.com/smarterwithgartner/a-data-and-analytics-leaders-guide-to-data-literacy

459 *What is Digital Transformation? Why Is It Important.* (n.d.). Salesforce. https://www.salesforce.com/products/platform/what-is-digital-transformation/

460 Kagan, J., Boyle, M. J., & Rathburn, P. (2021, September 2). *What Is a Fiduciary?* Investopedia. https://www.investopedia.com/terms/f/fiduciary.asp

461 OnBoard Meetings. (2022, February 11). *What Is a Board of Directors, Its Structure, Roles, and Responsibilities?* OnBoard. https://www.onboardmeetings.com/blog/board-director-structure-roles-responsibilities/

462 Board of Directors. (n.d.). Corporate Finance Institute. https://corporatefinanceinstitute.com/resources/careers/jobs/board-of-directors/

463 Conmy, S. (2022, August 30). *What is a Board of Directors? Corporate Governance Institute?* https://www.thecorporategovernanceinstitute.com/insights/lexicon/what-is-a-board-of-directors/

464 *Board of Directors.* (n.d.). Corporate Finance Institute. https://corporatefinanceinstitute. com/resources/careers/jobs/board-of-directors/

465 Chen, J., Brock, T., & Perez, Y. (2022, April 14). *Board of Directors.* Investopedia. https:// www.investopedia.com/terms/b/boardofdirectors.asp

466 *Board of Directors.* (n.d.). Corporate Finance Institute. https://corporatefinanceinstitute. com/resources/careers/jobs/board-of-directors/

467 International Finance Corporation. (2015). *A Guide to Corporate Governance Practices in the European Union.* IFC. https://www.ifc.org/wps/wcm/connect/506d49a2-3763-4fe4-a783-5d58e37b8906/CG_Practices_in_EU_Guide.pdf?MOD=AJPERES&CVID=kNmxTtG

468 Price, N. J. (2019, January 9). *The Role of Board Committees.* Diligent Corporation. https://www.diligent.com/insights/board-committee/the-role-of-board-committees/

469 Aguilar, L. A. (2014, June 10). *Boards of Directors, Corporate Governance and Cyber-Risks: Sharpening the Focus.* U.S. Securities and Exchange Commission. https://www.sec.gov/news/speech/2014-spch061014laa

470 Hayn, S. (2022, April 20). *Seven Priorities for EMEIA Boards to Transform Their 2022 Agenda.* EY. https://www.ey.com/en_gr/board-matters/seven-priorities-for-emeia-boards-to-transform-their-2022-agenda

471 Forrest, W., Li, S., Tamburro, I., & van Kuiken, S. (2021, April 30). *Four Ways Boards Can Shape the Cloud Agenda.* McKinsey & Company. https://www.mckinsey.com/business-functions/mckinsey-digital/our-insights/four-ways-boards-can-shape-the-cloud-agenda

472 A Dictionary of Law. (n.d.). *Definition of Fiduciary.* Oxford Reference. https://www.oxfordreference.com/view/10.1093/oi/authority.20110803095816799#:%7E:text=Quick%20Reference,position%20of%20trust%20or%20confidence

473 *Board of Directors Structure.* (n.d.). CFA Institute. https://www.cfainstitute.org/en/advocacy/issues/board-structure

474 *Fiduciary Responsibilities.* (2019, October 28). BoardSource. https://boardsource.org/resources/fiduciary-responsibilities/

475 Wex Definitions Team. (n.d.). *Definition of Fiduciary Duty.* Cornell Law School, Legal Information Institute. https://www.law.cornell.edu/wex/fiduciary_duty

476 Wire, A. (2022, March 3). *Living the Board of Directors Duties of Care & Loyalty.* OnBoard. https://www.onboardmeetings.com/blog/board-of-directors-duties-of-care-loyalty/

477 California Law. (2009). *California Corporation Legal Code, Article 3. Standards of Conduct Code 5231(a).* California Legislative Information. https://leginfo.legislature.ca.gov/faces/codes_displayText.xhtml?lawCode=CORP&division=2.&title=1.&part=2.&chapter=2.&article=3

478 Slaughter, J. (n.d.). *Board of Directors – Standards & Liabilities.* Law Firm Carolinas. http://www.lawfirmcarolinas.com/Directors-Standards-Liabilities.cfm

479 *The Director's Duty to Inquire.* (n.d.). Stimmel Law. https://www.stimmel-law.com/en/articles/directors-duty-inquire

480 Corporate & Business Services Group. (2016, May 18). *Pennsylvania Directorial Duties: What Directors and Officers Need to Know.* Reger, Rizzo, Darnall LLP. https://www.regerlaw.com/corporate-directional-duties.html

481 Oxford University Press. (n.d.). *Fit for Purpose.* Lexico. https://www.lexico.com/definition/fit_for_purpose

482 PricewaterhouseCoopers & The Conference Board. (2021, November). *Board Effectiveness: A Survey of the C-Suite.* PwC. https://www.pwc.com/us/en/services/governance-insights-center/library/board-effectiveness-and-performance-improvement.html

483 Huber, C., Sukharevsky, A., & Zemmel, R. (2021, June 21). *5 Questions Boards Should Be Asking About Digital Transformation.* Harvard Business Review. https://hbr.org/2021/06/5-questions-boards-should-be-asking-about-digital-transformation

484 Forrest, W., Li, S., Tamburro, I., & van Kuiken, S. (2021, April 30). *Four Ways Boards Can Shape the Cloud Agenda.* McKinsey & Company. https://www.mckinsey.com/business-functions/mckinsey-digital/our-insights/four-ways-boards-can-shape-the-cloud-agenda

485 PricewaterhouseCoopers & The Conference Board. (2021, November). *Board Effectiveness: A Survey of the C-Suite.* PwC. https://www.pwc.com/us/en/services/governance-insights-center/library/board-effectiveness-and-performanceperformance-improvement.html

486 Huber, C., Sukharevsky, A., & Zemmel, R. (2021, June 21). *5 Questions Boards Should Be Asking About Digital Transformation.* Harvard Business Review. https://hbr.org/2021/06/5-questions-boards-should-be-asking-about-digital-transformation

487 Perkowski, M. (n.d.). *Can You Talk the Talk? Cloud Jargon 101 for Executives.* Security Roundtable by Palo Alto Networks. https://www.securityroundtable.org/can-you-talk-the-talk-cloud-jargon-101-for-executives/

488 Venables, P., & Godfrey, N. (2022, January 13). *10 Questions to Help Boards Safely Maximize Cloud Opportunities.* Google Cloud Blog. https://cloud.google.com/blog/products/identity-security/10-questions-to-help-boards-safely-maximize-cloud-opportunities

489 National Audit Office. (2021, April 30). *Guidance for Audit Committees on Cloud Services.* https://www.nao.org.uk/report/guidance-for-audit-committees-on-cloud-services-2/

490 Newman, C. A. (2019, January 23). *Lessons for Corporate Boardrooms From Yahoo's Cybersecurity Settlement.* The New York Times. https://www.nytimes.com/2019/01/23/business/dealbook/yahoo-cyber-security-settlement.html

491 White and Williams LLP. (2019, January 30). *The $29 Million Yahoo Derivative Data Breach Settlement: What Next?* JD Supra. https://www.jdsupra.com/legalnews/the-29-million-yahoo-derivative-data-15252/

492 *Altaba, Formerly Known as Yahoo!, Charged With Failing to Disclose Massive Cybersecurity Breach; Agrees To Pay $35 Million.* (2018, April 24). U.S. Securities and Exchange Commission. https://www.sec.gov/news/press-release/2018-71

493 White and Williams LLP. (2019, January 30). The $29 Million Yahoo Derivative Data Breach Settlement: What Next? JD Supra.https://www.jdsupra.com/legalnews/the-29-million-yahoo-derivative-data-15252/

494 Benesch Attorneys at Law. (2021, December 7). *Shareholders Seek to Hold Current and Former SolarWinds Officials Liable for Massive 2020 Security Breach.* JD Supra. https://www.jdsupra.com/legalnews/shareholders-seek-to-hold-current-and-2113517/

495 Berger, M. (1997, November 7). *Isaiah Berlin, Philosopher And Pluralist, Is Dead at 88.* The New York Times. https://www.nytimes.com/1997/11/07/arts/isaiah-berlin-philosopher-and-pluralist-is-dead-at-88.html

496 Sheldon, R. (2022, February). *What is Cloud Washing?* TechTarget. https://www.techtarget.com/searchstorage/definition/cloud-washingcloud-washing

497 Chen, B. (2022b, January 18). *What's All the Hype About the Metaverse?* The New York Times. https://www.nytimes.com/2022/01/18/technology/personaltech/metaverse-gaming-definition.html

498 Clark, P. A. (2021, November 15). *The Metaverse Has Already Arrived. Here's What That Actually Means.* Time. https://time.com/6116826/what-is-the-metaverse/

499 *Sicilian Proverbs: Don't Celebrate Promises, and Don't Rear Threats.* (n.d.). Inspirational Stories. https://www.inspirationalstories.com/proverbs/sicilian-dont-celebrate-promises-and-dont-fear-threats/

500 *Utopia - Definition* (n.d.). Oxford Advanced Learner's Dictionary. https://www.oxfordlearnersdictionaries.com/us/definition/english/utopia

501 Kwik, J. (2020, April 7). *Limitless.* Kwik Learning, LLC. https://www.limitlessbook.com/

502 Levitas, R. (1990). *Educated Hope: Ernst Bloch on Abstract and Concrete Utopia.* Utopian Studies, 1(2), 13–26. http://www.jstor.org/stable/20718998

503 *Chaos Definition.* (n.d.). Cambridge Dictionary. https://dictionary.cambridge.org/us/dictionary/english/chaos

504 Cecci, H. (2020, February 25). *Move From Cloud First to Cloud Smart to Improve Cloud Journey Success.* Gartner. https://www.gartner.com/en/conferences/hub/cloud-conferences/insights/cloud-smart-best-practices

505 Baker, J. (2011). *The Technological-Organization-Environment Framework.* In Dwivedi, Y., Wade, M. and Schneberger, S. (Eds). *Information Systems Theory: Explaining and Predicting Our Digital Society.* Springer, New York, NY, pp. 231–246.

506 Ibid.

507 *The Future Depends on What You Do Today.* (n.d.). Quotespedia. https://www.quotespedia.org/authors/m/mahatma-gandhi/the-future-depends-on-what-you-do-today-mahatma-gandhi/

508 World Economic Forum. (2020, October 20). *The Future of Jobs Report 2020.* https://www.weforum.org/reports/the-future-of-jobs-report-2020/digest

509 Bianzino, N. M., & Srinivasan, P. (2022, February 14). *Metaverse: 5 Questions Shaping the Next Frontier of Human Experience.* EY. https://www.ey.com/en_cn/digital/metaverse-5-questions-shaping-the-next-frontier-of-human-experience

510 Linthicum, D. (2022, March 8). *Cloud Computing and the Metaverse.* InfoWorld. https://www.infoworld.com/article/3652496/cloud-computing-and-the-metaverse.html

511 Smith, B. (2022, February 9). *Adapting Ahead of Regulation: A Principled Approach to App Stores.* Microsoft. https://blogs.microsoft.com/on-the-issues/2022/02/09/open-app-store-principles-activision-blizzard/

512 Clement, J. (2021, October 13). *Cloud Gaming Market Size Worldwide 2019–2024.* Statista. https://www.statista.com/statistics/932758/cloud-gaming-market-world/

513 Microsoft. (2022, January 18). *Microsoft to Acquire Activision Blizzard.* Microsoft News Center. https://news.microsoft.com/2022/01/18/microsoft-to-acquire-activision-blizzard-to-bring-the-joy-and-community-of-gaming-to-everyone-across-every-device/

514 Chen, B. (2022, January 18). *What's All the Hype About the Metaverse?* The New York Times. https://www.nytimes.com/2022/01/18/technology/personaltech/metaverse-gaming-definition.html

515 Ryan, J. (2022, February 2). *Bungie to Join the PlayStation Family.* Sony Interactive Entertainment Blog. https://www.sie.com/en/blog/bungie-to-join-the-playstation-family/

516 Netflix Investor Relations. (2022, January 22). *Netflix Quarter 4 2021 Earnings Interview.* YouTube. https://www.youtube.com/netflixir

517 *Comparing 5G vs. Wi-Fi 6.* (n.d.). Intel. https://www.intel.com/content/www/us/en/wireless-network/5g-technology/5g-vs-wifi.html

518 Statista. (2021a, March 8). *IoT and non-IoT connections worldwide 2010–2025.* https://www.statista.com/statistics/1101442/iot-number-of-connected-devices-worldwide/

519 Statista. (2021, June 7). *Amount of data created, consumed, and stored 2010–2025.* https://www.statista.com/statistics/871513/worldwide-data-created/

520 Friedman, T., & Judah, S. (2016, June 30). *Data Risks in the Internet of Things Demand Extensive Information Governance*. Gartner. https://www.gartner.com/en/documents/3362117/data-risks-in-the-internet-of-things-demand-extensive-in

521 IBM Cloud Education. (2021, September 16). *What is Artificial Intelligence?* IBM. https://www.ibm.com/cloud/learn/what-is-artificial-intelligence?lnk=hpmls_buwi

522 European Commission. (2021, April 21). *Proposal for a Regulation Laying Down Harmonised Rules on Artificial intelligence*. https://digital-strategystrategy.ec.europa.eu/en/library/proposal-regulation-laying-down-harmonised-rules-artificial-intelligence

523 *Algorithmic Accountability Act of 2022*. (2022, February 3). U.S. Congress. https://www.congress.gov/bill/117th-congress/house-bill/6580/text?r=2&s=1

524 Jones, R. (2013, August 18). *A Wicked Cloud*. Poem Hunter. https://www.poemhunter.com/poem/a-wicked-cloud/

525 Camillus, J. C. (2008, May). *Strategy as a Wicked Problem*. Harvard Business Review. https://hbr.org/2008/05/strategystrategy-as-a-wicked-problem

526 Rittel, Horst. (1973). *Dilemmas in a General Theory of Planning*. Policy Sciences, 155–169.

527 Camillus, J. C. (2008, May). *Strategy as a Wicked Problem*. Harvard Business Review. https://hbr.org/2008/05/strategystrategy-as-a-wicked-problem

528 Blanton, N. (2021, November 10). *What is the Future of Wearable Technology in Healthcare?* Baylor College of Medicine. https://blogs.bcm.edu/2021/11/10/what-is-the-future-of-wearable-technology-in-healthcare/

529 Center for Devices and Radiological Health. (2021, December 22). *Cybersecurity*. U.S. Food and Drug Administration. https://www.fda.gov/medical-devices/digital-health-center-excellence/cybersecurity

530 U.S. GAO. (2012, September 27). *Medical Devices: FDA Should Expand Its Consideration of Information Security for Certain Types of Devices*. https://www.gao.gov/products/gao-12-816

531 U.S. Cybersecurity & Infrastructure Security Agency. (n.d.). *Stop Ransomware*. CISA.Gov. https://www.cisa.gov/stopransomware

532 *What is Edge Computing?* (2021, March 31). RedHat. https://www.redhat.com/en/topics/edge-computing/what-is-edge-computing

533 Marr, B. (2021, July 13). *The Amazing Ways Tesla Is Using Artificial Intelligence And Big Data*. Bernard Marr. https://bernardmarr.com/the-amazing-ways-tesla-is-using-artificial-intelligence-and-big-data/

534 Ferris, D. (2021, November 30). *Chip Shortage Threatens Biden's Electric Vehicle Plans, Commerce Secretary Says*. Scientific American. https://www.scientificamerican.com/article/chip-shortage-threatens-bidens-electric-vehicle-plans-commerce-secretary-says/

List of Figures

https://doi.org/10.1515/9783110755374-022

List of Tables

https://doi.org/10.1515/9783110755374-023

About the Authors

Steven Mezzio, Ph.D. is a results-driven business executive with experience spanning governance, accounting, auditing, financial reporting, Sarbanes-Oxley, COSO / controls, enterprise risk management (ERM), technology, and ESG. Steven is an Associate Dean, Professor of Accountancy and ESG, and Executive Director of the Center for Sustainable Business for the Lubin School of Business at Pace University in NYC. He publishes practice-oriented articles and speaks on a range of topics, including executive education, the cloud, robotics, sustainability, governance, internal controls, auditing, Sarbanes-Oxley, the future of work, and the future of accounting education. Previously, Steven was a Partner with PwC, serving in the Audit Practice, the National Audit Quality Group, and the Governance Advisory Services Practice. He also served as the Global Leader of Governance, Risk, and Compliance Services and Co-Leader of the Key Client Management Group for Resources Global Professionals, a NASDAQ-listed $1 billion company. In 2017, Steven earned a Ph.D. in Higher Education and Human Capital Development from NYU. He also holds a master's degree in Accountancy from the University of Miami, a Graduate Certificate in Information Systems Auditing from NYU, and a bachelor's degree in Business from Pace University.

Meredith Stein, CPA, has substantial and diverse experience in the domain of governance, including designing, operationalizing, and assessing governance structures, including ERM, COSO / internal controls, and external audits of financial statements. The design and deployment of governance-related executive education and training programs have been central to her various roles. Meredith works for the National Institutes of Health (NIH), a U.S. Federal Government agency. She improves program management and performance by organizing, aligning, assessing, remediating, monitoring corporate and program risk, and ensuring program integrity and compliance. Meredith is also actively involved in governance-related, learning and development initiatives. Previously, Meredith worked for the Pension Benefit Guaranty Corporation. Prior to that, she worked in KPMG's audit and advisory practices as a manager where she conducted audits and led Sarbanes-Oxley and governance-related consulting projects. Meredith received her degree in Accounting from the American University Kogod School of Business.

Vincent Campitelli is a practitioner with a specific focus on technology, governance, and risk management. Over the last 10 years, Vincent has focused on developing guidance and best practices for the adoption and use of all models of cloud computing and related emerging technologies such as AI, Big Data, IoT, and Blockchain. Vincent is a consultant to the president of the Cloud Security Alliance (CSA). He serves as an enterprise-wide cloud security specialist internationally, providing support, and advice on all aspects of cloud security, research, education, and practice guidelines. Previously, Vincent was a VP with McKesson

https://doi.org/10.1515/9783110755374-024

Corporation, responsible for the creation, implementation, and centralization of the IT risk management and security function, including the design, development, and delivery of training associated with cloud service providers. Vincent began his career with PwC, where he served as a regional technology partner. He received an undergraduate degree in mechanical engineering from Penn State University and an MBA in Operations Research from the University of Maryland.

Index

https://doi.org/10.1515/9783110755374-025